Robert Cox
March, 1962

Methuen's Old English Library

General Editors : A. H. SMITH, D.Lit.
                F. NORMAN, M.A.

EARLY MIDDLE ENGLISH
LITERATURE

METHUEN'S OLD ENGLISH LIBRARY

General Editors : A. H. Smith, D.Lit., Reader in English, University of London ; and F. Norman, M.A., Professor of German, University of London.

A—POETIC TEXTS

1. THREE NORTHUMBRIAN POEMS : Cædmon's Hymn, Bede's Death Song, The Leiden Riddle. Edited by A. H. Smith, D.Lit.
2. DEOR. Edited by Kemp Malone, Professor of English, Johns Hopkins University, Baltimore.
3. WALDERE. Edited by F. Norman, M.A.
4. THE DREAM OF THE ROOD. Edited by Bruce Dickins, M.A., Professor of the English Language, University of Leeds ; and A. S. C. Ross, M.A., Lecturer in English, University of Leeds.
5. WIDSITH. Edited by Kemp Malone.
6. THE BATTLE OF MALDON. By E. V. Gordon, M.A., late Smith Professor of English Language, University of Manchester.

B—PROSE SELECTIONS

1. THE PARKER CHRONICLE : 832–900. Edited by A. H. Smith, D.Lit.
2. ÆLFRIC'S COLLOQUY. Edited by G. N. Garmonsway, M.A., Lecturer in English, King's College, London.
3. SERMO LUPI AD ANGLOS. Edited by Dorothy Whitelock, M.A., Fellow and Tutor in English Language, St. Hilda's College, University of Oxford.

C—STUDIES

1. EARLY MIDDLE ENGLISH LITERATURE. By R. M. Wilson, M.A., Lecturer in English, University of Leeds.

EARLY MIDDLE ENGLISH
LITERATURE

BY

R. M. WILSON

METHUEN & CO. LTD.
36 ESSEX STREET W.C.2
LONDON

| First published | . | . | October 12th 1939 |
| Second edition | . | . | 1951 |

CATALOGUE NO. 7715/U

PRINTED IN GREAT BRITAIN

TO

MY MOTHER

AND

THE MEMORY OF

MY FATHER

PREFACE

DURING recent years much important work has been done on various aspects of early Middle English literature, and the time seems to have come when some attempt should be made to present the general results of this research. In dealing with an early period such as this it is inevitable that what may seem a disproportionate space should be devoted to questions of authorship, provenance, etc., which are still unsettled and for which, in many cases, it is doubtful whether sufficient evidence will ever be available for a definite conclusion. It was obviously impossible to deal in detail with all the theories which have been brought forward at one time or another. Only those which have received a support so general that they may be considered established, together with the more plausible or more interesting of the remainder, could be dealt with at all fully; a brief reference is all that has been possible for the majority. Nor did this seem to be the occasion on which to bring forward any individual views of the author for the first time. In a synthesis such as this it is essential that the theories and opinions included should have been subjected elsewhere to the approval or criticism of other workers in the same field.

The period dealt with extends from 1066 to 1300. Not because either of these dates has a special significance in literary history; rather because they definitely have none. In dealing with early Middle English literature it is necessary to discuss the transition between Old and Middle English, and 1066 provides a convenient date at which to begin, since then, so far as we can tell, the traditional forms and subjects are still in indisputable possession. Since the period dealt

vii

with is that in which English is only one of the vernaculars in use in this country it will naturally close with the beginning of the fourteenth century, at a time when Anglo-French is beginning to decay and English has once again become the chief literary language of the country.

A book such as this must necessarily owe much to the work of other students and scholars on the same subject. Particular indications of the debt will be found throughout the book, and more especially in some of the footnotes. It owes perhaps most to the stimulating and suggestive work of Professor R. W. Chambers, who, more than any other scholar, has made clear the importance of this period in the history of English literature. In common with all students of Middle English I owe a great debt to the invaluable *Manual of the Writings in Middle English* of Professor J. E. Wells, which has done much to lighten the unavoidable drudgery of all mediæval literary historians; it may be recommended here to all readers desiring a fuller bibliography on any of the Middle English texts mentioned in this work. Finally I have to express my gratitude to various colleagues and friends who have been kind enough to read through portions or the whole of the typescript of this book: to Professor I. D. O. Arnold of Leeds University for valuable criticism and suggestions on the chapter dealing with the Anglo-French Background; to Dr A. H. Smith for his careful guidance and help in preparing the book for the press; and above all to Professor Dickins of Leeds University for his constant kindly encouragement and help. All who have enjoyed the benefit of his wide learning and accurate scholarship will easily realize the debt which this book must owe to his generous assistance. Nevertheless it must be emphasized that any mistakes, whether of omission or commission, are the sole responsibility of the author himself.

CONTENTS

EARLY MIDDLE ENGLISH
LITERATURE

I

THE EFFECTS OF THE CONQUEST

PROBABLY one of the most obscure periods in the history of English literature is that which immediately precedes the Conquest. Little has been preserved which we can definitely say was composed during the reign of the Confessor, and, most illogically, this has been taken to indicate that little was produced. The political bankruptcy of Anglo-Saxon England has long been a cherished theory, and it was perhaps an inevitable assumption that cultural and political history had followed the same lines of development. For all that there could be no doubt that it was essentially an English nation which survived the Middle Ages. And so it was assumed that the Norman Conquest alone saved England from a premature decline and fall, and that all that was best in the later England was due to the Conquest. There were doubters, but they received little attention. Sir Charles Oman had indicated some points in which the influence of the Conquest was not necessarily for the better,[1] and, more recently, Professor Chambers has exposed the fallacy of the whole argument.[2] No doubt in some respects the Conquest was beneficial; there can be even less doubt that in others it took England the better part of the following five centuries to recover. Old theories, un-

[1] C. W. C. Oman, *England before the Norman Conquest* (8th edn., London 1938), pp. 650 ff.
[2] R. W. Chambers, *On the Continuity of English Prose* (London 1932), and *Man's Unconquerable Mind* (London 1939), pp. 80–85.

3

fortunately, die hard, and in a recent work on Anglo-Norman literature we still read :

' Au milieu du XIᵉ siècle, l'Angleterre se trouvait dans une période de décadence générale. . . . La littérature latine, qui au temps de Bède, d'Aldhelm et d'Alcuin avait brillé d'un bel éclat et qui, au début du XIᵉ siècle encore, avait eu dans l'abbé Ælfric un représentant très honorable, était maintenant presque absolument négligée. D'un autre côté, l'inspiration populaire et nationale paraissait épuisée, et l'initiative du roi Alfred le Grand, reprise par Ælfric, pour créer . . . une littérature savante en langue anglo-saxonne, était tombée en oubli. Comparée aux états continentaux, l'Angleterre, au milieu du XIᵉ siècle était un pays fort arriéré. . . .' [1]

Actually, as Professor Chambers has pointed out, there seems to be far more to be said for the view that the England of the time was far ahead of the rest of Western Europe in most of the arts of civilization :

English jewellery, metal-work, tapestry and carving were famed throughout Western Europe. English illumination was unrivalled, and so national that the merest novice can identify the work of the Winchester school. Even in stone-carving, those who are competent to judge speak of the superiority of the native English carver over his Norman supplanter. In building upon a large scale England was behind Normandy. But what little is left to us of Eleventh Century Anglo-Saxon architecture shows an astonishing variety. Its mark is ' greater cosmopolitanism, as

---

[1] E. Walberg, *Quelques aspects de la littérature anglo-normande* (Paris 1936), p. 6 ; but compare the views of R. R. Darlington, ' The Last Phase of Anglo-Saxon History ' (*History*, June 1937, pp. 1–13) : ' The Normans, a vigorous if somewhat crude race, were confronted in England with a highly developed civilization, older than and in many respects superior to their own. It is clear that the period which closed with the tragic events of 1066 can in no sense be regarded as an age of stagnation and decay, for, from whatever angle it is viewed, the last phase of Old English history is rich alike in achievement and promise.'

compared to the more competent, but equally more restricted and traditional architecture of the Normans '.[1]

Most important of all, Anglo-Saxon England had developed an official language in the vernacular centuries before the rest of Western Europe. During the tenth century the power of the West Saxon kings had advanced until the whole of England was united under one king, and in the same way the West Saxon literary prose had gradually become the standard literary language of the whole country. Initiated by Alfred this prose had reached a remarkable standard of development in the hands of the homilists Ælfric and Wulfstan. The volume of extant prose writings composed during the reign of the Confessor dwindles considerably, but this is not necessarily evidence of a smaller output. On the contrary the great number of prose writings preserved only in post-Conquest manuscripts suggests that the lack of material for the immediate pre-Conquest period may be due partly to accident. Certainly in the little that remains there is no question of decadence. The *Old English Chronicle* is still being carried on by competent writers. Though prose on other subjects is not plentiful there is enough to show that trained writers of vernacular prose were not rare.

Throughout the Old English period, from the time of Alfred, there is a stream of prose texts, sometimes dwindling to a narrow brook, sometimes swelling to a broad river, but always continuous. The case is very different when we consider the poetry. At a casual glance Old English poetry seems to have decayed with the beginning of the eleventh century and to be no longer composed. But we

---

[1] R. W. Chambers, *contin.* p. lxxvii ; see also A. W. Clapham, *English Romanesque Architecture before the Conquest* (Oxford 1930), p. 77 : ' . . . in the minor arts the Norman conquest was little short of a catastrophe, blotting out alike a good tradition and an accomplished execution, and setting in its place a semi-barbaric art which attempted little and did that little ill.'

must remember that, in the main, this poetry was not a matter of the written word. The greater part of it, and especially the more typically Old English part, was not composed for reading and would never be written down at all. The small part of it which did achieve a written existence would be fortunate to survive even long enough to be disposed of as waste paper at the dissolution of the monasteries. Throughout the greater part of the Middle Ages the monasteries were the only libraries, and non-didactic or non-religious poetry should have been ejected by any conscientious librarian. The religious poetry itself, with the disuse of the West Saxon literary dialect after the Conquest, would rapidly become unintelligible. It is significant that the Exeter Book, to which we owe so much of our knowledge of Old English poetry, finds a place, if at all, in the fourteenth-century catalogue of the library of Exeter Cathedral only as one of a number of worthless and anonymous volumes in Latin, French and English.[1] During the centuries following the Conquest many Old English manuscripts must have been ruined to provide material for Latin treatises. As it is the ravages of time have made it almost impossible to attempt a description of the state of Old English poetry at any given period. Our knowledge of it depends almost entirely on the accidental preservation of four great codices, all written round about the year 1000. Nor can these be regarded as providing a corpus of the poetry of the preceding period. So far as we can tell they merely provided an anthology, and not necessarily an anthology based on merit. Apart from these codices Old English poetry is represented by a comparatively small

[1] Incidentally it may be noted that the *Peterborough Chronicle* finds no place in the late fourteenth-century catalogue of the monastic library. In the fragmentary catalogue of the same library, drawn up early in the twelfth century, it may perhaps have been the item 65, *Elfredi regis liber anglicus.*

number of odd pieces, preserved in a variety of ways, and, significantly enough, only very rarely duplicating the poems preserved in the manuscript collections. Since no similar anthology for the eleventh century happens to have been preserved we should expect the poetry of that period to be represented only by a few isolated pieces, and that, in fact, is what we find. This is not proof that little poetry was being composed; much that was written down must have been lost, and much was probably never written at all and so had little chance of survival. The net result is that we know very little of the state of Old English poetry towards the end of the period. Nevertheless, we can say that, in the few poems remaining from the eleventh century, there is no evidence of any decline in technical skill. A poem on the death of the Confessor, which has been incorporated in the *Chronicle*, one on the *Site of Durham* written just after the Conquest, and one or two other examples, show that the old technique was still practised, and that alone presupposes a continuous tradition. On the whole, whatever may have been the case politically, there is no reason to suppose that literature was decadent in eleventh-century Anglo-Saxon England. The prose was certainly vigorous enough and, though we can speak less confidently of the poetry, the little evidence available suggests that the present lack of texts is due largely to accident.

It is certain that Norman influences were at work in England long before the Conquest, and the insularity of the Old English kingdoms has often been greatly exaggerated. Kent, of course, was always in comparatively close touch with continental culture, and the other kingdoms, at the height of their power, were far from being isolated. The Mercia of Offa and the Wessex of Alfred were in continual diplomatic and commercial contact with the Frankish empire. The court of Athelstan

was the refuge of youthful princes from abroad. One of them

was to wear the crown of France, and to be called Louis d'Outremer in memory of his exile across the sea ; another was Alan, K. Athelstan's god-son, waiting to be old enough to fight his way back to his lost inheritance of Brittany ; and a third was young Haakon, of Norway, also training for a crown. When we recall, besides, the foreign embassies which brought magnificent presents to a king famed for his splendour and bounty, we may conjecture what intercourse England then had with the continent. . . . Hither also came Howell the Good, wisest of Welsh kings ; and sometimes the treacherous Constantine, king of the restless Scotland.[1]

Æthelred II married the daughter of Richard of Normandy, and it was to Normandy that he fled when driven out of England by Swegen. Under Canute London was the centre of a great maritime empire, one without equal in ancient or mediæval times.

For at London the ways crossed : the ancient route which led from Rome to York and the North, and the Viking sea-route which stretched, by the Baltic, through Russia to Byzantium. In the streets of early Eleventh Century London, a man who had visited Rome might easily have met a man who had visited Micklegarth by the way through Ryzaland, who also might have talked with a man who had stepped upon what is now the territory of Canada and the United States.[2]

English merchants frequented Italy, and there is evidence of a considerable body of trade with the south coast of the Channel from Flanders to Normandy, with the cities of Lorraine along the Meuse, and with the Imperial dominions.[3] The sons of Æthelred were brought up at the Norman court, and the Edward who was elected king of England was more Norman than Saxon. Throughout his reign Normans were welcomed at a court where Norman influence was paramount. In fact the number of Normans settled in

---

[1] J. Armitage Robinson, *The Times of St Dunstan* (Oxford 1923) p. 83.

[2] R. W. Chambers, *op.cit*. p. lxxvi.

[3] R. R. Darlington, *loc.cit*. p. 12.

England during this period was great enough to demand special mention by the Conqueror who, in one of his statutes, speaks of ' omnis Francigena qui, tempore regis Eadwardi propinqui mei, fuit in Anglia. . . .' [1] The national reaction under Godwine was aimed at the leaders and does not appear to have been followed by any considerable expulsion of foreigners from the country. The only indication of this pre-Conquest Norman influence is to be found in the introduction of some half-dozen French loan-words into the language. No signs of it appear in the literature, due probably to the paucity of the extant remains and the fact that the Conquest followed before any influence could become apparent.

It is difficult to give any reasonably accurate estimate of the influence of the Conquest on the spoken language of the country. An appreciable amount of evidence on the subject exists, but it is often apparently self-contradictory and capable of very different interpretations. It has been assumed by some scholars that, during the two and a half centuries following the Conquest, French was extensively spoken in England and a knowledge of English confined almost exclusively to the lower classes; and even here French influence was often perceptible. The evidence available hardly seems to warrant such a conclusion. It rather suggests, as indeed we might have expected, that French always remained a foreign language in this country. Its later use in literature in England does not necessarily indicate a similar development as a spoken language. No doubt French was almost exclusively spoken at court during most of the Middle Ages, but after all the royal family, because of dynastic marriage policies, was likely to be more continental in language and culture than the rest of the country. Even so there is evidence for a knowledge of

[1] A. J. Robertson, *The Laws of the Kings of England from Edmund to Henry I* (Cambridge 1925), p. 238.

English by some of the Norman and Angevin kings. The Conqueror himself had tried to learn it—apparently with no great success. Henry I probably spoke it and Henry II almost certainly understood, though he could probably not speak, the language. For most of the other kings there is no evidence one way or the other; [1] the first and third Edwards appear to have been able to speak English, and by that time there can be no doubt that it had become the usual language of those born in this country. The evidence available for the language spoken by the other classes of society is apparently, though not necessarily actually, contradictory. Although French seems to have been commonly spoken, or at any rate understood, by the upper classes, a knowledge of English amongst them was certainly not exceptional. This is natural enough, since the Norman conquerors formed only a small, and not particularly homogeneous, class. In other countries where they settled the Normans showed little power of resistance, either linguistically or culturally, to the native element and there seems no reason to suppose that they preserved their individuality better in England. Intermarriage, especially between Normans and Englishwomen, was common and we should expect that, in the second generation, the speech of the mother would prevail. French, as an almost international language, the language of culture and of polite society, would be a necessary accomplishment to be learned later, but there is no reason to suppose that it would entirely displace English as the language of everyday life. Indeed, whatever may have been the case at court, for the ordinary country landowner engaged in the cultivation of his estates,

---

[1] Though apparently Richard of Cornwall, brother to Henry III, must have spoken English since one of the reasons given for his election as King of the Romans by the German magnates was the similarity in sound of the English and German languages. See Matthew Paris, *Chronica Majora* (Rolls Series 57, v. 603).

a knowledge of English would be necessary and natural. Even in large towns, many of which received a considerable influx of foreigners, French was not particularly frequent. In the course of an anecdote told by Richard of Devizes we learn that in such rich and important towns as Durham, Lincoln and Norwich, French was rarely heard, and if this were the case in places where a large group of foreigners might have been expected, how much less likely is the continuance of a native French in the widely-scattered halls of the nobles at a time when intercommunication was slow and difficult. The number of foreigners in England, despite later immigration, was never great enough for the formation of any considerable and homogeneous French-speaking class except at the court itself, nor does there seem to have existed any particular hostility between the two races such as might have prevented fusion. The legend of the long-continued hostility between English and Normans seems, indeed, to derive most of its authority from the popularity of Scott's *Ivanhoe* and to have little foundation in fact. On the whole the evidence suggests that, during the twelfth and thirteenth centuries, most of the upper classes were bilingual ; many of the middle class, especially the commercial and mercantile part of it, probably understood French, but the lower classes, the great majority of the people, spoke English and English alone. English seems to have been the natural speech of the lower clergy, though they presumably knew some Latin too. It is probable enough that some of the higher clergy, especially the foreigners who had received preferment in England, knew only French and Latin ; amongst the higher clerics of native birth there is abundant evidence for trilingualism. The position seems to have been that, as early as the twelfth century, for anyone born in England English was the natural language, but that French or Latin, less frequently both, was a not uncommon, though far from inevitable accomplishment.

If there was little likelihood that Anglo-French would supersede English as the language of everyday speech, there was even less chance that it would displace it as the language of literature. It must be remembered that Anglo-French as a literary language was developed entirely on English soil and not imported, already flourishing, in the wake of the conquering army. Works in it begin to appear towards the end of the first quarter of the twelfth century, yet during the greater part of that century it is Latin rather than Anglo-French which is the chief literary rival of English. No doubt some of the Anglo-French literature produced during the twelfth century has been lost, and the extant remains may be only a small part of what was actually composed. Even more certainly a considerable proportion of the English literature of the century has perished. If we are to judge from what has actually survived—and it is probable enough that the extant remains give a fairly true picture of the respective proportions—it would appear that, after 1200, much more literature was being written in Anglo-French than in English. But during the thirteenth century English, too, is increasing in importance as a literary language. Its period of least production during post-Conquest times is apparently about the middle of the twelfth century at a time when Anglo-French is as yet comparatively unimportant. It is outstripped by the latter, not because of any decline in the number of English works produced, but simply because of the increase in the number of works written in Anglo-French. The two literatures exist side by side and for essentially different classes of readers.

This becomes clear when we examine the versions of some of the romances which are to be found in both languages. Those in Anglo-French are obviously written for a higher class than are the English versions of them. Whatever may have been the case with regard to the spoken language Anglo-French was the usual literary language of the upper classes during the thirteenth century. But this is not due to the displacement of English ; English as the literary language of the aristocracy had already been abolished by the Conquest which had replaced the Anglo-Saxon thegnage by foreigners. When a literary language is evolved for this class the increasing cultural importance of French, and their own continental affiliations, will inevitably lead to the development of a French literary language. Throughout the Middle Ages Anglo-French is the literary language of a comparatively small class ; as that class gradually becomes anglicized Anglo-French declines in importance and its place is taken by the English which had developed side by side with it.

Though there is no reason to suppose that the Conquest might have resulted in the disappearance of English as a literary language, its influence, direct and indirect, on English literature was considerable. More especially the effects of it on the traditional alliterative poetry are quickly perceptible and apparently decisive. Only one or two poems in the strict alliterative line still remain which seem to have been written after the Conquest. The longest is a poem of some twenty lines, *The Site of Durham*. It is written in the Old English tradition and quite uninfluenced by French. The opening lines seem to be vaguely reminiscent of some of the earlier elegies, and the poem is completely traditional in vocabulary, phraseology and metre. As literature it is comparatively unimportant ; after a few lines at the beginning describing the site of the city, it passes into a list of the relics to be found in the cathedral church. In addition there are one or two other pieces such as *The Grave* and the *Worcester Fragments* which retain much of the Old English phraseology and metre. Though probably copied from Old English originals the language of the latter is, however, no longer the standard West Saxon literary dialect but Middle English. These are the only extant post-Conquest poems in which the traditional alliterative line is still in use. It may be that they form only a very small proportion of what was actually composed, but it is more probable that such poetry practically ceased to be written down after the Conquest. The class for whom it was written was precisely that class which felt the fullest effects of, and was almost exterminated by, the Conquest. Nevertheless, alliterative poetry must have continued to be composed. This is evident from the sporadic appearance of alliterative verse throughout the Middle English period and its eventual culmination in the alliterative revival. It was a type of poetry which depended for its existence on a continuous tradition. Once that tradition was broken it could never have been revived so that the alliterative revival alone is evidence for a continuous, if restricted, use. Further evidence can be gathered from the works of Giraldus Cambrensis. In his *Descriptio Kambriae*, he tells us that the Welsh

make use of alliteration in preference to all other ornaments of rhetoric, and that particular kind which joins by consonancy the first letters or syllables of words. So much do the English and Welsh nations employ this ornament of words in all exquisite composition, that no sentence is esteemed to be elegantly spoken . . . unless it be fully polished with the file of this figure.

He goes on to give examples in English of regular alliterative lines. Evidently to him alliteration was as characteristically English as Welsh. Practically no examples of alliterative poetry composed at this time still remain, but they must have existed and been known to Giraldus.

The alliterative verse that appears after the Conquest is very different from the strict Old English type. Some changes are due to the loss of the old poetic dialect. The actual spoken speech has to be used and this differs considerably from the old literary language. Other changes are probably due to the influence of a different alliterative tradition. In all probability the strict metrical system was of purely literary growth and knowledge of it existed chiefly in the monasteries. This was the type of verse which would be most affected by the Conquest and which early disappeared. But side by side with it, during the Old English period, there seems to have existed a popular type of alliterative poetry in which quantity was neglected and the rhythm had become purely accentual. Since such poetry was purely popular and oral it is not surprising that few examples of it still exist. Some of the *Charms* and some of the poetical entries in the *Chronicle* may be examples of it. After the Conquest the survival of the alliterative line depended entirely on oral tradition, so that this popular type of poetry inevitably came to the fore. In some parts of the country there were monks who carried on the strict alliterative tradition until the middle of the twelfth century. But on the whole Middle English alliterative poetry seems to have been considerably influenced by, if not entirely derived from, the more popular type. For some time the exact line of development which it would take was doubtful. Occasionally the long line breaks up and, with the addition of rhyme, a couplet is formed which becomes more and more syllabic until it is written side by side with the French couplet and becomes indistinguishable from it. This line of development is exemplified by Laȝamon's *Brut, The Proverbs of Alured* and *King Horn*. In Laȝamon we find occasional rhyme and the failure of the alliteration. In the *Proverbs of Alured* we find the short rhyming couplet side by side with the alliterative line, whilst in *King Horn* the rhyming couplets are invariable. The long line, how- ever, still remains and, when rhyme is not added, shows little sign of becoming syllabic. Finally it shakes off both rhyme and assonance and in the fourteenth century we find a much purer form of the alliterative verse, existing more especially in areas where national feeling had always remained strong.[1] The influence of the Conquest on the poetry, then, was decisive, though possibly not altogether unfortunate. It meant the end of the specifically literary Old English poetry which thus died comparatively young and, if we can judge from such examples as *Maldon*, whilst still vigorous. But it was becoming more and more artificial and conventional. The conventional battlefield with the wheeling eagles and the wolves ' eager for carrion ' has already been completely standardized, and most of the kennings have become little more than synonyms. By its early death it was, at any rate, saved from the painful ingenuity which overtook the Old Norse skaldic poetry. It was brought into contact with the popular poetry, was reinvigorated, made less artificial and, by the changes which it underwent, it took on a new lease of life.

There can be no doubt that the displacing of alliteration by rhyme was mainly due to the Conquest. Occasional rhyme is found in Old English poetry and occurs long before any French influence can be postulated. It is characteristic of the Cynewulfian poems, and found occasionally elsewhere. It is even quite regular in the *Rhyming Poem*, though this is an isolated example. The influence here is presumably from the early Latin hymns, and it is possible enough that rhyme would have developed in English even without French influence. Certainly the later supremacy of rhyme is not necessarily due to the Conquest. The importance of French literature during the later Middle Ages was such that it must, in any case, have made its influence felt on English poetry. The Conquest made that influence more direct, and gave an impetus to the use of rhyme whereby its later supremacy was assured more easily than might otherwise have been the case.

---

[1] On the continuity of the alliterative tradition see especially J. P. Oakden, *Alliterative Poetry in Middle English* i. (Manchester 1930), pp. 153 ff.

On poetry, then, the influence of the Conquest was considerable, immediate and probably not altogether harmful. On prose, on the other hand, French influence, though slow to take effect, was eventually deadly. The development of a literary prose in the vernacular, some centuries ahead of the rest of Western Europe, was the especial achievement of Anglo-Saxon England. The reasons for the disuse of the traditional poetry in the years succeeding the Conquest would not apply to the prose and, in fact, the standard West Saxon prose continues in general use for over a century. It is in use, moreover, not only in didactic literature but also in theological, official and historical works. The fact is not generally realized because much of the late eleventh- and early twelfth-century prose consists of copies of much earlier works. In any case it carries on the traditions of the Old English prose and is usually classed together with it. A great part of our knowledge of Old English, more especially of Old English prose, is due to manuscripts written after the Conquest.

The translations of Alfred and other Old English versions of mediæval classics continue to be copied ; some of the extant manuscripts of Boethius, of the pseudo-Alfredian Bede, and the only manuscript of the translation of the Flowers of St Augustine, were copied in post-Conquest times. The work of Alfred, in this as in other respects, had been carried on by Ælfric, and his translations, too, are still being copied. Moreover, the tradition of the translation of Latin works into the vernacular, initiated by Alfred, continues to be carried on. Towards the end of the eleventh century Honorius of Autun had written a theological work under the title of the *Elucidarium* which immediately became popular. It was translated into most of the Western European languages, and fragments of a translation into West Saxon still exist. It is not a particularly good translation and we do not know who the author may have been. Whoever he was he was carrying on the tradition of Alfred and of Ælfric. Translations of the Scriptures into West Saxon continue to be copied. Four of the seven surviving manuscripts of the Old English version of the *Heptateuch* were written after the Conquest. Similarly with the translations of the Gospels.

Made, perhaps, in the troublous times of Æthelred the Unready, it is being copied, perhaps, in the even more troublous times of Stephen. This copy was again transcribed in the latter half of the Twelfth Century, and some gaps in it were filled up by a new translation by the late Twelfth-Century scribe.[1]

The works of the great homilists, Ælfric and Wulfstan, together with the homilies of other unknown writers, remained popular. Some of them are extant only in post-Conquest manuscripts and, long after the West Saxon literary prose has been lost, they are still being modernized and adapted in Middle English. Nor was this prose employed only in religious works. During the Old English period a technical legal vocabulary had been developed which remained in use in post-Conquest times, while in historical writing the West Saxon literary prose continues until well into the twelfth century. The quasi-scientific treatises which begin to appear towards the end of the Old English period continue to be copied, and much of the material collected in Cockayne's *Leechdoms* is extant only in post-Conquest manuscripts.

And so, in spite of the Conquest and the consequent discouragement of a foreign aristocracy in church and state, works in the West Saxon literary prose are still being written until well into the following century. The reasons for its later decline are obvious enough. Despite a certain amount of modernization it gets further and further away from the spoken language. Consequently it is entirely dependent on

[1] R. W. Chambers, *op.cit.* p. xcii.

a literary tradition. If that tradition is once broken it can never be recaptured, and a new prose must be developed based on the actual spoken language. In post-Conquest England the influence of Latin and of Anglo-French gradually increases, and their increasing use means a decrease in the use of the vernacular. In this connexion the influence of Latin is undeniable, but it is not until the middle of the twelfth century that English prose had to face any competition from Anglo-French.

> In fact, of the two vernacular tongues in England, English, as a language of record in competition with Latin, seems to have been much more important than French. What is true of writs, charters and laws is true of the Chronicles of this period ; they are in Latin or English—chiefly the former—not in French. . . . The disuse of English was not because of the introduction of French, but because of the increased use of Latin by a body of churchmen trained to consider Latin the superior tongue for literary purposes. To the historian of the time, French no less than English was a ' vulgar ' tongue as compared with Latin.[1]

The vernacular prose depended for its existence on its use in the monasteries and as an official language. The official language of the Normans was Latin, and the reform of the monasteries meant an increased knowledge of Latin and a decrease in the use of English. In the first place the development of an English prose had been due to the decay of learning so bitterly lamented by Alfred, and in the same way its later decline was due to a revival of learning in the church.

One of the chief results of the Conquest, and of the consequent loss of the Old English literary prose, was the inordinate use of verse in the later Middle English period. The popularizers of learning, carrying on the Old English tradition of translation into the vernacular, are fatally in-

[1] P. V. D. Shelly, *English and French in England 1066–1100* (Philadelphia 1921), p. 90.

fected by French influence. Before the Conquest such translations would have been made in prose, after the fashion initiated by Alfred the Great. A French prose was not developed until comparatively late in the mediæval period, and the result was that the French popularizers had to do their work in verse. This reacts on English literature and the result is the interminable rhymed chronicles, romances and popular theology of the Middle English period. At one time it had seemed possible that mediæval England might attain a prose equal to that developed in Iceland. There its development had been due, in great part, to the isolation of the country ; in England the opportunity was lost because of that closer connexion between England and the continent which was one of the vaunted results of the Conquest. English prose lingers on for some time but it eventually dies, and centuries have to pass before a new prose can be evolved for most of the subjects for which it is the natural vehicle. In one subject only does prose retain its position throughout the Middle English period. Under special conditions and in a different dialect the Old English homiletic prose continues to flourish until the prose of Alfred develops into the prose of the Authorized Version, and so becomes the foundation of the modern prose style. Eventually this prose makes its way into other subjects ; into theology with the earlier translators of the Bible, and into history with Capgrave, until poetry is able to take its proper place and need no longer usurp the functions of prose.

No doubt the Conquest facilitated the growth of mediæval romance in England. Equally certainly French subjects would have made their way into Middle English literature whether the Conquest had intervened or not. The attraction of French subjects and of French models was all-pervading during the twelfth and thirteenth centuries, and is to be found in most European countries. Nor are signs wanting that subjects other than religious and those dealing with the old Germanic heroes were making their way into Old English literature. Fragments exist of an eleventh-century translation into West Saxon of the tale of Apollonius of Tyre—perhaps the manuscript which we find entered as *Apollonium, anglice* in the twelfth-century catalogue of the library of the abbey at Burton-on-Trent. In another manuscript we find a tract on the *Wonders of the East* and a translation of the *Letter from Alexander to Aristotle*, works of a type which was later to become popular. It seems that already in Late Old English romance was beginning to take the place of epic. But if, on the one hand, romance is found in the earlier period, on the other the old subjects continue to be popular, though the tales are usually remodelled under the influence of French romance. Wade and Weland the Smith are long remembered—vague tales of Wade were even known to Leland—and, though no separate tale of their adventures has been preserved, the numerous allusions to them in Middle English literature indicate that their legends must have been quite familiar. Much of the later matter of England is essentially pre-Conquest in origin. It has been affected considerably by the influence of French romance ; some of the extant romances are in fact translations from the French, but the subjects themselves are taken from Anglo-Saxon history and legend and were probably extant orally long before they came into the hands of French authors., Moreover, the surviving romances are only a small proportion of those which were actually composed. We know of some which were certainly written down, though the English versions have not been preserved. *Waldef* is extant only in a French version which, the author tells us, is translated from an English original ; the *Gesta Herewardi* was translated from the English of Leofric ; Robert Mannyng of Brunne knew of a work by a certain Thomas of Kendal which told of the exploits of Scarthe and Flayn, the supposed founders of Scarborough and Flamborough. Others, such as the *cantilenae* dealing with the legends connected with Athelstan and Edgar known to William of Malmesbury and Henry of Huntingdon, the exploits of Eadric the Wild and the legend of Godwine, possibly never had a written existence. Nevertheless, there can be no doubt that, throughout most of the mediæval period, tales based on Anglo-Saxon history and legend comprised an appreciable proportion of Middle English romance.

It is difficult to decide exactly how far the Conquest was responsible for these various changes. The pre-eminence of French literature in the Middle English period, which may have owed something to the political supremacy of the Normans in England, would in any case have left a considerable mark on English literature. Probably the importance of French as the language of government and culture in England made these changes swifter and more widespread than would otherwise have been the case.

II

THE ANGLO-LATIN BACKGROUND

THROUGHOUT the Middle Ages [1] Latin remained a living language, though the Latin spoken in mediæval monasteries was a very different language from classical Latin. In order to express new ideas it had assimilated a large number of loan-words, especially from the Germanic languages, and, in addition, had undergone considerable phonological changes. Nevertheless mediæval writers of Latin looked back to ancient models ; they strove to imitate them, though they often differed much in vocabulary and showed certain syntactical simplifications. The mediæval Latin which was thus developed remained an international medium for literature until modern times, and it was natural enough that original works should almost invariably be first published in it. Its international aspect made possible a much wider circulation than would have been available for a work written in any of the vernaculars. It was the language of the church and of the schools and so an indispensable accomplishment for all literate people. The result was, that throughout the Middle Ages, any contribution to science,

[1] For the Latin background during the Middle Ages, see especially Max Manitius, *Geschichte der lateinischen Literatur des Mittelalters* (München 1911–31) ; F. A. Wright and T. A. Sinclair, *A History of the Later Latin Literature* (London 1931) ; H. O. Taylor, *The Mediæval Mind* (London 1911) ; M. de Wulf, *A History of Mediæval Philosophy* (London 1926). For the revival of learning during the twelfth century see C. H. Haskins, *The Renaissance of the Twelfth Century* (Harvard 1928).

art, philosophy or theology was first published to the western world in Latin. The vernacular might be used for the literature of entertainment, or for the somewhat self-conscious popularization of knowledge, but Latin invariably remained the literary language of the scholar.

Only in a single country of Western Europe during the Middle Ages was there ever any prospect that a vernacular might take the place of Latin as the language of original scholarship.[1] This was in Anglo-Saxon England where the decay of learning, consequent on the Danish invasions, had led to the precocious development of a native prose. But the ravages of those same invasions also brought it about that, after the age of Alcuin, few great scholars were produced in a country which had once been a centre of Latin learning in the West. The scholars of the later period were concerned rather with the enlightenment of their ignorant flock than with original speculation, and for this purpose the vernacular provided a more convenient medium for instruction. However, one of the most important effects of the Conquest was the reform of the church which led to an increased knowledge and importance of Latin.

The great Latin writers of the earlier part of the period, Lanfranc and Anselm, have little to do with English literature. They were not English themselves and were already famous as scholars and writers long before they came to this country. Consequently, important as they undoubtedly are in the political and ecclesiastical history of England, their writings belong rather to the history of Latin literature on the continent. The earliest important and distinctively English writers of Latin are the group of Anglo-Latin historians who came into prominence during the twelfth century, at a time when the vernacular historical prose was

---

[1] That is, of course, with the exception of Iceland where the special conditions later led to the development of a vernacular prose, which was used as a language of original scholarship.

at last beginning to disappear. As far as number and general standard of excellence go they form a company which is without equal in any other country of Western Europe. Although they use Latin their works are written from a purely national standpoint; they are histories of England, more especially valuable, as we should expect, for their record of contemporary happenings. Even when they deal with events of which they could have no first-hand knowledge they preserve traditions which would otherwise have perished. The modern student of the period, who has discovered that these chroniclers have not in every instance succeeded in freeing themselves entirely from the ideas and conventions of their own time, is apt, perhaps, to underestimate their value. No doubt their chronology is not always so trust-worthy as that of official documents, but they clothe the bare facts with a life which it is impossible for the latter to give. Their anecdotal method may occasionally lead to irrelevance, but it presents the life of the times with considerable vividness and increases the interest of the narrative both to the modern and mediæval reader. Many start their histories at the beginning of the Christian era, even occasionally at the Creation, with the result that the earlier parts of their chronicles are too often mere compilations from other historians and devoid of either interest or value. Even so historians such as William of Malmesbury, Ordericus Vitalis or Henry of Huntingdon preserve twelfth-century traditions of these earlier periods which are not without their importance. All of them try to be readable and strive for a symmetry and proportion of narrative very different from the patchwork performances of the earlier annalists. For their literary models they look back to the classical Latinists and are fond, sometimes too fond, of adorning their writings with classical tags and allusions. As their model in historical writing they look back to Bede and, like him, whenever possible quote documentary evidence and attempt to discriminate between that which they have seen for themselves and that for which they have to depend on the evidence of others. Often enough they have taken part in the events which they are describing, for the best of them, William of Malmesbury, William of Newburgh and Roger of Hoveden were men who had travelled widely or even spent part of their lives in the service of the crown.

It would be out of place to deal fully here with all the twelfth-century Latin chroniclers. Almost without exception, from Eadmer to Gervase of Tilbury, they are of abiding interest and not a little value to the later historian of the period. Here we can deal in comparative detail only with the most important and the most interesting of them. Undoubtedly the greatest of the earlier historians is William of Malmesbury, one of the numerous class who, beginning with the Christian era or the Saxon invasions, carry the story down to their own times. He was by no means the earliest of the Latin historians ; that distinction belongs, in the south to Florence of Worcester [1] and in the north to Simeon of Durham,[2] whilst on the continent the history of the Normans had been written by Ordericus Vitalis [3] whose chronicle, for all its inconsequential rambling, is important for the history of the Normans in England. But William was a greater historian and a better writer than any of these, and in his avowed intention of filling in the gap between Bede's history and the work of his contemporary

[1] *Chronicon ex chronicis* ; based mainly on the Chronicle of Marianus Scotus. Ends with 1117 but continued by various hands to 1295.

[2] Wrote between 1104 and 1108. Especially valuable as preserving material from older Northumbrian sources now lost.

[3] *Historica Ecclesiastica* continues to 1141. Ordericus was the son of a Norman priest and an Englishwoman, but spent his life from the age of twelve onwards in the Norman monastery of St Evroult. Especially valuable for conditions in Normandy during the eleventh and twelfth centuries.

Eadmer he enjoyed considerable success. He was educated in the monastery of Malmesbury and, after a life the greater part of which was spent as monk and librarian there, died in 1143. His fame as a historian rests mainly on three works —the *De Gestis Regum Angliæ*, dealing with the history of England from the Saxon invasions to 1127; the *Historia Novella*, which carries the account down to 1142 in three short books unfortunately little more than notes; and the *De Gestis Pontificum Anglorum*. In addition he wrote a life of Wulfstan of Worcester, a tract *On the Antiquity of Glastonbury*, which proved too tempting to the monks of that monastery and suffered a great deal of interpolation from them, and he is responsible also for a number of minor writings and compilations. He has been justly called the most enlightened of English historians since the Venerable Bede, and, it might be added, he is in many ways the most interesting too. He is as fond of anecdote as were his readers and he has all the contemporary belief in the supernatural. Nevertheless he possesses all the qualifications of the historian: industry, an insight into character, a critical judgment which leads him to sift and select his material, and a sanity of mind allowing him to control his credulity. He seems to have travelled widely and was very different from the cloistered and secluded historian usually accounted as typically mediæval. His wide scholarship is indicated by the fact that, so far as can be gathered from incidental allusions, only John of Salisbury, amongst other twelfth-century scholars, surpassed him in the breadth of his reading. He is possessed of a power of vivid description which enables him to bring to life the history of earlier periods, whilst, for his own times, his accuracy and honesty are beyond question. Whenever possible he investigated facts for himself and, if he must depend on hearsay evidence, he is always careful to warn his readers of the fact. In dealing with the events of an earlier age he is not satisfied with the available written sources but quotes contemporary traditions, though always with the clear warning that these are merely traditions and not ascertained facts. In his descriptive power, mastery of significant detail, skilful arrangement and honesty of purpose he is a worthy predecessor of Matthew Paris, the greatest of all mediæval Latin historians.

At the same time it must be remembered that William was only one of a number of historians, many of whom, in their own day, approached him in popularity, and each of whom has his own individual interest and importance. Such were Henry of Huntingdon,[1] more concerned with style than history, thoroughly unreliable and credulous but preserving twelfth-century traditions of the earlier periods, and, at the end of the century, Roger of Hoveden [2] and Ralph of Diceto.[3]

Of the historians who were content to write only, or mainly, of contemporary events the earliest was Eadmer,[4] a monk of Canterbury, who wrote a history of the period between the Conquest and 1122, but undoubtedly the most interesting of them is William of Newburgh. He seems to have been born of a good family at, or near, Bridlington, and

[1] Archdeacon of Huntingdon. His *Historia Anglorum* begins with 55 B.C. and continues to 1154, having been revised and brought up to date several times ; in it he includes a translation into Latin prose of the Old English poem on the Battle of Brunanburh.

[2] *Chronica*, 732–1201. Roger was a justice itinerant of the Forests under Henry II and Richard I and so is especially interested in legal matters. The last part of his work gives a fairly comprehensive history of Europe for the last decade of the twelfth century.

[3] *Imagines Historiarum*, Creation–1202. Ralph was Archdeacon of Middlesex and Dean of St Paul's. Invaluable from 1188 and illustrated by documents to which his position gave him special means of access.

[4] *Historia Novorum*, 960–1122. The interest is mainly ecclesiastical but not exclusively so. It is full of vivid and trustworthy detail and distinguished by its design and sense of proportion. Eadmer also wrote a life of Anselm whose friend and confidant he was.

to have received his education at the Augustinian Priory of Newburgh, of which his brother Bernard later became prior. His marriage with an heiress brought him extensive property in the south, but in 1182/3 he left her and became a canon of Newburgh priory. There he wrote his chronicle in which the last recorded event to be dated is in 1198 and, being at that time elderly and in poor health, he probably died soon afterwards. His *Historia Rerum Anglicarum* deals with events from the Conquest onwards, but the earlier parts are summarized and its chief interest begins only with the accession of Henry II. For the second half of the twelfth century it is by far our best authority for English history, William being no mere annalist but a careful and painstaking historian, an acute critic of men and events. His scathing attack on the fictions of Geoffrey of Monmouth probably leads the reader to look for a more modern type of historian than he has any right to expect, and to be correspondingly disappointed when William fails to escape entirely from the faults of his period. He has the same honesty, love of accuracy and independence of judgment which we find in William of Malmesbury, and, though less ambitious of literary ornament, possesses a clear and straightforward style. His fondness for anecdotal digression has filled his work with the legends of the countryside, and so made it one of the most interesting of all the mediæval chronicles. But these digressions are never allowed to usurp the place of history or to distract the author from his clear, well-ordered presentment of historical events.

A number of chroniclers deal only with a single topic, and of these the earliest is probably St Ailred of Rievaulx,[1] who, however, owes his fame to other than historical writings. His account of the battle of the Standard is an ambitious production, but neither so full nor so trustworthy as that

[1] See F. M. Powicke, ' Ailred of Rievaulx and his Biographer ' (*Bulletin of the John Rylands Library* vi. 310, 452).

by Richard of Hexham.[1]   A remarkably graphic account of
the crusade of Richard I is given by Richard of Devizes [2]
in a modest and unassuming essay, which, nevertheless,
shows him to have been an excellent historical writer.   But
the most interesting of all these shorter works is the *Chronica*
of Jocelin of Brakelonde who, in his account of the community of St Edmund's, has given us a unique picture of
monastic life in the twelfth century.   A vivid picture of
Abbot Samson emerges from his pages, learned and able
but proud and overbearing, a typical example of the great
mediæval abbot.   We see the daily life of the monastery,
the petty intrigues and jealousies of the monks side by side
with their sincere devotion to the monastic ideal ; the internal
economy and daily routine of the house are pictured with
intimate knowledge.   We obtain a clear picture of the
relation of the monastery to the social and industrial life
of the people, and it is impossible to overestimate the charm
and interest of this unpretentious chronicle.   The work of
Jocelin is worth many a more ambitious production from
which we learn much less of the actual life of the people.

Finally mention must be made of an historian who owes
his fame, not to any outstanding historical qualities, but to
an almost complete lack of them.   Somewhere about 1136
Geoffrey of Monmouth, a Welshman, Archdeacon of Monmouth and later Bishop of St Asaph, published his *Historia
Regum Britanniæ*, which purported to tell the history of the
kings of the Britons from the landing of Brutus, the great-
grandson of Æneas, to the death of Cadwallader, whom the
Britons regarded as the last British king of England.   Geoffrey
claimed to have drawn his material from a certain British
book which had been lent to him by Archdeacon Walter of
Oxford, but no one else seems to have known anything of

---

[1] *Historia de gestis Regis Stephani*, 1135–9, continued to 1154
by Richard's son John.

[2] *De Rebus Gestis Ricardi Primi*, 1189–92.

this book, and its existence has been doubted. Actually his material seems to have been drawn from certain well-known Welsh sources, Gildas and Nennius, from oral legends, and from his own vivid imagination. The result is an historical novel rather than a history, valuable in that it gives us the Welsh traditions of the Saxon invasions, but even more valuable as the source which gave currency to themes later to become famous in romance and drama. He is the first to claim a Trojan descent for the Britons and from him are ultimately derived the stories of Lear, of Cymbeline, of others only slightly less famous, and most important of all, of Arthur and his knights. He is the first to invest Arthur with an historical personality, to surround him with some of the knights later to become famous, and to give a full-length description of him and of his career. Many of the characteristic people and episodes of later romance are absent; there is no Lancelot, Tristram and Iseult have not yet joined the court, and the Round Table and the Quest of the Grail are missing. But the outline of the story is already there: Guanhumara is in name, though not yet in character, the later Guinevere, Gawain is there as Walganus; the widespread conquests of Arthur, the treachery of Mordred and the final departure to Avallon are all there.

The popularity of Geoffrey's work was immediate and its influence on later literature immense. William of Newburgh might thunder against his vain fictions, and Giraldus tell cynically how a certain Melerius, being afflicted by devils, obtained relief when the Gospel of St John was placed on his breast, but when, as an experiment, Geoffrey's history was substituted, the devils gathered in even greater numbers than usual and perched not only on the unfortunate youth but also on the book itself.[1] All such protests were

---

[1] But incidentally it is Giraldus who, in his *De Instructione Principis* and in a slightly different form in the *Speculum Ecclesiae*, tells us of the discovery in his own days of the bodies of Arthur

useless. Geoffrey had pictured the earlier history of the country as his contemporaries wished it to be ; they found his work more interesting than that of more orthodox historians and they preferred to believe him rather than his critics. Some of the contemporary historians, as for example Henry of Huntingdon, who would have believed anything if it were interesting enough, accepted it, and its influence on the later chroniclers was considerable. Whatever we may think of its historicity there can be no doubt that it was one of the most important and influential of all mediæval writings.

These are only the more important of the Anglo-Latin historians who made the twelfth century the golden age of historical writing in England. There were others ; occasionally, like William FitzStephen who prefixed to his life of Becket a valuable description of contemporary London, we know their names and something of their lives, more frequently, like the author of the *Gesta Stephani*, their name has been lost and only their work remains. Almost without exception, whether anonymous or not, their work is of great importance to the historian. Most of them, even those who were monks, were men who had travelled widely and had often taken a part in the events which they described. The following century, on the other hand, is the age of the essentially monastic historian. It was a time when most of the greater monasteries were compiling, revising and adding to their stores of historical knowledge and the results, the annals of Burton, Winchester, Waverley, and others are invaluable to the historian though of little interest to literature. Most of these chroniclers are quite unknown ; only at St Albans do we know the names of some of that

and Guinevere at Glastonbury. He himself claims to have seen the bones and the inscription on the coffin, ' Hic jacet sepultus inclitus rex Arthurus cum Wenneveria uxore sua secunda in insula Avallonia '. [RS. 21, viii, 126 ; 21, iv, 47.]

school of brilliant historians which culminated in Matthew Paris.[1] A regular historiographer seems to have been established there by Abbot Simon (d. 1183), though the first whose work has come down to us is Roger of Wendover, whose *Flores Historiarum* is based on a work of John de Cella, abbot from 1195 to 1214, extending to 1188 and continued by Roger to 1235. On his death he was succeeded as official historian by Matthew Paris, of whose life previous to his admission as a monk in 1217 we know little. Most of his life, apart from a journey to Norway in 1248 to reform the abbey of Holm, seems to have been passed in the monastery. His best-known historical works are the *Chronica Majora* (–1259), and the *Historia Anglorum*, or *Chronica Minora*, a history of England after the Conquest, mainly abridged from the larger work, but he was also responsible for parts of other composite chronicles, for numerous hagiographical works in French and Latin, and for a life of Stephen Langton. He was a man of varied gifts who, in addition to his literary work, seems to have attained considerable fame as an artist.[2] The earlier parts of his historical works are based on Wendover, but from 1235 onwards they are original works and in them he shows himself to have been probably the greatest of all mediæval Latin historians. For the quarter of a century before his death in 1259 he gives us a comprehensive and well-digested history, not only of England, but of Europe. More especially the struggle between the empire and the papacy receives considerable attention, many of the documents that issued from both sides being preserved only by him. Matthew Paris was a born historian; his position in an important monastery near the capital brought him into touch with the court and, in addition, he seems to have relied for the collection of facts, in the verification of which he took

---

[1] See especially C. Jenkins, *The Monastic Chronicler and the Early School of St Albans* (London 1922).

[2] See Walpole Society, xiv. 1–26 and plates.

considerable pains, on the help of a host of correspondents both at home and abroad. The remarkably vivid descriptive qualities of his writing have always received full recognition, and he was a fearless and impartial critic of the persons and events of the day. He was not entirely free from the bias of the monkish historian, as is shown by some of his references to the secular clergy and the friars. Nevertheless he can still recognize the greatness of those of whom he disapproves, as witness his treatment of Bishop Grosseteste; he is not above repeating the scandal spread by the Bishop's enemies, but he realizes and does full justice to his fearless honesty and intellectual ability. The greatness of Matthew as an historian was recognized in his own lifetime, and his reputation has always remained high.

Naturally enough other thirteenth-century historians, important though they often are for historical fact, fade into insignificance as compared with Matthew Paris. Historical writing was continued at St Albans long after his death, but none of his followers had the literary distinction or historical skill of their predecessor. The same is true of other historians such as Walter of Hemingburgh,[1] Thomas of Wick [2] and John of Tayster.[3] Probably the most interesting of these is Thomas of Eccleston, one of the earliest of the English Franciscans, who, in his *De Adventu Minorum in Angliam*, tells of their hardships, their adventures and their unaffected humility. But, tempting though the subject is, we cannot deal at any greater length with the Anglo-Latin historians. They have been discussed in comparative detail because they are after all the most distinctively English of

[1] Canon of Guisborough; his *Chronicon* extends from 1048 to his death, which probably took place soon after 1313.

[2] Known as a poet, but the ascription to him of a *Chronicon* (1066–1289) and of a share in the contemporary *Osney Chronicle* is not so certain.

[3] A monk of Bury St Edmund and author of a *Chronica Abbreviata* (–1265).

all the mediæval Anglo-Latin writers. Others, even though of much greater importance in the history of mediæval thought, must be dealt with more summarily.

Greek learning was almost unknown to the early Middle Ages, which derived its knowledge almost exclusively from Latin sources, and, after the Scipionic age, there had been little direct translation from Greek into Latin. More especially the development of Greek science after the triumph of Rome was unknown to the West, though a slight acquaintance with Greek medicine seems to have lingered on in Southern Italy. However the Greek tradition lived on in the Eastern Empire ; from there it made its way eastward by translation into Syriac and Arabic, and it was through these intermediaries that Greek science made its way into Western Europe during the twelfth century.[1] There were two main channels by which the new learning reached the West ; through the Norman kingdom of Sicily, which still retained a considerable Mahommedan population, and from the Spanish peninsula, though the translations made in Sicily were not only less numerous but also less influential than those which came from Spain. These translations were carried out by scholars who, attracted by the brilliance of the Sicilian court and the fame of the Spanish schools, gathered there from every country in Western Europe. Many of the famous English scholars of the twelfth and thirteenth centuries visited the Norman court in Sicily and some of them found a career there. In fact English scholars took a distinguished part in the diffusion of the new learning to the West, as is shown by such names as Adelard of Bath, Walcher of Malvern, Robert of Chester, Daniel of Morley, Roger of Hereford, and, in the following century, Alfred of Shareshull and Michael Scot. Of these the earliest was Adelard of

[1] For a full description of the introduction to the West of Greek and Arabic science see C. H. Haskins, *Studies in the History of Mediæval Science* (Harvard 1924).

Bath, a pioneer of scientific enquiry and the greatest name in English science before Bacon and Grosseteste. We know little of him personally, but from his writings we can gather something of his originality and versatility, and it was to him that the West was indebted for the introduction of the new astronomy and the new Euclid. He is one of the most interesting and significant figures in mediæval science. Robert of Chester, by his translation of the *Algebra* of al-Khwarizmi, introduced the name as well as the processes of that science to Western Europe. Alfred of Shareshull was a philosopher and interested mainly in the natural philosophy of Aristotle. In his works he displays an acquaintance with that author such as is shared by no other Latin writer of his time. The later fame of Michael Scot as a wizard has overshadowed his earlier claim to fame as a translator who worked both in Spain and in Sicily. Nevertheless his translations of Arabic versions of some of Aristotle's works remained in use throughout the Middle Ages and, though condemned by Bacon, he received the praise of some of the greatest of the contemporary mathematicians. He was court astrologer to the Emperor Frederick II, and it was on his astrological writings that his principal fame rested during the mediæval period.

Undoubtedly the best classical scholar during the twelfth century was John of Salisbury, a pupil of Abaelard and educated at Paris and Chartres.[1] He was engaged under Henry II in constant diplomatic activities, especially in connexion with the papacy. A firm friend and moderating counsellor of Becket, he shared in his exile, was present at his death, and urged forward his canonization. He became Bishop of Chartres in 1176 and died four years later. He is one of the most attractive characters of the century with a unique knowledge of the classics and a distinctive and lively prose style of his own. In his extant Letters he shows

[1] C. C. J. Webb, *John of Salisbury* (London 1932).

himself to have been an able politician, and a zealous though far from narrow ecclesiastic, whilst in other writings he is always interesting and the master of a polished prose. His most important works are the *Polycraticus*, a miscellaneous encyclopædia reflecting the cultivated thought of the period and including the earliest of the mediæval theories on the nature and functions of the state, the *Metalogicus*, a defence of the method and use of logic containing an analysis of the whole series of Aristotle's treatises on that subject, and the *Historia Pontificalis*, an account of ecclesiastical history between the years 1148 and 1152. All bear witness to the unique width of his reading, to his experience of contemporary affairs and to a critical and independent mind ; on the whole he was probably the greatest scholar of a brilliant century.

Two of the most interesting of the Latin writers to be found at the court of Henry II were the friends Walter Map and Giraldus Cambrensis. Of these the former enjoyed in his lifetime a reputation such as is hardly borne out by his extant works. At various times Map has been credited with the authorship of most of the Goliardic poems and of a good deal of the Arthurian legend, but the only work certainly by him which still remains is a book of miscellaneous content with the title, borrowed from John of Salisbury, *De Nugis Curialium*.[1] As we have it the book apparently consists of a series of fragments, written by the author at different times, and put together after his death in a somewhat haphazard fashion. Map himself was born somewhere on the Welsh Border about the middle of the century and after studying at Paris obtained preferment at the English court, eventually becoming Archdeacon of Oxford in 1197 and dying early in

---

[1] Edited by M. R. James in *Anecdota Oxoniensia* (London 1914). Two good translations into modern English exist, one by M. R. James in the Cymmrodorion Record Series ix, and another by F. Tupper and M. B. Ogle (London 1924).

the following century. His book is one of the most
entertaining of all mediæval writings ; it begins as a satire
on the court, but there is no real plan and it is simply an
attack on the various abuses of the time, illustrated with
equal facility by quotations from the Bible or the classics
and by illustrative stories from history and folk-tale. That
is the real interest of the book. It is full of tales drawn
from all kinds of sources, from history, from legend, and
above all from the folk-lore of both English and Welsh ; we
owe to him, for example, the only tale of Wade which has
survived in England. Map is a good hater and his command
of vigorous invective is well displayed whenever he has
occasion to refer to the court, to women, to the Cistercians
—a particularly bitter subject with him—or to Jews. In
addition his various references to contemporary figures,
especially his description of Henry II and his sons, afford
valuable information such as is not found elsewhere. A
similar and almost as interesting collection of folk-lore,
history and legend, though with a rather larger admixture of
politics and geography, is contained in the *Otia Imperialia*
written for the emperor Otto IV by Gervase of Tilbury, a
younger contemporary of Map and the author of other
similar and religious works.

Giraldus Cambrensis,[1] or Gerald de Barri, was descended
on one side from the royal families of Wales and on the other
from some of the greatest of the Norman lords of the Welsh
marches. The greater part of his life was spent in a vain
struggle for the independence of the Welsh church in which,
despite his failure, he had the consolation of knowing that
his opponents recognized his undoubted ability too well to
allow him to succeed his uncle as bishop of St David's.

[1] For full accounts of Giraldus Cambrensis see H. Owen, *Gerald
the Welshman* (London 1904) ; F. M. Powicke, ' Gerald of Wales '
(*Bulletin of the John Rylands Library* xii, 389), and H. E. Butler,
The Autobiography of Giraldus Cambrensis (London 1937).

Most of our knowledge of him comes from his own works, nor did any false modesty prevent him from allowing his readers to realize that he recognized in himself one of the most brilliant intellects of a brilliant century, an opinion for which he had considerable justification. Educated at Paris he acquired there a genuine love for literature which sustained him in the continued defeat of his ambitions. He became Archdeacon of Brecon in 1176 and a royal chaplain in 1184, in which capacity he accompanied Prince John on his journey to Ireland. Four years later he accompanied Baldwin of Canterbury on a mission preaching the crusade through Wales and he does not forget to inform us of the popularity and miraculous effects of his own oratory. In 1198 the bishopric of St David's fell vacant for a second time, but after a five years' fight, though supported by the chapter, he was compelled finally to resign his old ambition, and occupied himself with literature until his death somewhere about 1223.

Giraldus was a voluminous writer, his earliest works, apart from youthful poems, being the *Topographia Hibernica* and the *Expugnatio Hibernica*, material for which he had gathered during his visit to that country and in the conquest of which many of his kindred had taken a leading part. The former of these enjoyed a unique publication by being read aloud at Oxford in three successive sessions by the author himself. We may find the instantaneous popularity which he claims for it more credible when we read further that he provided splendid feasts at each of the public recitals. Not that its success need have depended entirely on this; it really is an interesting work and to it we owe much of our knowledge of mediæval Ireland. In it Giraldus shows himself to have been an acute observer with a keen and inquisitive mind. But he is one of the most credulous of authors, willing to repeat any flight of imagination so long as it makes a good story, and with an even lower opinion, if possible, of

4

the Irish than he has of any other race. The *Expugnatio* is a much more critical work. Though he has hardly made the most of his unique opportunities it still remains one of the most important of our sources for the conquest of Ireland. The two books which resulted from his Welsh journey, the *Itinerarium Kambriae* and the *Descriptio Kambriae*, are full of the same kind of interest as the *Topographia*. There is the same fondness for irrelevant digression, but his love for marvels is kept within reasonable bounds. As a patriotic Welshman he naturally makes the most of the country and its people, though he is not too prejudiced to acknowledge their faults—and no doubt felt a justifiable glow of pride at his own impartiality. The favourite amongst his many writings was the *Gemma Ecclesiastica*, a copy of which he presented to the Pope. It was written for the instruction of the Welsh clergy, and he reinforces his teaching by numerous illustrations of their ignorance and of the vices of the monks, subjects which he developed still further in the *Speculum Ecclesiae*, for he shared to the full the dislike of his friend Walter Map for monks.

These are only the more important of Giraldus' works; others of them such as the *Libellus Invectionum*—an attack on his old enemy, Hubert of Canterbury, which one imagines he thoroughly enjoyed writing—his autobiography *De Rebus a se Gestis* and the *De Instructione Principis*, are often equally entertaining but can only be mentioned here. Giraldus is always an interesting writer, with a love for illustrative stories, a weakness for amusing and occasionally valuable digression, and a command of vituperative Latin which is remarkable, even for the twelfth century. Granted he was vain, garrulous and careless of accuracy, but his vanity, however it may have annoyed his contemporaries, only adds to his charm for the modern reader. With all his faults he was one of the most learned of a learned age, and, if he was unable to view the controversies of the time with an unprejudiced eye, he brought to them a keenness of intellect and a readiness of invention which makes him more interesting than many a more impartial observer.

Other twelfth-century scholars worthy of more than the brief note, which is all that is possible here, are Adam du Petit-Pont, a lexicographer in Paris during the early twelfth century and one of the teachers of John of Salisbury, and Peter of Blois, a pupil of the latter into whom he had succeeded in instilling some of his own love for the classics. A more important figure is Alexander Nequam, canon and abbot of Cirencester, a voluminous author who distinguished himself at Paris and Oxford, dying in 1217. Judging from the numerous stories told of him he seems to have impressed his contemporaries, and certainly he had considerable influence on later English thought, both in arts and theology. His numerous writings in verse and prose include fables, popular science and scriptural commentary. Probably the most characteristic and certainly the best-known of his works, the *De Naturis Rerum*,[1] consists of two books of moralized science and three of scriptural commentary, including numerous anecdotes of animals and an attack on the methods of teaching logic at Paris.

During the thirteenth century the chief interest in the literary history of the period centres in the friars. The small parties of Dominican and Franciscan friars who arrived destitute in England in 1221 and 1224 set on foot a movement whose success surprised even themselves. Within a generation of their arrival the English branch of the Franciscan order comprised six wardenries containing forty-nine foundations, with Scotland as a separate province.[2] But success brought prosperity; the original strictness of the

---

[1] Of especial interest here in that it seems to have been used extensively by the author of the *Owl and the Nightingale*.

[2] The early history of the Franciscans is fully dealt with by A. G. Little, *Studies in English Franciscan History* (Manchester 1917).

rule was relaxed and, despite the constant reforms of the superiors, the order degenerated rapidly. Nevertheless they long remained popular, and certainly performed a great service in England by their missions to the poor and the part which they took in the development of popular preaching. Recruited from the educated classes the Franciscans at an early date disregarded the prohibition of St Francis and began to emulate the learning of the Dominicans. One of the earliest of the English convents was that founded in Oxford where Agnellus, the first of the English provincials, founded a lectureship which he persuaded Grosseteste, then Master of the Schools, to undertake. Robert Grosseteste,[1] Bishop of Lincoln, was not himself a Franciscan, but his relations with the English Franciscans were so close, and he himself influenced them so greatly, that he is better dealt with here. He was born of a poor Suffolk family somewhere about 1170, and is said to have received his first schooling at Lincoln, afterwards studying at Oxford. By 1221 he had become Magister Scolarum, but later resigned most of his preferments and became master of the Franciscan school. He was elected Bishop of Lincoln in 1235 and died twenty years later. His numerous writings include theological and philosophical works, commentaries on the Scriptures, an allegorical poem in French, and translations into English of practical works on husbandry. Few scholars have exerted a greater influence on succeeding literature, though today he is overshadowed by his greater pupil Roger Bacon. He wrote in English, French and Latin, and knew Greek and Hebrew as well, the beginnings of Greek learning at Oxford being due to him. It was from Grosseteste that Bacon received his training in the sciences, as he gratefully records. 'No one,' he says, 'knew the sciences save Lord Robert, Bishop of Lincoln, from his length of life and experience,

---

[1] See F. S. Stevenson, *Robert Grosseteste, Bishop of Lincoln* (London 1899).

and studiousness and industry, and because he knew mathematics and optics, and was able to know all things ; and he knew enough of the languages to understand the saints and philosophers of antiquity ' ; nor was Bacon accustomed to praise anyone unduly. There can be no doubt that Grosseteste was one of the foremost scholars of his time, though to-day he is of more interest because of his influence on his successors than because of his own writings. In addition he occupied an important position as patriot, statesman and reformer, struggling against the interference of the papacy. Even the monks, though they resented his reforming zeal, recognized his greatness and, in the person of Matthew Paris, paid tribute to his piety, fearlessness and ability.

The first of the Franciscans to become lector to the convent at Oxford was Adam Marsh, a friend of Grosseteste and a scholar whose attainments were warmly praised by Bacon. His Letters show him to have been a competent Latinist and one whose advice was valued by people of widely differing outlook, but his remaining extant works give no special indication of the qualities attributed to him by his traditional title of Doctor Illustris. The claims of the Doctor Irrefragabilis, Alexander of Hales, are more evident, though Roger Bacon did not think very highly of him. He was the first of the Franciscans to become doctor of theology at Paris, the author of the first *Summa Theologiae*, and the first of the schoolmen to show full acquaintance with the works of Aristotle. But the greatest of the Franciscans, and undoubtedly the greatest scholar of the century, was the Doctor Mirabilis, Roger Bacon (1214–92).[1] A student of linguistics, mathematics, astronomy, optics, chemistry, and an advocate of the experimental method in science, he was in many

---

[1] Bacon's achievements in the different branches of knowledge are summed up authoritatively in *Roger Bacon Commemoration Essays*, ed. A. G. Little (Oxford 1914).

respects far ahead of his times, though in others, as for example in his subordination of the sciences to theology, he was but too closely bound up with them.[1]   His life was a tragedy spent in struggling vainly against the stranglehold of the scholastics, a contest embittered by his own violence, intellectual arrogance and scathing criticism.   His caustic contempt for contemporary scholarship made him many enemies, and their success condemned him to a silence which must have seemed to him the cruellest of punishments.   He was born in England and studied at Oxford under Grosseteste, from whom he derived his interest in languages and love of science.   His scientific studies were continued in Paris under Peter de Marincourt, an experimental scientist of whom he had a great opinion, but by 1250 he was again in Oxford. Soon afterwards he came under the suspicion of his superiors, was removed to Paris and kept under supervision, condemned to a silence from which he only escaped on the receipt of a letter in 1266 from Pope Clement IV asking for copies of his works.   Unfortunately Clement died in 1271, and under his successor, a strict Franciscan, Bacon's attacks on the vices of the clergy and on the obscurantism of the scholastics soon got him into trouble again.   In 1277 he was condemned to an imprisonment which may have lasted until his death somewhere about 1292.

Despite the difficulties of imprisonment and continual suspicion under which he laboured Bacon was a voluminous writer, the best known of his works being the *Opus Maius*, *Opus Tertium*, *Compendium Studii Philosophiae* and a Greek grammar.   The first of these, his most important work and written at the request of the Pope, consists of seven parts of unequal length.   It begins with an account of the chief causes of the errors which he found in contemporary scholarship, and passes on to the relation of science and theology.

[1] Though it must be remembered that by the mediæval scholar Theology was always accounted Queen of the Sciences.

The third part is concerned with languages, the fourth with mathematics, astronomy and geography, and the fifth with optics. Part VI deals with experimental science and Part VII with moral philosophy. Much the same ground is covered with more or less detail in others of his writings. Throughout his life Bacon's object was the pursuit of knowledge, a pursuit which he maintained despite all the hardships and persecution which he suffered. He was perhaps the most outstanding genius of the Middle Ages, the earliest of the natural philosophers of the West and in the knowledge of science centuries ahead of his time. He revived the study of mathematics, accomplished a considerable advance in optics, and was a notable linguist. Occasionally in his writings he shows a distortion and confusion of method due to his inability to free himself entirely from the conventions of his day, but on the whole the originality and insight displayed is amazing. Moreover, great as he was as an original thinker, he was even greater as a synthesizer of the knowledge of the period. Bacon left no disciples to carry on his work ; he was as lonely in death as he had been in life and his true greatness was hardly recognized until two centuries later.

The last of the great Franciscans of the thirteenth century is John Duns Scotus,[1] the Doctor Subtilis. Little is known of his life ; born in Scotland somewhere about 1270 he was educated at Oxford and passed the greater part of his life there as a student and teacher. In 1307 he was at Paris where he became a Doctor, and died a somewhat mysterious death at Cologne in the following year. Like Bacon, but with better fortune, he attacked the work of Aquinas, with such success indeed that the scholastics of the following generation were divided into Scotists and Thomists. A man of wide knowledge and acute philosophical insight, a master of theology, philosophy, astronomy and mathematics, he

[1] C. R. S. Harris, *Duns Scotus* (Oxford 1927).

nevertheless represents the beginning of the end of the scholastic system. Lacking his powers his disciples turned his subtlety into sophistry and scholasticism deteriorated into hair-splitting technicalities.

Bartholomew Anglicus was a Franciscan whose popularity arose from a totally different type of work. His most important book, the *De Proprietatibus Rerum*,[1] is an immense encyclopaedia of mediæval science which was finished about 1250. It remained popular throughout the Middle Ages and was translated into English during the following century by John of Trevisa. The material is gathered from all kinds of sources, ancient and modern, from the standard authorities, from personal observation, and from such typically mediæval sources as the bestiaries and lapidaries. Today it is exceptionally valuable for the light which it throws on the scientific beliefs and legends of the Middle Ages, and many of the mediæval fables perpetuated by later writers appear in Bartholomew's compendious work.

Although the most important scholars of thirteenth-century England were Franciscans that order by no means enjoyed a monopoly of learning. In France the Dominicans were supreme and the followers of St Francis could produce no one to compete with the two great Dominicans, Albertus Magnus and St Thomas Aquinas. In England too the order produced theologians of importance such as Robert Bacon (d. 1248), Richard Fisacre (d. 1248) and Robert Kylwardby (d. 1279), Archbishop of Canterbury. From the older monastic orders and from the secular clergy came a number of capable scholars, many of them of considerable importance in their own time, and some who are of interest even today. Of these mention may be made of Stephen Langton, theologian and historian, but more famous today as statesman and diplomat; Simon Langton, archdeacon of Canterbury,

---

[1] R. Steele's *Medieval Lore* (London 1893) consists of translated extracts from Bartholomew's work.

likewise of some importance as a theologian, but better known as the diplomatic representative of his more famous brother ; Archbishop Edmund Rich (d. 1240), perhaps better known as St Edmund of Abingdon, the author of much devotional literature, both in Latin and in French, some of which was exceptionally popular in later times ; Odo of Cheriton (d. 1247), the author of a number of didactic and religious pieces including commentaries on the scriptures, collections of fables and numerous *exempla* ; John of Garland (d. *circa* 1260), professor at Paris and a competent classical scholar, was the author of a wide variety of works both in prose and in verse.

Of the Latin verse written during this period probably the best, whether religious or secular, is the occasional verse, hymns, satires and lyrics, which are usually anonymous.[1] Many of the writers already mentioned were the authors of verse works as well as prose, but it is usually on their prose works that their fame rests. The earliest of the Anglo-Latin poets was probably Reginald of Canterbury, who, though born in France, crossed to England sometime before 1092 and spent the remainder of his life at St Augustine's, Canterbury. He was an industrious and ingenious versifier, composing a long poem on the life of the hermit Malchus, and numerous shorter works of a personal nature. Lawrence of Durham, always a readable and pleasant poet, was responsible for the *Hypognosticon*, a versification of scriptural material, and for some more interesting poetic dialogues directed against the Scotch intruder William Cumin, who had attempted to possess himself of the see of Durham. His *Consolatio de Morte Amici* is a mixture of prose and

---

[1] On Mediæval Latin poetry see especially F. J. E. Raby, *A History of Christian-Latin Poetry* (Oxford 1927), and *A History of the Secular Latin Poetry* (Oxford 1934) by the same author ; for the Goliardic poetry see H. Waddell, *The Wandering Scholars* (6th edn. London 1932).

verse in imitation of Boethius, and in it he shows some skill in the use of lyric metres. But probably the most important of the twelfth-century writers of personal verse is Serlo of Wilton, a friend of Walter Map and known to Giraldus. In fact the latter has a characteristic anecdote in which he tells how his youthful beauty once struck Serlo with amazement. In his youth he wrote a number of secular poems many of which are surprisingly original and, though the morality is frequently questionable, the technical achievement is remarkable. However, he underwent a conversion which later became one of the most popular of the mediæval *exempla*. A dead friend, a logician, appeared to him from the fires of purgatory and touched him with a scorching finger as a foretaste of the everlasting flames of hell. Serlo joined the Cistercians, eventually becoming Abbot of L'Aumône, and henceforth occupied himself with didactic and religious poems. Here too mention may be made of the Englishman Hilarius, a pupil of Abaelard, whose verse plays give him a more important place in the history of the drama than his somewhat pedestrian lyrics can claim for him in that of poetry. Giraldus Cambrensis and Walter Map are also responsible for a certain amount of verse of the kind fashionable in their youth, and many of the Goliardic poems have been at various times attributed to the latter.

These Goliardic poems are a typical product of the twelfth century, when a mass of poetry was being produced, mainly satiric and lyric, which modelled itself closely on, and often actually parodied, the lyric poetry of the church. But it concerned itself, not with religion, but with the more worldly delights, and with the satirizing of the vices and corruptions of ecclesiastics, taking its name from a certain Bishop Golias, the personification of the evil and worldly prelate. The authors are usually unknown, wandering scholars roaming from university to university in search of knowledge, claiming the privilege of clergy but escaping from its restraints.

The poetry which they produced is probably the most interesting of all mediæval Latin poetry to the modern reader. It has as a rule a wonderful freshness and lyric quality, and the authors show surprising technical skill and ease of mastery in the handling of complicated metres and rhyme schemes. It is fairly certain that Walter Map was not the author of any of these extant poems—the attribution was presumably due mainly to his oft-expressed hatred for the monks—but it is equally certain that many of them were composed in twelfth-century England. Probably the best known of such satirical poems is the *Apocalypse of Golias* in which the author dreams that he meets with Pythagoras and with him passes to another world where he finds Aristotle, Cicero, Lucan, and most of the great Latin poets. An angel then appears with seven candles, and the remainder of the poem, which contains some 400 odd lines in all, is taken up with a fierce attack on the seven orders of the clergy from the Pope downwards. This, however, is only one of a number of similar works which have been preserved, on such themes as the greed of the higher clergy, the duplicity of the monks and the corruption of the Roman Curia.

It is probable that many of the anonymous poems on such subjects which are preserved in English manuscripts were actually written in this country, though naturally any kind of certainty is impossible. However, there was a considerable amount of satirical Latin poetry produced in England during the twelfth century by known authors. Godfrey of Cambrai, Prior of St. Swithin's, Winchester, and Henry of Huntingdon composed epigrams in the style of Martial. John of Salisbury, better known for his prose writings, composed also an elegiac poem, *Entheticus de Dogmate Philosophorum*, which covers much the same ground as his *Metalogicus*, deriding the claims of the new learning and attacking the abuses of the time. But the greatest of the satirical poets is Nigel Wireker, precentor of Christ Church, whose *Speculum Stultorum* is directed against the usual objects of mediæval satire—scholars, ecclesiastics and monks. It is a long elegiac poem on the adventures of the ass Brunellus, a satire on the ambitious monk as he is careful to explain in the preface. Brunellus, desiring a longer tail, consults Galen and is sent off to Salerno with a prescription for it. On the way he is so plundered by thieves that he loses even half of the small tail which he already has. Being ashamed to return home he joins the English ' nation ' at Paris, and after seven years has learned only to say ' ya ', something which he knew before he joined the University. He then tries all the monastic orders in turn, meets Galen again, and with him discusses the general corruption of society. Finally his old master reappears and claims him and Brunellus thereupon returns to his former life. This is one of the most interesting of the mediæval Latin poems. Nigel writes clearly and entertainingly and he has taken pains to make his satire, though fairly obvious, not too offensive to the objects of his attack. Inside the main framework of the story are digressions and illustrative tales of all kinds, and from widely different sources, such as delighted the contemporary reader. It is not surprising that his poem immediately became, and long remained, popular.

A more pretentious, but much less interesting, work is the *Architrenius* of John de Hanville, a long allegorical poem in hexameters, badly constructed and written in a somewhat obscure style. The hero, a young man, laments his wasted life and goes in search of Nature for a remedy. On his way, having visited the palace of Venus and the hall of Gluttony, he arrives in Paris and comments satirically on the life and studies of the students. He reaches the mount of Ambition, inhabited by kings and courtiers, the hill of Presumption, a haunt of monks, and finally finds Nature who, by the gift of Moderation as a bride, remedies all his troubles.

Alexander Nequam was probably the most popular of the

twelfth-century didactic writers. His long elegiac poem, *De Laudibus Divinae Sapientiae*, covers much the same ground as his prose *De Naturis Rerum*, and in addition he produced two books of versified fables, the *Novus Aesopus* and the *Novus Avianus*. Nequam uses the elegiac couplet skilfully and was competent enough as a composer of rhythmical verses. In his scientific works he was essentially a popularizer rather than an original thinker, and edification is as much his object as is the imparting of information. Nothing is known of Geoffrey de Vinsauf except that he was an Englishman who visited Rome and composed his *Poetria Nova* somewhere about the year 1210. A number of other poems have also been attributed to him but the evidence is inconclusive. The *Poetria Nova*, a technical handbook on the art of poetry, though it deals only with hexameter verse, was one of the most popular works of its type during the Middle Ages and is well known from Chaucer's ironic reference to it in the Nun's Priest's Tale.[1] Actually it is simply a treatise on rhetoric as applied to poetry, concerning itself with the different ways of beginning a poem, methods of amplification and abbreviation, ornaments of style, etc., with examples of his own composition.

Epic poetry does not seem to have been in any great favour amongst the Anglo-Latin writers, and only two authors of such poetry are known. Geoffrey of Monmouth, in addition to his *Historia Regum Britanniae*, composed an epic of some 1,500 hexameter lines on the life of Merlin. In it he displays all the fondness for anecdotal digression so characteristic of the contemporary historians. Though the

[1] F. N. Robinson, *The Complete Works of Geoffrey Chaucer* (Oxford), p. 244, lines 3347 ff. But see *Troilus and Criseyde* i, 1065 and note. Professor Dickins also compares *Troilus and Criseyde* v, 813–14, ' And, save hire browes joyneden yfere, Ther nas no lak, in aught I kan espien ', with Geoffrey de Vinsauf lines 565–7 ' vaccinia nigra coaequet/forma supercilii : geminos intersecet arcus/lactea forma viae '.

material is not very well arranged, it is at any rate a welcome change from the eternal weak imitations of the classics and the conventional moralizings which are so frequent. The second of the epic poets is Joseph of Exeter, one of the ablest of the many brilliant men who were gathered together round Archbishop Baldwin of Canterbury. He accompanied him on the crusade, but after his death returned to England to compose an epic, the *Antiocheis*, on the deeds of Richard I, of which nothing remains today except two fragments preserved by Camden. He seems also to have composed a panegyric on Henry II and a versified *Cyropaedia*, but the only complete work of his which has survived, and on which his fame rests, is the *De Bello Troiano*,[1] an epic in six books based mainly on Dares. It is an extraordinary production in which he displays a wide knowledge of the classics and a true appreciation of the epic form. He had all the characteristics of the rhetorical epic at his fingers' end, was a competent versifier and possessed of an inexhaustible inventiveness. He had soaked himself thoroughly in the atmosphere of his ancient models and was no mere imitator of the classics, but one who had made himself completely master both of his language and of his material. Perhaps too much so ; he has not learned to carry his learning lightly and is apt to display it somewhat ostentatiously, so that there is a certain ponderousness about it all which impresses, rather than charms, the reader. For all that his attainments and success are considerable and he has a unique place in the literature of the period.

The political struggles of the thirteenth century had their effects on the Latin poetry of the period. A great deal of verse, almost invariably anonymous, celebrated the victory of the baronial party under Simon de Montfort. After his

---

[1] Joseph of Exeter's work seems to have had great influence on Chaucer, see especially *Troilus and Criseyde* v, 799 ff, and the notes to them in Robinson's edition.

death he was venerated as a saint, an office was composed for his commemoration, and hymns compared his death with the martyrdom of St Thomas of Canterbury. Similarly the enthusiasm aroused by the coming of the friars had its effects on the religious verse, and, just as the greatest scholars of the century were Franciscans, so the greatest religious poet was also a follower of St Francis. John of Garland, in addition to such didactic works as a versified *Accentuarium* and the *Exempla Honestae Vitae*, composed also a number of religious poems. The longest and most important of these, the *De Triumphis Ecclesiae*, is valuable for its references to contemporary events, but the theme is obscured by numerous irrelevant and uninteresting digressions, and the poem as a whole betrays a painful lack of any sense of form or structure. The best of his poetic works are probably some of his sequences, but it must be admitted that neither his didactic nor his religious poetry has anything to raise it above the general level of mediocrity. Fortunately thirteenth-century England had better religious poets than he; indeed, it is possible that one of the greatest of the sequences, *Veni, sancte Spiritus*, the Golden Sequence, may have been the work of Stephen Langton, though there are other claimants. In any case a more important figure than John of Garland in this field of literature is his namesake John of Hoveden, who died about 1290 leaving behind him the reputation of a saint. He was the author of much religious verse, celebrating more especially the praise of the Virgin. On the whole he is rather disappointing and seems to promise something more than he ever succeeds in accomplishing. Probably the best of his works, the *Philomena*, a poem on the Passion, is apt to be confused with a work of the same name and on the same subject by his contemporary John Peckham, a much greater artist and one of the greatest of the mediæval religious poets. John Peckham was born about 1230 and studied at Oxford and under Bonaventura at Paris. He became lector at Oxford in 1270, Provincial of the English Franciscans five years later, and was appointed Archbishop of Canterbury in 1279, which office he held until his death in 1292. His greatest work, the *Philomena*, is a purely lyrical poem on the Passion in which the death of the nightingale signifies the pious soul living through a mystical day, the hours of which correspond with the stages of man's redemption. It is one of the best expressions of the spirit of personal devotion to Christ which was typical of the early Franciscans. In it the devotional fervour of the author is expressed with consummate poetic skill. He wrote, too, other religious poems none of which, despite their frequent excellencies, can be compared with the *Philomena*, ' one of the loveliest of all the poems of the Passion '.

III

THE ANGLO-FRENCH BACKGROUND

THE third, and in some respects the most important, of
the literary languages in use in this country during the
twelfth and thirteenth centuries was Anglo-French.[1] This
is the literary language which developed from the spoken
speech of the conquerors, a language based mainly on
Norman-French but with an admixture of forms and words
from other French dialects, from English and from Flemish.
It was natural enough that it should influence, and be influenced by, English, and it was also inevitable that non-
Norman characteristics should make their way into it. In
the first place the army which William led at Hastings, and
which received its full share of English manors after the
victory, was far from being a purely Norman array. William
had realized that the strength of Normandy alone was too
weak for the conquest of England, and some of his barons,
distrusting the project, took small share in it. No doubt
the main strength of the army consisted in the Norman
magnates and their followers, but to them had been added
adventurers from the greater part of France and from some
of the surrounding countries, urged on by the blessing of

[1] For a fuller treatment of the history of Anglo-French literature
see J. Vising, *Anglo-Norman Language and Literature* (London
1923) ; E. Walberg, *Quelques aspects de la Littérature Anglo-
Normande* (Paris 1936) ; U. T. Holmes, *A History of Old French
Literature* (New York 1937).

the pope against the perjured usurper Harold Godwinesson, and still more by their hope for a share in the riches of England. Moreover many of the later French immigrants were from other French provinces than Normandy, and the Angevin empire of the Plantagenets would lead to the introduction of other non-Norman elements into the language. Nevertheless, so long as Normandy remained a part of the English dominion, the connexion between the two countries remained close and the dialects developed along much the same lines, so much so that it is often difficult to distinguish between texts written in Normandy and those written in England. But though this is true of the written language the well-known reference of Walter Map to ' Marlborough French ' suggests that already the spoken language is following its own line of development. In any case the loss of Normandy in 1204 inevitably led to the isolation of Anglo-French. The immediate results of that event were probably beneficial to the dialect since it led to the settlement in England of numbers of Normans and Poitevins who were not prepared to accept the new conditions, or who preferred their broad English lands to their narrower Norman estates. This was the last extensive influx of Norman-speaking Frenchmen, later influences being rather from the southern and central French dialects. There is a definite separation between Norman and Anglo-French, and henceforth the latter develops along its own lines. The period of its flourishing was brief, and its gradual decline seems to have started soon after the middle of the thirteenth century. This is usually reckoned as one of the consequences of the outburst of national feeling aroused by the French favourites of Henry III, when a coalition of the English lower and middle classes, led by the descendants of the old Norman aristocracy, resulted in the expulsion of the French, and in the consequent encouragement of English. No doubt, too, the increasing cultural importance of the central French dialects contributed largely to the decay of Anglo-French, which, during the fourteenth century, comes to be regarded rather as the language of the country gentleman and of the lawyer than as the language of the court and of society.

The literary language, then, used by French writers in England is, in the earlier period, characterized mainly by the dialectal forms of Normandy, and as time goes on it is also recognizable by an increasing unfamiliarity with the idiom among writers, and especially among scribes. The earliest extant works written in it probably date from the first quarter of the twelfth century, but it is of comparatively little importance before the second half of the same century. At first its main use is in the literature of edification and entertainment ; only very gradually, and comparatively late, does it displace Latin as the language of government. As an official language the Old English of English and early Norman kings is replaced by Latin probably towards the end of the eleventh century, and it was probably a century later before Latin was in turn replaced by Anglo-French. Fourteenth-century writers, indeed, claimed that the Conqueror had ordered that all pleading in the law-courts should be in French, but there is no contemporary evidence for such a statement and it is most improbable. However, once established as the legal language it proved remarkably tenacious. In 1362 an act of parliament ordered that all pleas should be conducted in English, but the act seems to have had little effect, since Fortescue, over a hundred years later, informs us that the judges were still accustomed to conduct legal proceedings in French.[1] Though abolished for a time under Cromwell Anglo-French as a legal language was reintroduced under Charles II, and remained the language of legal record, until

---

[1] Though we may note that there are examples of the quotation of English proverbs in the law-courts towards the end of the thirteenth and the beginning of the fourteenth century ; cf ' Hwo so boleyth myn kyn ewere is the calf myn ', ' Selde erendeth well

its final abolition in 1731. Laws and decrees were drawn up in Anglo-French from the second half of the thirteenth century until the introduction of English under Richard III. English is used for the first time at the opening of parliament in 1363, and it is clear that by this time English as well as French was used in the debates. As the language of the schools French remains in use from the twelfth until the second half of the fourteenth century. The significant change by which instruction was given in English instead of in French is noted in a famous passage by the translator John of Trevisa. Commenting on Higden's statement that the pupils were obliged to learn French and neglect English, he tells us :

This was the custom before the first plague (1348), but things have changed now. For John Cornwall, a schoolmaster, changed the methods of teaching and made his pupils construe into English instead of French ; and Richard Pencrych, and other men of Pencrych, learned that way of teaching from him, so that now (1385) in all the grammar schools of England children have given up French and construe and learn in English.

Many a less important man is better known to English litera- ture than are John Cornwall and Richard Pencrych. But already by 1322 it had been decreed that the students of Oxford should use only French or Latin in conversation, sufficient evidence that their usual language must have been English.

The greatest period of Anglo-French literature is during the thirteenth century. In the twelfth century it is still struggling against the established power of Latin and English, and by the fourteenth century Anglo-French writers are

the lothe and selde pledeth well the wrothe ', ' Bothe thei schellen out of this house benedicite and dominus '. W. C. Bolland, *The Year Books* (Cambridge 1921), pp. 76 ff. With the second of these proverbs compare the *Owl and the Nightingale*, lines 943–4.

already making excuses for their ignorance, the first symptoms of decay. During the intervening period there can be little doubt that in interest and volume writings in Anglo-French are almost as important as those in Latin and much more important than those in English. Not that it displaces either of the others. Latin is still the language of the scholar and of the thinker, and the edification and entertainment of the common people are still carried on in English. But side by side with them a literary language has been developed devoted mainly to the edification and entertainment of the upper classes and of those who aped them.

The greater part of the surviving Anglo-French literature is religious or didactic. This is not surprising since, as was the case with other languages, it was the type of literature which stood the best chance of a written existence and so of subsequent preservation. It consists chiefly in translations from the Latin, compilations of edifying reading, and versified sermons ; however important it may be in other ways, comparatively little of it is of much interest to the modern reader. Translations of parts of the Bible are fairly frequent, the earliest of them, the so-called *Oxford* and *Cambridge Psalters*, being written probably during the first quarter of the twelfth century. The former of these is of interest in that it is said to have remained in use, with some modification, until the sixteenth century. Other biblical books were translated at various times during the period, sometimes into prose, but more frequently into verse. The book of *Proverbs*, always a popular subject, was translated, along with a commentary, into skilful octosyllabic verse during the reign of Stephen by a certain Samson of Nanteuil, of whom we know nothing except that he wrote at the request of Lady Aaliz de Cundé, of Horncastle in Lincolnshire. Anonymous versions are those of the four books of *Kings* translated into prose, but with occasional rhyme, somewhere about 1170. Translations of other books, both canonical and apocryphal, also exist from the thirteenth century. Amongst others are versions of the *Apocalypse* and the *Gospel of Nicodemus*, both works which were remarkably popular in the Middle Ages.

It was not enough, however, to provide translations of the Bible. The chief tenets of the Christian faith also had to be expounded and the result was that there appeared, especially during the thirteenth century, various theological encyclopaedias usually of considerable length but comparatively little interest. Such works, it must be noted, were almost invariably in verse, and verse remains the most popular medium for didactic and religious works throughout the Middle Ages. No doubt in the earlier period, before an Anglo-French prose had been developed, this was inevitable, and there was the added attraction of presenting instruction in a form associated with entertainment. It was an old trick ; in the same way Aldhelm, disguised as a minstrel, had gradually mingled salutary words with the epic lays by which he attracted his audience, and Ælfric had made extensive use of rhythm and alliteration. Old English, however, had early developed a didactic prose and rarely needed to make use of verse for this purpose ; in Anglo-French verse remained popular long after the development of an adequate prose. Amongst others we may note, from the first half of the thirteenth century, the 20,000 verses of the *Evangiles des domnees* by Robert of Gretham, an exposition of the Sunday gospels dedicated to a certain Dame Aline, the wife of Alain. Rather more interesting are the 15,000 lines of the *Lumiere as lais* composed in 1266–7 by Peter of Peckham, also known as Pierre d'Abernum. It is a series of questions and answers on theology based largely on the *Elucidarium* of Honorius of Autun and the *Sententiae* of Peter Lombard. The 11,000 lines of the *Manuel des Pechez* of William of Waddington discuss such subjects as the Commandments, the Creed, and the Seven Deadly Sins ; the work is more interesting than it sounds because the author includes a number of illustrative stories. An English translation, with the addition of further tales, was made early in the following century by Robert Mannyng of Brunne.

More important are the allegorical poems of which the best is probably the *Chasteau d'Amour* of Robert Grosseteste, a poem in praise of the Virgin. In it the castle, the fortifications and its defenders are all allegorized and help to make clear the essential points of the Christian faith—especially those dealing with the Redemption. The poem is a pious, and not unsuccessful, predecessor of the *Roman de la Rose*. In it appears for the first time the allegory of the four daughters of God, Mercy, Truth, Justice and Peace, a theme elaborated by Grosseteste in a later poem to which has been given the title *The Four Daughters of God*. A similar allegorical poem is *Le Char d'Orgueil* by Nicholas Bozon. The author is one of the most mysterious figures in mediæval literature. He seems to have been a voluminous writer both in prose and verse, his works including religious, satirical and lyrical pieces, and collections of *exempla*. We know nothing of him beyond the facts that he was a Franciscan and lived towards the end of the thirteenth century, possibly later. *Le Char d'Orgueil*, directed against the vanity of women, is an allegorical poem of the usual type. Orgueil is the queen of sin and daughter of Lucifer ; all the different parts of the chariot signify different vices, as also the horses, the harness, and even the different parts of their bodies.

Undoubtedly by far the most interesting section of the Anglo-French religious literature is that which deals with the legends of the Church and the lives of the saints. If we are to judge from the comparatively large number of works still extant on these subjects they also found considerable favour amongst contemporary readers. Nor is it surprising ; the best of them are very different from the usually dry and conventional Latin originals on which they are based.

Historically, unless the author is dealing with comparatively modern times, they are usually worthless, and indeed, whatever the supposed period, usually provide vivid descriptions of life during the twelfth and thirteenth centuries. Some of them are as full of incident, and often the same kind of incident, as the romances, and inevitably the fascination of the marvellous is given free play. To a mediæval reader many of them must have possessed all the fascination of the contemporary romances, together with the added attraction of being after all pious reading encouraged by the church. No special type of saint seems to have been particularly popular, all came alike to the Anglo-French versifier—and apparently to his audience too. Saints from the near east, Catherine of Alexandria, Margaret, George, the Seven Sleepers, are found side by side with French saints such as Giles and Faith, English saints, Edmund, Edward, Alban, Osyth, Audrey, and even specifically Celtic saints such as Brendan and Modwenna. Of more historical value are the lives of a group of almost contemporary saints, Thomas Becket, Edmund Rich, and Richard of Chichester. Many of them are anonymous, but of a surprisingly high proportion we know at any rate the name of the author, though that is frequently all that we do know of him. Amongst others we may mention the names of Clemence of Barking (c. 1160), author of a celebrated life of Catherine of Alexandria ; Denis Piramus, who between the years 1170 and 1180 wrote *La Vie seint Edmund le Rei*, in which he makes considerable use of English sources. He may have been identical with the Magister Dionisius mentioned at various times in Jocelin's *Chronicle* as a monk of Bury St Edmunds. The eastern legends were utilized by Chardri in his poems on the *Set dormanz* and *Barlaam et Josaphaz*. Angier, a canon of St Frideswide's at Oxford, translated the *Dialogues of Gregory* in 1212, and a few years afterwards wrote the life of the saint. Henry d'Arci, a Templar of Temple Bruer in

Lincolnshire, wrote a life of Antichrist, a life of Thais, and translated part of the *Vitae Patrum* during the first half of the thirteenth century.

One of the most interesting, and certainly the oldest, of the legends of the saints in Anglo-French is the *Voyage of St Brendan*, written by a certain Beneeit, sometime after 1121, for Aaliz of Louvain, the second wife of Henry I. It is dependent on a ninth-century Latin narrative, the *Navigatio Sancti Brendani*, and tells of the marvels seen by Brendan and his companions during their search for the Earthly Paradise. They see sheep as big as stags, the birds' Paradise, a battle between a dragon and a griffon, Judas Iscariot, and other wonders such as the Middle Ages loved. The whole legend is obviously borrowed from the secular type of Celtic literature known as the *immram*, in which is described a difficult quest by the hero and the various adventures with which he meets by the way, a type which may have been influenced by classical literature. The versification is unique, the poem being written in strophic form, each strophe containing two octosyllabic couplets in which the feminine -*e* is counted as a syllable. In language, versification and interest, there can be no doubt that it is one of the most important of the Anglo-French religious works. Of the remaining lives of the saints the most interesting are probably the *Vie Saint Gilles* of Guillaume de Berneville, possibly Barnwell in Cambridgeshire, written *c.* 1180, and, despite its subject, containing some remarkably vivid descriptions of twelfth-century life and manners, and the life of St Modwenna with its peculiarly Celtic miracles. Some of the others are often interesting, but in them the entertainment takes a minor place and they are essentially pious reading. The lives of some of the modern saints are occasionally of value historically. One of the two extant Anglo-French versions of the life of Becket, that written by Benet of St Albans between the years 1183 and 1189, is interesting in that its source seems to have been a Latin *Vita* by Robert of Cricklade, known otherwise only as one of the sources of the Old Norse *Tómássaga erkibiskups*. Peter of Peckham wrote a life of St Richard of Chichester in 1267–8, and a thirteenth-century life of St. Edmund Rich has been attributed to Matthew Paris, who is also said to have written the lives of saints Alban and Thomas Becket. If the extant versions of these lives are indeed by him they are hardly likely to enhance his reputation, the French being often incorrect and the versification poor.

Visions and legends telling of visits to the otherworld were as common and popular in Anglo-French as in other vernaculars. The *Vision of St Paul* and the *Purgatory of St Patrick* were perhaps the most common of such legends, and from them are derived many of the mediæval ideas of Hell. The former of these, telling how St Paul, accompanied and guided by the archangel Michael, visited Hell, of the sights which he saw there, and of how he obtained from God repose from their torments for the wicked souls on the Sabbath, is Greek in origin but early made its way into the West and became remarkably popular. The subject is dealt with in English in one of the *Lambeth Homilies*, and there are three Anglo-French versions from the thirteenth century. The *Purgatory of St Patrick* derives from a Latin treatise written *c.* 1185 by an English Cistercian, Henry of Saltrey. Whilst St Patrick was preaching in Ireland there was revealed to him the existence of a cave through which it was possible to enter into Purgatory. Henry of Saltrey tells how an Irish knight, Owen, penetrated through this cave to the otherworld, of the torments which he saw there, and of the joys of Paradise of which he was permitted a glimpse. The various Anglo-French versions of these two important texts are not in any way remarkable, the only point worthy of note being that Marie de France was the author of one of the six extant versions, or fragments, of the *Purgatory*.

The earliest Anglo-French writer whose name we know is Philippe de Thaon, the author of various didactic works including a *Cumpoz*, a *Bestiaire*, and probably two *Lapidaires*. We know very little about him personally ; he was presumably a cleric of some kind and he or his family must have come originally from the Norman village of Thaon, near Caen. His earliest work, the *Cumpoz*, is dedicated to his uncle Hunfrei, the chaplain of Eudes, seneschal of Henry I, and various specific references in the text indicate that it was probably written in 1119. It is simply a versified calendar written especially for the clergy, describing the various measures of time, the year and its subdivisions, the determination of the movable feasts of the church, and similar matters. The works of former writers on the subject such as Bede, Gerland and Helperic, are cited, though possibly only at second-hand. The author apparently intended his work, not only as a practical handbook but also as pious reading, since he allegorizes whenever possible, the names of the months, for instance, being given a Christian signification. He uses a six-syllable verse rhyming in couplets, no doubt an excellent aid to the memory, but a metre which the dry and uninteresting style of the poet makes very monotonous. As literature the work is of little value, but linguistically, since it is the oldest extant Anglo-French work, its importance is considerable. The most famous work of Philippe is his *Bestiaire* dedicated to Aaliz of Louvain, and probably written by 1125. It is the earliest translation of the *Physiologus* into a French dialect, but is not otherwise of any special significance. The latter part of it includes a *Lapidaire* in which the author has abandoned his hitherto invariable six-syllable lines for octosyllabic couplets. Two other *Lapidaires*, treatises on the miraculous and symbolical qualities of precious and semi-precious stones, are also attributed to Philippe de Thaon. It was a similar type of literature to the *Bestiary* and like it became extremely popular during the Middle Ages. Most mediæval *Lapidaires* derive ultimately from the Latin poem *De Lapidibus* of Bishop Marbod of Rennes.[1]

Philippe de Thaon is the first writer of Anglo-French didactic literature but he is far from being the last. A number of other *Lapidaires* was produced, as well as various collections of proverbs, the most famous of the latter being the *Disticha Catonis*, a favourite mediæval school-book really composed during the third or fourth century and having nothing to do with Cato the Censor. It was translated into six-syllable couplets by Everard de Kirkham and into octo-syllabic couplets by Elias of Winchester, also by other anonymous writers. There are treatises on medicine, falconry and manners, and prose tracts on Geometry and Geomancy dating from the thirteenth century. The *Disciplina Clericalis*, an important and influential collection of moral stories written by the Spanish Jew, Petrus Alphonsi, was translated into Anglo-French towards the end of the twelfth century. The *Secreta Secretorum*, a book of moral and scientific content composed originally in Syriac during the seventh century but popularly ascribed to Aristotle, was translated by Peter of Peckham, also known as Pierre d'Abernum, a thirteenth-century lawyer and a voluminous writer on religious and didactic subjects. The earliest of the vernacular books on venery is the *Art de Venerie* of Guillaume Twich, written about 1300. More practical is a work on *Husbandry* by Walter of Henley, of whom we know nothing except that he must have lived about the middle of the thirteenth century, seems to have served for a time as a bailiff, and may have been the author of an Anglo-French *Art of Love*.

---

[1] He wrote towards the end of the eleventh century, his principal sources being the Bible, Pliny, Isidore, and a Greek work commonly called the *Damigeron* which had been translated into Latin probably as early as the first century A.D.

As is the case with the Anglo-Latin literature, the most characteristically English productions of the Anglo-French writers are those of the chroniclers and historians. Partly from political reasons, and partly to enhance their own achievements, the Norman conquerors took a lively interest in the history and traditions of their adopted country. This is evident from the way in which Anglo-Saxon traditions were utilized and popularized by Anglo-French poets, and by the comparative importance of the versified histories produced by them. The earliest Anglo-French historian seems to have been a certain David, of whose life we know nothing. He is said to have written the life of Henry I at the request of his widow, Aaliz of Louvain. The work itself, which must have been completed before 1139 since Aaliz was already remarried by that year, is lost, and its former existence is known only from references to it in Gaimar's *Estoire des Engleis*. The latter apparently found the *Life* by David decidedly unsatisfactory. He declares that its descriptions of the dead king's pleasures, his feasts, his hunts, and his various loves, are much too brief; though the last seems rather a strange complaint to make when we consider that the biography had been ordered by Henry's widow. In any case Gaimar announces his intention of rewriting and completing it, though whether he ever carried out his intention we do not know ; if so his work, like his original, has disappeared.

The earliest historical work in Anglo-French which has survived is the *Estoire des Engleis*, composed between 1138 and 1140 by Geoffrey Gaimar. As extant it contains some 6,500 octosyllabic verses, but it is evidently far from complete. We know nothing of the author except what he himself tells us in an epilogue, apparently genuine, which is to be found in one of the four manuscripts in which his poem has been preserved. From it we learn that his work was composed at the request of Custance, wife of Robert

FitzGislebert, who seems to have owned land both in Hampshire and Lincolnshire. Apparently the history started originally with the expedition of the Argonauts and the Trojan war, and amongst the sources were Geoffrey of Monmouth, one of the manuscripts of the *Old English Chronicle*, and other chronicles as yet unidentified.[1] The first part of the work, if indeed it was ever written and there seems no reason for doubting Gaimar's word, has entirely disappeared, a loss which is usually ascribed to the popularity of Wace's *Roman des Bretons*, published soon afterwards and covering practically the same ground. The surviving part of Gaimar's work contains, in the first 800 lines, a version of the Havelok tale, after which the author contents himself with what is essentially a mere paraphrase of the *Old English Chronicle*, relieved occasionally by the insertion of Old English traditions and legends. The *Estoire* ends with the death of Rufus in 1100, just when it might have become an original work of some historical importance.

We know rather more of Wace, perhaps the greatest vernacular chronicler of the century. Strictly speaking he has no place in this chapter since he neither wrote in Anglo-Norman, nor so far as we know spent much of his life in England. Nevertheless his *Roman de Brut* formed the chief source of Laȝamon's *Brut* so that he has an important place in the history of English literature. He was born, probably about the year 1100, on the island of Jersey, and of gentle parents. He was educated at Caen, whence he probably proceeded to Paris, but during the early years of Stephen's reign was back at Caen again employed as a *clerc lisant* and apparently earning his living by the composition of works, mainly devotional, in the vernacular. Only three of these early compositions seem to have survived,

---

[1] Such as *le livere Walter Espec*, a *bon livere de Oxford*, and *de Wassinburc un livere engleis*.

a life of St Nicholas, *La Conception Nostre Dame*, and fragments, known as the Tours fragments, of a life of St Margaret. The first of these, preserved in five manuscripts, seems to have been extremely popular, whilst the second appears to have been propaganda for the establishment of the Feast of the Immaculate Conception in Normandy, a feast which was definitely authorized in 1145. Lives of other saints have also been attributed to him, but with little proof. How long this period lasted we are unable to say ; by 1155 he had completed his translation of Geoffrey of Monmouth's *Historia Regum Britanniae*, the *Geste des Bretons*, or more commonly the *Roman de Brut*. The 15,000 octosyllabic couplets of Wace are rather more than a simple translation of Geoffrey ; he includes material from other sources—the first appearance of the Round Table in Arthurian romance, a subject developed still further by Laȝamon, is due to Wace—and amplifies and abridges his sources whenever he considers it necessary. In addition, by his power of detailed description, he vivifies the whole story considerably ; the various events are described as by an eyewitness, and an emotional colouring is imported into the more sober Latin prose of Geoffrey. As an historian, despite the fact that he uses the most unhistorical of sources, he takes great pains to verify his facts whenever possible. He seems to have visited a good many of the places mentioned in his source ; certainly he made a special visit to the fabled forest of Broceliande and the fountain of Berenton, returning a disillusioned man, ' a fool I went and a fool I returned ', as he tells us.[1]

The popularity of Wace's *Roman de Brut* seems to have been immediate, and may have led to his being commissioned by Henry II and Queen Eleanor in 1160 to write a verse chronicle of the Dukes of Normandy from Rolf down to his own times. The first 700 lines of the resulting work were

[1] But this episode comes from the *Roman de Rou*.

written in octosyllabic couplets, but the author then changed to monorhymed *laisses*. After about 5,000 of these he ceased work, giving lack of financial support as his reason, and addressed to Henry and Eleanor a short poem of some 300 lines giving a brief survey of his work, afterwards inserted in his chronicle as the *Chronique ascendante*. The purpose of this was obviously to secure funds, an object in which it seems to have been successful, since this was probably the period when Wace received a canonry at Bayeux. At any rate he resumed his work, reverting to the original octo-syllabic couplets, and occupying some eight or nine years in completing another 12,000 lines. This seems to have been too slow for the king and he turned to a more facile writer, a certain Maistre Beneeit (possibly Benoit de Sainte-More), whom he commissioned to write the whole work anew. As soon as he was superseded in the royal favour Wace seems to have lost all interest in his work and he never finished it. Consequently the *Roman de Rou* ends with a description of the battle of Tinchebrai, just when Wace's habits of patient investigation might have made him an invaluable historical source. Even as things are his work is often of interest historically, especially when he treats of the invasion of England by the Normans, an event which is dealt with in great detail. He is not satisfied to depend entirely on his written sources ; he verifies them whenever possible and adds to them from popular tradition. He is always a careful and conscientious worker, and though his work may rarely rise to any great height, it equally rarely falls below a high level of accomplishment. He is a careful versifier, occasionally dull but never slovenly. In his works there is little of that lyrical quality which was being developed by contemporary French poets, but he is a master of vivid and imaginative description. We know nothing of the later years of his life, not even the date of his death, which seems to have taken place somewhere about 1184.

Neither Gaimar nor Wace, nor even Wace's rival, Maistre Beneeit, ever got as far as their own times, but there were Anglo-French historians who dealt with contemporary events in which they themselves had taken a part. The earliest of such works which has survived is the *Chronicle* of Jordan Fantosme, a learned clerk who, in his youth, had studied under the famous Gilbert de la Porrée. He became Chancellor of the Cathedral Chapter of Winchester during the episcopacy of Henry de Blois, brother of King Stephen, and after the death of the bishop in 1171 he seems to have been employed by Henry II. In 1173 Henry and Richard, the sons of the king, in alliance with the kings of France and Scotland and with the Count of Flanders, revolted against their father. During July of the following year William of Scotland was surprised and captured by loyal barons whilst ravaging in Northumberland. Fantosme seems to have accompanied the English troops who had been sent North against the Scots, and in a poem of some 2,000 lines he describes the principal events of the campaign. Judged from the versification he was far from being a great poet, but he has succeeded in presenting the course of events in a lively and picturesque fashion. His chronicle was obviously composed soon after the events which he describes had taken place, certainly before the death of the Young King Henry in 1183 since he is spoken of as still alive. It is one of the best of our historical sources for the events of the war with Scotland in 1173–4.

Another important source for contemporary events is the *Rei Dermot*, or *Conqueste d'Irlande*. It was apparently composed about 1226 by some unknown author who seems to have received his information from Maurice Regan, the interpreter of Dermot, King of Leinster, and a witness of the events described. It has survived only in a single manuscript of which both the beginning and the end have been lost. The poem is of little literary value, but

6

historically it is of considerable importance since it, and the *Expugnatio Hibernica* of Giraldus, provide practically the only contemporary sources for our knowledge of the conquest of Ireland.

Equally important historically, and much better as literature, is *L'Histoire de Guillaume le Maréchal*, the biography of William Marshal, Earl of Pembroke and regent of England during the minority of Henry III. Its 19,000 lines of octosyllabic verse have been preserved in a single manuscript, and the epilogue informs us that the work was undertaken at the request of the Earl Marshal's eldest son by an author who was probably a professional trouvère. It seems to have been completed somewhere about 1226, and the author, who claims to have been present at some of the events which he describes, informs us that it is based mainly on the memoirs of John of Earley, the squire of the Earl Marshal from 1186 onwards. Consequently from that date until the death of the Earl in 1219 we have a first-class historical work based on the account of an eye-witness, and, though the earlier period is vaguer, the author freely confessing to a lack of accurate knowledge, it still contains much of value. The author was more concerned with giving a faithful presentation of his material than in attempting any literary graces, and formally the work is rather a succession of connected episodes than a perfect whole. For all that he possessed a clear and straightforward style, was a very competent poet, and had a remarkable gift for the delineation of character. The Marshal is the only one of whom he attempts a full-length picture, but he had a quick eye for the essential characteristics of other important figures who occur in his narrative such as Stephen, Henry II, the Young King, Richard, John and Philip Augustus. Other thirteenth-century historical works of comparatively little importance are the prose *Livere de reis de Britannie et le livere de reis de Engletere* of Peter of Ickham, a monk of Christ Church,

Canterbury, who died *c.* 1289, and a continuation of 1,200 verses which was added to Wace's *Brut* by an unknown author about the middle of the century.

The works of the historians form a connecting link between the religious and didactic productions and the literature of entertainment. Though the greater part of the extant Anglo-French literature is of a pious or didactic nature we cannot assume from this that such was the favourite literature of the upper classes. The fact that the most popular section of the edifying reading seems to have been the lives of the saints—the nearest approach of the church to romance—is probably significant. But didactic and religious works were those which stood the best chance of preservation and, though undoubtedly the volume of such literature was great, it is probable that the comparative scarcity of a lighter and more secular literature is due rather to the accidents of a later loss of texts than to any specifically serious or pious strain inherent in the Norman race.

If we accept the theories of a propagandist and monastic origin it is not perhaps surprising that the ' Matter of France ' should have received no addition in Anglo-French.[1] Certainly there was no lack of interest in the theme, and no active hostility towards a specifically French hero, since romances on the subject by continental authors were read and copied in this country. The best manuscript of the *Chanson de Roland*, the most famous of all the chansons de gestes, was written in England between 1130 and 1150 and is still preserved at Oxford. Versions of the *Chanson de Guillaume*, the *Pèlerinage de Charlemagne*, and others, were copied in England, but the only example of a chanson de geste written in Anglo-French is the *Amis et Amilun*, a story which essentially has nothing to do with the Charlemagne legend, but has been very superficially attached to it by the author.

[1] On the origins of the Charlemagne romances see p. 199.

It seems to have been written towards the end of the twelfth or the beginning of the thirteenth century, contains just over 1,200 lines of octosyllabic couplets, and is a relatively short version of a well-known romance of friendship. Amis and Amilun are two friends who pledge themselves to help each other at all times. The former of them, having seduced the daughter of his overlord, is accused by the steward. The truth of the charge makes it impossible for Amis to defend himself in the ensuing trial by battle and his life is saved by Amilun, who impersonates his friend and succeeds in killing the steward. But, as a punishment for his deceit, Amilun is stricken with leprosy and becomes a beggar. Amis finds him and in obedience to a vision sacrifices his children so that Amilun can be cured by their blood. This Anglo-French version served as the basis for the fourteenth-century English *Amis and Amiloun*.

The ' Matter of Britain ' seems to have been much more popular amongst Anglo-French poets.[1] The earliest extant version of the story of Tristram and Iseult is the *Tristan* of the Anglo-French poet Thomas. The greater part of it has been lost and the surviving 3,000 lines, from five different manuscripts, are not continuous.[2] Though the earliest extant romance on the subject it certainly had predecessors which have since been lost, but which are necessarily inferred by the various theories concerning the origin of the legend. In addition the author himself informs us that numerous stories were told of Tristram and mentions an unknown

---

[1] On the origins of the Arthurian romances see p. 201.

[2] The substance of Thomas's poem is to be found in the Norwegian *Tristans Saga ok Isondar* written by a certain Brother Robert for the benefit of Hakon V of Norway ; in addition Gottfried von Strassburg and Eilhart von Oberge used it as the foundation for their own poems on the same subject. The work of Brother Robert and the extant fragments of Thomas are translated into modern English by R. S. Loomis, *The Romance of Tristram and Ysolt* (New York 1923).

writer called Breri [1] as the source of his poem. The work
of Thomas, fragmentary as it is, is one of the finest achievements of Anglo-French literature. Though the primitive
vigour of the legend has been to a certain extent softened
down, and so perhaps weakened, much of the moving
beauty of the original tale still survives. Despite the
occasional prolixity of style the emotions of the lovers have
been described with much poignancy and poetic insight.
This work by Thomas formed the basis of the Northern
Middle English *Sir Tristrem* written during the fourteenth
century. Towards the end of the twelfth century a single
episode of the theme was dealt with in Anglo-French in
La Folie Tristan by an unknown author, who bases his
work on the poem by Thomas, and perhaps makes use too
of the somewhat later version in continental French by
Béroul. [2] The Tristram story was not, however, the only
subject from Arthurian romance which was treated of in
Anglo-French. One of the earliest versions of the Grail
story is to be found in the *Roman de l'estoire dou Graal*—
also often called *Joseph d'Arimathie*—by the Anglo-French
knight Robert de Boron, a work which may have been
inspired by the *Conte del Graal* of Chrestien de Troyes.
In it Robert gives the early history of the Grail, identifying
it with the cup used at the Last Supper, in which Joseph of
Arimathea had caught the freshly-flowing blood from
the body of Christ. In a second poem, the *Merlin*,
only a small part of which has been preserved, he con-

[1] Probably identical with the *Bleheris* cited as an authority in
the *Conte del Graal*, and with the *famosus ille fabulator Bledhericus,
qui tempora nostra paulo praevenit* cited by Giraldus in his *Descriptio Kambriae* ; see E. K. Chambers, *Arthur of Britain* (London
1927), pp. 149 ff.

[2] Episodes from the Tristan legend are also found in the
Chievrefueil of Marie de France and in the *Donnei des amanz*, a
debate between a lady and her lover, written in England towards
the end of the twelfth century.

nected the early history of the Grail with Arthur's court.

The Norman invaders had early appropriated to themselves the traditions and legends of their adopted country —so much so that most of the romances of the ' Matter of England ' make their first appearance in literature in Anglo-French. No doubt they had been current orally, presumably in English, long before, but the extant English versions were not written down until some time after the initial use of the material by Anglo-French authors. The earliest of such romances is the *Horn et Rimel*, written somewhere about 1180 and forming the basis of the later Middle English *Horn Childe*, the thirteenth-century English *King Horn* being more independent. The author, who calls himself Mestre Thomas, tells us that he had already written a romance on Aaluf, the father of Horn, which has been lost, and in his conclusion promises that his son Gillimot will treat of the deeds of Hadermod, the son of Horn ; that work too, if it was ever completed, has long since disappeared. The poem is written in alexandrines, rhyming in tirades, and the author seems to have rewritten a Viking saga of the tenth century as a chanson de geste. He seems to have been influenced too by the *Tristan* of Thomas, and it has been suggested that the two authors may be identical. In any case, whoever Mestre Thomas may have been, he had a command of narrative and a vivid, descriptive power which raise him above the ranks of the majority of mediæval chroniclers. A late twelfth-century romance on *Waldef*, incomplete though containing over 20,000 lines, is remarkable in that it is the only one of the romances of the ' Matter of England ' of which no English version remains. On the other hand it enjoyed the distinction of being turned into Latin by a fifteenth-century monk, John Bramis of Thetford. The Anglo-French romance has not yet been edited, but, if we can judge from the Latin of John Bramis, the story would seem to be of comparatively little interest. It is full of folk-lore material and the usual incidents of mediæval romance, and depends for its interest on an abundance of fighting and fantastic adventure. It tells of the fortunes, not only of Waldef, but also of his father, his nephew and his sons. An interesting point is that the author definitely states that he is translating from an English original. This must have long since disappeared, though it was apparently known to John Bramis, since he informs us that he used it to complete his translation of the Anglo-French poem into Latin prose. From the first half of the thirteenth century are found versions of the Anglo-French romances of *Gui de Warewic* and *Boeve de Haumtone*, two of the most popular of mediæval romances, translated later into English as well as into most other European vernaculars. Since they celebrate English champions they are usually included in the ‘Matter of England’, but, although Gui is said to have rescued England from the Danes by slaying their champion Colebrant in single combat, there is no evidence for any historical basis such as is to be found in the Horn and the Havelok legends. They are simply romances of adventure, celebrating the piety of the heroes and their adventures in various European and eastern countries. Extant only in a prose version of the early fourteenth century is the romance of *Foulques FitzWarin* celebrating a famous and nobly-born outlaw who lived at the beginning of the thirteenth century. It is apparently based on an earlier rhymed version of the legend, composed between 1256 and 1264, which has since been lost.

The ‘Matter of Antiquity’, or more accurately the Alexander legend, is represented in Anglo-French by the *Roman de toute chevalerie* of Eustache (or Thomas) of Kent, an author who seems to have written at the beginning of the thirteenth century, but of whom nothing is known beyond the name. Like so many of the mediæval historical themes of romance the Alexander legend was based, not on the available historical sources, but on later fictions. During the third century A.D. an account of his Asiatic campaign was composed and ascribed to Callisthenes, an actual personage whose genuine work on the subject has long since perished. This Pseudo-Callisthenes was translated into Latin during the fourth century by Julius Valerius, and an epitome of the Latin translation was made during the ninth century. In the following century a full-length account of Alexander was given by the Archpriest Leo, who seems to have obtained additional material during an embassy to Constantinople, in his *Nativitas et victoria Alexandri Magni regis*. The earliest version in a western vernacular appears to have been that of Alberic of Besançon (or possibly Briançon or Piançon), which was certainly written by 1130 at which date a Middle High German adaptation was made by the priest Lamprecht. Only 105 lines of Alberic's original remain, and we know his name only from the version by Lamprecht. During the twelfth century the most famous of all treatments of the legend, the *Roman d'Alexandre*,[1] was composed by various authors, the most important of whom seems to have been a certain Lambert le Tort, the composite version later being revised by Alexandre de Bernai. Eustache makes use of the *Roman d'Alexandre*, but for the youth of the hero, the war against Darius and the expedition to India, he relies on Latin sources, especially on the *Epitome* of Valerius and on the *Letter of Alexander to Aristotle*. Though a competent versifier he seems to have possessed no great literary talent, and the main interest of his poem, as yet unedited, lies in the fact that it served as a source for the fourteenth-century English *King Alisaunder*.

Amongst the miscellaneous themes of romance are the *Ipomedon* and the *Prothesilaus* of Hue de Rotelande, who flourished towards the close of the twelfth century. We

[1] Incidentally it is this romance which has given the name *Alexandrine* to the twelve-syllable line.

know nothing of him except that he lived at Credenhill, near Hereford, that he is said to have been a friend of Walter Map, and that he wrote under the patronage of Gilbert Fitz-Baderon of Monmouth. His extant works are simply a patchwork of incidents and themes borrowed from or suggested by contemporary romance. They are full of reminiscences, not only of the Troy Tale and the Story of Thebes, but also of Arthurian romance and of the *Lais* of Marie de France. The former tells of Ipomedon, son of Hermogenes, King of Apulia, who loves the daughter of the duke of Calabria, and after the usual type of chivalrous adventures eventually wins her for his wife. It seems to have been popular in England and three English versions still exist. The second romance continues the story and describes the various adventures of Prothesilaus, son of Ipomedon, unjustly deprived of his heritage by his elder brother Daunus after the death of his father. Extant only in a fragment of some 300 lines is an Anglo-French version of the famous love story of *Amadas and Idoine* ; it seems to have been written about 1160 and thus is the earliest of the extant Anglo-French romances.

The most interesting of the shorter types of narrative verse are the so-called Breton *lais*. As extant these are short tales written in octosyllabic couplets, dealing mainly with love and containing a considerable admixture of the supernatural. This, however, seems to be a comparatively late development of the genre and, despite discussion and conjecture, we are still uncertain of the original form or provenance of the *lais*. They are evidently Celtic in inspiration, though not all of them have Celtic themes, but it is impossible to decide whether they are to be derived mainly from Brittany or from Wales. In some of them the personal names seem to be purely Welsh, in others purely Breton ; the probability is that both countries played an almost equal part in the development of the later stories.

The evidence available suggests that the original *lais* were pure lyrics, presumably in some Celtic language, telling of emotional moments in the lives of Celtic heroes, either real or imaginary, and sung to the accompaniment of a small harp called a *rote*. The meaning of such lyrics, though clear enough to the singer, must have been quite incomprehensible to the audience. Consequently they would be introduced by an explanation of the story, or of the circumstances under which the *lai* came to be composed. In the same way the Irish minstrels interpreted in story form the cryptic lyric utterances of their bards, and the later Icelandic saga-tellers introduced in prose the complicated kennings of the ancient skaldic poems. The story itself appears to have been known as the *conte*, in distinction to the lyric, which was the *lai*. Such an origin, prose tales enclosing lyrics, explains several allusions in the extant French *lais*, which seem to have been very different from the compositions of the Welsh and Breton minstrels on which they were based. The extant *lais* were essentially meant to be read and have nothing musical about them ; there is no attempt to give even the substance of the original *lai*, but only of the circumstances which led up to its composition. They were rhymed versions of the prose *contes*, which had originally been simply a framework for the lyric *lais*. Mediæval poets in France and England took these *contes* and developed them into narrative poems, usually in octo-syllabic couplets, and to these poems also—romances in miniature—contemporaries applied the word *lai*, partly because it was the lyric which especially attracted the French audience, and partly because they also were in lyric form. Today, of the original songs, whether Welsh or Breton, not a single verse remains, but only vague scraps of evidence in the shape of proper names and three Breton titles. Such seems to have been the origin and development of the extant Breton *lais* in France and England, but it must be emphasized that the question is still unsettled and the above is only one, perhaps the most probable, of a number of theories.

The Breton *lais* first appear in literature during the twelfth century, and became remarkably popular, so that it soon became common for tales of a very different origin to be rewritten in imitation of them. By the fourteenth century their vogue was exhausted and their place taken by the romances which they had helped to develop. The word itself loses its earlier meaning and becomes simply a synonym for a *fabliau* or *dit*, the latter a very vague term indicating a short poem, often narrative, and usually with a moral tendency. The best known of the adaptors of the original Breton *lais* is a certain Marie de France, whose work seems to have been especially influential in fixing their form. She was the author of twelve of them, and in the prologue she speaks of herself as a literary pioneer, though it remains uncertain whether or not she were the first to contrive the narrative, as distinct from the lyric, *lai*. Some of the other *lais* have been assigned to an earlier period and, though the dating is largely tentative, it is quite possible that the narrative *lai* was introduced into French independently by two or more poets. In addition to her *lais* Marie was also responsible for the translation, from English into French, of a collection of fables, and, from Latin into French, of the *Purgatory of St Patrick*. Apart from a reference by Denis Piramus in his *Vie seint Edmund*, where he speaks of a ' Dame Marie, who turned into rhyme and made verses of *lais* which are not in the least true ', we know nothing of her life beyond what can be gathered from her own works. She seems to have lived during the second half of the twelfth century, to have been born and to have spent at least part of her early life in France. We have no means of knowing when, or why, she left that country, but most of her literary works seem to have been produced in England. At any rate she knew English, which at that time she could have learned only in England, and she occasionally uses English words in her works. Since Denis Piramus calls her *Dame* she must have been a lady of noble birth, and there is much in her work to confirm such a supposition. The king to whom she dedicated her *Lais* was almost certainly Henry II ; her education, the tone of her dedications and the persons to whom they were addressed, her representation of courtly love, all indicate an author of some rank. She was certainly well-educated for her time. She knew Latin and English well enough to translate from those languages, and she may possibly have known something of Welsh and Breton. Some scholars would identify her with Mary, the half-sister of Henry II, who became Abbess of Shaftesbury. Others suggest that she may have been Marie, daughter of Count Waleran of Meulan, who married a Hue Talbot and presumably lived in Hereford and Devon. There is no proof of these and similar theories ; most of the evidence is conjectural and either proof or disproof is equally impossible.

Since her originals have all disappeared it is difficult to give any reasonable estimate of Marie's literary abilities ; we are unable to say which qualities were due to Marie herself rather than to the material upon which she was working. Undoubtedly the *Lais* give an impression of considerable charm, due mainly to the vivid descriptions and the fitness of the phrasing to the idea. But structurally they leave much to be desired. They display that lack of unity so common in mediæval narrative : the various elements of the plot are often badly combined and the centre of interest is at times shifted unskilfully. The characters, too, are largely conventional ; there is a fixed type of physical and mental qualities for hero, heroine and villain. On the whole it was probably the scantiness of her material, rather than any particular skill in the handling of it, that saved Marie from many of the literary faults of her contemporaries. But when every possible disparagement has been made there still remains a balance in her favour. At times we find flashes of insight into human nature, usually unimportant in the tale and so probably due to Marie herself. She was a competent versifier, had a considerable poetic instinct, a feeling for the right word, and an astonishing gift for miniature painting. In addition she has remodelled her material skilfully and conscientiously. The dozen *lais* which she translated into French had a remarkable influence on mediæval literature.[1] They were in the drift of the tendencies of the time and caught the fancy of her contemporaries, all of them being translated into German and Old Norse. Translations of only two of them have survived in Middle English, *Lanval* and *Lai le Fresne*, both from the fourteenth century, but it is not improbable that these are only the fortunate survivors of a larger number.

Apart from the works of Marie de France only three of these short narrative poems have been preserved in Anglo-French, and only one of them is a true *lai*. This is the *Lai del desirré*, written during the second half of the twelfth century, and dealing with the same theme as the *Lanval* of Marie de France. It tells of the love of a knight for a fairy ; by speaking of his supernatural mistress he loses her and is pardoned only after much hardship and many adventures. The unknown author seems to have had much less literary talent than Marie, and the points in which his work differs from hers are nearly always unfortunate. The second of the *lais*, and probably the earliest since it may even precede those of Marie, is the *Lai du cor*, written about the middle of the twelfth century by an Englishman of the name of Robert Biket. It tells how a drinking-horn,

---

[1] The following are the twelve *lais* certainly by Marie de France : *Milon, Deus amanz, Le Fresne, Chaitivel, Equitan, Guigemar, Lanval, Chievrefueil, Laostic, Bisclavret, Yonec, Eliduc* ; a thirteenth, *Tydorel*, is also occasionally attributed to her.

which had the magic property that only a husband whose wife is faithful could drink out of it, was brought to the court of King Arthur. With the exception of the hero, Arthur and all his knights fail in the attempt. The action takes place at Arthur's court and the hero is Caradoc, one of his knights, but for all that the work is a *fabliau* rather than a *lai*, since it is not properly speaking a tale of love and the supernatural interest is confined to the horn. The theme is a common one and is found elsewhere in later *fabliaux* and romances. The third of the *lais*, the *Lai d'Haveloc*, is simply a reworking of the Havelok episode as told by Gaimar. Despite a mention of Arthur and the presence of supernatural incidents it has little in common with the true *lai*. The continental forms of language, and the correctness of the author's versification, suggest that he may have been a Frenchman who had only recently settled in England.

There is little that need be said concerning the remaining literature of entertainment. There are a number of Anglo-French *fabliaux* from the twelfth and thirteenth centuries, but they do not differ materially from the type of work produced in France. The same is true of the lyric poetry ; the content is small and mainly religious, hymns and poems in praise of the Virgin being especially popular. More notable are two verse debates, the *Geste de Blancheflour e de Florence* and *Melior et Ydoine*, both of which are independent treatments of the same subject, whether a knight or a clerk is to be preferred as a lover, a question often debated in mediæval literature. The former, exceptional in that the verdict is given in favour of the knight, contains seventy-two six-line stanzas, whilst the latter is of about the same length but written in octosyllabic couplets. *Blancheflour e Florence* is of especial interest in that we are told in the last stanza that it was translated into French by Brykhulle, an author otherwise unknown, from the English of Banastre. The English original has long since disappeared, but in any case resemblances between the Anglo-French text and continental poems on the same subject indicate that the English author probably derived his inspiration from abroad. A debate on a different subject, the *Estrif de l'iver et de l'esté*, in octosyllabic couplets, also seems to have been composed in England.

A considerable amount of Anglo-French literature was produced during the fourteenth century, but by 1300 its greatest period was past. Unfortunately comparatively little work has been done on the subject; some of the texts, whose length it must be admitted is often daunting, are still unedited, and until the whole matter has been dealt with in greater detail it is impossible to estimate the exact significance of Anglo-French writers in the history of English literature. There can be no doubt of their importance; they were the first to utilize the Anglo-Saxon traditions of the ' Matter of England '; because of their contact with Wales they probably greatly influenced the development of the Arthurian legend; the development of the *lai* owes much to them, and the earliest examples of vernacular drama seem to be due to them. In addition French literary influence probably first made itself felt to any great extent in this country through the medium of Anglo-French writings.

IV

LEGAL AND HISTORICAL SURVIVALS

THERE can be little doubt of the great importance of the Norman Conquest in the history of English law, but its exact significance is not so easily described.[1] It is not a case of the Anglo-Saxon being replaced by a foreign legal system, nor even of a compromise between two rival systems. English law, as it appears during the reign of Henry II, seems to be a particular development of the Anglo-Saxon law due to the characteristics of the ruling family. The fact that that family was of Norman descent is of less importance than the fact that it produced a line of strong rulers able to make the royal power feared and respected. On the whole there is comparatively little evidence for the legal activity of the Norman—especially of the earlier Norman—kings. What there is suggests that they were content, in the main, to govern the country by the old laws. In the earlier period the existence of two hostile peoples living side by side introduced some difficulties necessitating special legislation. But there was already such a diversity of national laws, Mercian, West-Saxon, Kentish and Danelaw, that the introduction of a Norman law would have little effect.

[1] See especially F. Pollock and F. W. Maitland, *The History of English Law* (Cambridge 1898) ; T. F. T. Plucknett, *A Concise History of the Common Law* (2nd edn. London 1936) ; J. E. A. Jolliffe, *The Constitutional History of Medieval England* (London 1937).

The Conqueror himself has often been accused of introducing the feudal system—a convenient generalization for a state of society which varied according to time and place. Probably some of the peculiarly feudal institutions found in later times were introduced as a direct result of the Conquest, but in so far as, by the term feudal system, we refer to the system by which men of inferior status commended themselves to the protection of their superiors, and the holding of land by various services and rents, there can be little doubt that Anglo-Saxon society was rapidly becoming feudalized before the Conquest. On the other hand some aspects of feudalism were repugnant to the Conqueror and to his successors, and they did their best to keep them out of England, as witness the great assembly on Salisbury Plain. In his own eyes William I did not reign over England as a conqueror; rather was he the legal successor of the Anglo-Saxon kings, though before he could reign he had to put down a rebellion due to the ambition of Harold Godwinesson. On his accession to the throne he promised to respect the laws of the Confessor, and, in fact, it was to his interest to do so. Anglo-Saxon law granted to him, as king of England, far greater powers than he possessed under Norman law as Duke of Normandy.

So far as we know William himself seems to have enacted few new laws.[1] One of the few was, however, highly significant. He decreed that pleas dealing with ecclesiastical discipline should henceforth be judged according to canon law, and not according to the law of the hundred as had previously been the case; a decree which led to the institution of separate church courts. Another law, in attempting to protect isolated Normans from murder, led to the

[1] For the laws of the early Norman kings, see A. J. Robertson, *The Laws of the Kings of England* (Cambridge 1925), pp. 221 ff.

long-lived Presentment of Englishry.[1] With these two exceptions the surviving laws of the Conqueror were all such as might have been enacted by preceding Saxon kings —some of them in fact had been. The English land-law seems, in the main, to have been retained after the Conquest and 'for the purpose of taxation the Frenchman succeeded to the duties of his English *antecessores*'.[2] William is determined that the royal rights shall not be diminished. So the old land tenures are retained in order that the new lord shall receive only the same jurisdiction, the same fines and forfeitures, as his predecessor has received. Domesday Book is compiled so that the rights of the crown may be definitely determined and the old Danegeld rigorously exacted. Here the most important innovation of William seems to have been the introduction of the probably Frankish inquest, later to become the germ of trial by jury.

On the whole the main significance of the Conquest seems to have consisted in the establishment of a strong central government. There seems to have been little direct legislation ; the local courts of the hundred and the shire continued to function in the old way, and a group of treatises, written during the reign of Henry I, indicate that it is still the Anglo-Saxon law which is being administered.[3] So far as we can judge from the extant written records the real

---

[1] If a Norman were slain and his murderer not arrested by the men of the hundred within eight days, then the whole hundred was liable to a fine. This led to the later theory by which any unknown man found slain was presumed to be Norman, and the hundred fined accordingly, unless it could be proved that he was English. Englishry, if established, excused the hundred from the fine. It was abolished in 1340.

[2] Pollock and Maitland, *op.cit.* i, 69.

[3] Plucknett, *op.cit.* pp. 15, 228. Probably the most important of the treatises are the *Leges Henrici Primi* and the *Leges Edwardi Confessoris.*

change takes place during the reign of Henry II, though it is possible enough that in many respects he is simply carrying on the work of his grandfather and continuing policies initiated by him. It is under the Plantagenet that the law of the King's Court becomes supreme. English law is centralized and unified by the institution of a permanent court of professional lawyers, and by the frequent mission of itinerant judges. The old local courts begin to fall into disuse, and the variety of local laws is displaced by the common law of the King's Court. Other changes in the history of English law are to be ascribed, either directly or indirectly, to the Norman Conquest, but this is not the place in which to discuss them in detail. We are not concerned here with legal history, but rather with the language in which the law is expressed. The important point to be noted is that the reign of Henry II, rather than that of William I, marks the division between the Old and the Middle English legal systems.

The great advantage of English after the Conquest was that it had long been employed as a legal language. Almost from the earliest appearance of writing in England the laws of the Anglo-Saxon kings seem to have been written down in the vernacular.[1] Consequently, by the time of the Conquest, we find that Old English possesses a legal vocabulary and a tradition of legal writing in the vernacular, though those writings are, of course, as yet little more than the bare laws themselves ; no commentary on them has yet been seen to be necessary. After the Conquest this legal language could not, at first, be subjected to any pressure from French, since French did not yet exist as a legal language. The official language of the Normans was Latin,

---

[1] The Old English laws are edited by F. Liebermann, *Die Gesetze der Angelsachsen* (Halle 1903–16). See also F. L. Attenborough, *The Laws of the Earliest English Kings* (Cambridge 1922), and Robertson, *op. cit.*

and Latin is therefore the competitor of English. About a dozen of the laws issued by the Conqueror still remain. They were apparently published in both Latin and English, though the two versions have not, in every case, been preserved. Apart from these there seems to have been little legal activity before the reign of Henry I. Under him we find the laws of the Anglo-Saxon kings being translated into Latin in the *Quadripartitus*, the *Leges Henrici*, the *Instituta Canuti* and the *Leges Edwardi Confessoris*. In addition the Old English versions of these laws continue to be copied out. The manuscript known as the *Textus Roffensis*, a manuscript to which we owe much of our knowledge of Anglo-Saxon law, seems to have been written during this reign. Other manuscripts are being copied, too, and some of the pre-Conquest laws are known to us only from these post-Conquest copies. It is possible that the local laws were now written down for the first time. Previously they must have depended almost entirely on oral tradition. We remember the numerous inquests, summoned in the reign of William I, to discover and swear to the law. Ethelric of Chichester, ' a man very learned in the law of the land ', is brought to Penenden Heath in a cart in order that he may testify to that law.[1] Very probably this outburst of legal writing is an attempt to formulate the ' lagam Edwardi ' which Henry, in his coronation charter, had promised to restore. It is not until the middle of the twelfth century that we find the Old English laws being translated into French in the *Leges Willelmi Conquestoris*, and it is not until the second half of the thirteenth century that laws are ordinarily drawn up in Anglo-French. Until that time, whatever may have been the actual language spoken in the courts, the language of legal record is Latin. It is only when Anglo-French is already beginning to decline in importance that it takes the place of

[1] H. Wharton, *Anglia Sacra* (London 1691), i. 335.

Latin as the legal language, English itself having been displaced by Latin during the reigns of the first two Williams.

In all the legal writings produced under Henry I it is still, in the main, the Anglo-Saxon law which is being considered. The aim of the writers is to state it in a form suitable for the new Norman age, and the fact that they are not very successful in their enterprise is far from surprising. In attempting to write a text-book on a law which is neither Roman nor Canon, they are engaged in a task so new that the very attempt is noteworthy ; but the diversity of local law and the confusion of competing systems proves too much for them. Not until fifty years later are documents available to show the widespread changes which must have been going on during the period between these writings and the appearance of the *Tractatus de Legibus*, usually ascribed to the justiciar Ranulf Glanville. The appearance at about the same date of the *Dialogus de Scaccario* of Richard FitzNigel shows that it was already possible to write separate treatises about administration and the law. It is probably impossible to overestimate the importance of the *Tractatus de Legibus*. It settled the method of legal writing for centuries to come, and Glanville is the first exponent of the new common law, which, in due course, was to supersede completely the old legal institutions. The significant feature of the new law is that it is now royal and derived from the King's Court. The tangled masses of local custom, certainly still in force, are completely ignored and local variations receive little sympathy. The law is strongly procedural and based on writs, the treatise itself taking the form of a commentary on these writs. The appearance of Glanville marks the end of the Anglo-Saxon law. Some of its features are carried over into the newer system which has arisen from it, and many of the local laws still continue in use, but henceforward the new common law of the King's

Court is steadily gaining ground and taking the place of the older systems of law.

The writs and charters of the early Norman kings differ little from those of their predecessors.[1]   Under the successors of Alfred the decay of learning and the advance of West Saxon as the official language had led to the use of the vernacular in such documents.   By the end of the period legal documents, from whatever locality, are usually written in some form of the West Saxon literary dialect, and the usage is continued under the early Norman kings. Some kind of a Chancery, in fact if not in name, seems to have existed already at the court of the Confessor and to have been taken over by the Conqueror.   In it the English element was naturally strong, and the charters issued differ little from the pre-Conquest ones.   They are still occasionally drawn up by the persons in whose favour they were issued, and the normal writ is still a letter addressed to the magnates of the shire court.   But throughout the reigns of the two Williams the traditions of the royal chancery were changing rapidly.   In the early years of the Conqueror many of his writs and charters—even those of them addressed to Normans—are issued in English, or occasionally in both English and Latin.   French is never found in use in such official documents, though later on Latin becomes the usual language with English employed only very occasionally. During the reign of William II such documents in the vernacular become very rare, and Latin is almost invariable. We seem to see the gradual dying out or promotion of the clerks trained under the Confessor, and their replacement by clerics trained in the reformed Norman church to whom an official language was inevitably Latin.   Henceforth, until the end of the thirteenth century when French begins to

---

[1] These have been collected and calendared by H. W. C. Davis and R. J. Whitwell, *Regesta Regum Anglo-Normannorum* (Oxford 1913).

be used, Latin is the language of all official documents, with only a very occasional use of English. Moreover, after the reign of Rufus the English that is used is the actual spoken language of the period, not the standard West Saxon of the pre-Conquest kings. Much of the technical legal vocabulary that had been developed during the Old English period continues in use long after the old language has been forgotten. The charters of the Plantagenets still speak of ' saca et soca et toll et theam ' and ' infangenethef et utfangenethef ' ; occasionally a long list of such terms is given, ' et hamsoka et grithbrige et blodwita et ficthwita et flictwita et fredwita et hengwita et leirwita et flemenes-frith et murdro et latrocinio et ordel et oreste '.[1] It would be interesting to know if all these terms were still understood. The *Owl and the Nightingale*, a debate poem in English written towards the end of the twelfth century, is a dispute conducted with strict formality and full of technical legal terms. Most of these are taken from the Old English legal vocabulary, and the antiquity of many of them is evidenced by their alliterative character. The only exception is a reference to trial by battle, one of the few legal customs definitely introduced by the Normans.[2] No doubt the exact meaning of many of these legal terms was soon obscured, though this would not necessarily prove any draw-back to their continued use. Roger of Hoveden, writing at the beginning of the thirteenth century, thought it necessary to give a Latin explanation of the Old English legal terms and to translate them into French. Nevertheless, the vitality of the Old English legal vocabulary, and its continued use during the Middle English period, is shown by the number of words such

---

[1] Charter of the Hospitallers, *Rot. Cart.*, p. 15.
[2] *Owl and the Nightingale*, lines 1197–8 :

> ' ȝef men habbeþ bataile inume,
> ich wat hwaþer schal beon ouer-kume.'

as *saca*, *soca*, *atha*, *burlawa*, *danegeldum*, *dempstor*, *geld-abile*, *morgagifa*, which were borrowed into mediæval Latin.[1]

In historical, as in other departments of prose literature, the West Saxon literary language continues to be used for some time after the Conquest. Half a dozen manuscripts of the *Old English Chronicle* still remain and, for purposes of identification, are usually known as the A, B, C, D, E and F manuscripts of the *Chronicle* respectively.[2] Of these the three latter were all copied entirely after the Conquest. One of the remaining manuscripts, B, was written about the year 1000 and ends with the annal for 977, and neither A nor C are carried on for long after 1066. The A manuscript, written at Winchester and later given by Archbishop Parker to Corpus Christi College, Cambridge, was probably begun in the reign of Alfred and is carried on by various hands for nearly 200 years. But long before the Conquest the entries had become very jejune, consisting mainly of the obits of kings and bishops, and only two of its entries are of post-Conquest date. Under 1066 it notes very briefly the events of that year. A longer entry, s.a. 1070, is concerned with the consecration of Lanfranc to Canterbury and with his quarrel with Thomas of York, after which the manuscript is continued in Latin as the *Acta Lanfranci*. The C manuscript, probably written at Abingdon, ends abruptly in the middle of the entry for 1066 describing the battle of Stamford Bridge. A later scribe, writing probably at the beginning of the twelfth century, has completed the

---

[1] J. H. Baxter and C. Johnson, *Medieval Latin Word-List* (London 1934).

[2] The only complete edition of all the manuscripts of the *Old English Chronicle* is that by B. Thorpe, *The Anglo-Saxon Chronicle* (London 1861), but see also J. Earle and C. Plummer, *Two Saxon Chronicles Parallel* (Oxford 1892, 1899).

entry by adding the well-known account of the defence of the bridge by one of the Norwegians :

There was one of the Norwegians who withstood the English so that they could not pass over the bridge, nor complete their victory. Then one of the English shot an arrow, but it availed nothing, and another, passing under the bridge, stabbed him beneath his mail-coat. So King Harold passed over the bridge and his army with him, and there was a great slaughter, both of Norwegians and of Flemings.

Our knowledge of historical writing in English after the Conquest is almost entirely dependent on the D and E manuscripts. The D manuscript, apparently written somewhere in the diocese of Worcester, carries on the record until 1079 and ends mutilated, though little seems to have been lost. The post-Conquest entries were all written by one man, some time at the beginning of the twelfth century. Since the E manuscript, too, was copied out in one hand as far as 1121, there is no change of writing to tell us how many different writers may have had a hand in compiling the record. The only information to be obtained on the subject is that which can be derived from internal stylistic evidence, and the usual impersonal style in which the *Chronicle* is written is fatal to any chance of success. The E manuscript, written at Peterborough and given by Archbishop Laud to the Bodleian, carries on the tale until the middle of the twelfth century ; the last entry appearing under the date 1154. In 1116 there was a disastrous fire at Peterborough when the greater part of the monastery was completely destroyed. In this fire their copy of the *Old English Chronicle* seems to have perished. However, the tradition of historical writing must have been vigorous there for, in 1121, the monks appear to have borrowed another manuscript from some monastery in the south of England, possibly from St Augustine's, Canterbury. This was copied and then, presumably, returned to its southern home.

What became of it and how much longer it was kept up we can never know, since it has long disappeared. But the manuscript at Peterborough itself is kept up by various hands until the accession of Henry II.

Until D ends with the annal for 1079 the two manuscripts of the *Chronicle* tell much the same story. The events of the various years are told in a plain straightforward prose, and occasionally in some detail. The accounts differ only in the prominence given to matters of local interest. As we should expect the author of E is interested in Peterborough events and gives more detail concerning them. He has a much fuller account, for example, of the rising at Ely and the exploits of Hereward. D, on the other hand, is more interested in Northern happenings; compare for example his account of the adventures of Eadgar Atheling in Scotland, and the fuller details which he gives of the Scandinavian invasion in 1076. We may note, too, the fact that a twelfth-century scribe under the year 1080, miswritten for 1130, has added a note of the death of Angus, Earl of Moray, at the end of the D manuscript. If, as appears probable, this manuscript was written in the diocese of Worcester, the interest of the scribe in Northern events is not surprising. During the last century of the Old English period, and for some time after the Conquest, there seems to have been a close relationship between the York and the Worcester dioceses.

After the end of the D manuscript, E is the only survivor, and is continued in a similar impersonal style. The entries vary considerably in length, and we come across occasional vivid little descriptions, as in the tale of the slaughter of the monks of Glastonbury by the new Norman abbot in 1083 and the description of the compilation of Domesday Book in the following year. A distinct break in the even flow of the prose is found in the annal for 1086. This is evidently written by a different author and one who is probably the most individualistic and one of the best of the whole series of writers to whom we owe the *Old English Chronicle*. We owe to him a vivid description of the Conqueror, the impressions of one ' who had gazed upon him and for some time lived in his court '. He was evidently a man of some importance and no little learning. Latin constructions are found occasionally in the prose, and the personal and homiletic tendency of the preacher is evident as in his fondness for rhetorical questions, ' Who cannot grieve at such a time ? or who is so hard-hearted that he cannot weep at such misfortunes ', and again, ' What can I say ? Stern death which spares neither high nor low seized him '. In reporting the death of William he must pause, in the true Old English fashion, to reflect on the transitoriness of earthly things :

Alas ! how false and how transitory is the prosperity of this world. He who was formerly a powerful king and lord of many lands, of all his land he possessed now only seven feet. He who was formerly clothed in gold and gems lay now covered with earth.

He was obviously an Englishman, but though of a conquered race he can be just to the Conqueror, ' these things we have written about him, both of good and of evil '. General though the description is, the author succeeds in making clear the power and personality of William :

He was a wise man and very powerful, nobler and stronger than any of those who had gone before him. He was mild to honest men who loved God, but above all exceedingly harsh with those who withstood his will. On the place where God granted him the winning of England he raised a glorious monastery, and established monks there and endowed it well. In his days was the glorious monastery at Canterbury built and also many others throughout all England. This land was also filled full of monks who lived their life after the rule of St Benedict. . . . He was very noble ; three times a year he wore his crown as often as he was in England. At Easter he bore it in Winchester, at Pentecost in Westminster, and at midwinter in Gloucester. Then there were with him all the powerful men throughout England, archbishops and bishops, abbots and earls, thanes and knights. He was also a fierce man and cruel so that none dared act against his will. Bishops he removed from their bishoprics, abbots from their abbeys ; thanes he thrust into prison and spared not his own brother. . . .

The whole annal is a vivid reminder of the loss which Middle English literature sustained when the historical prose, fashioned amid the triumphs and disasters of the Old English period, at length disappeared. It is full of apt phrases which strike the imagination, ' there was not a hide of land in England but he knew who possessed it and what it was worth ', ' he loved the tall deer like a father ', ' so fierce was he that he cared not for the hatred of them all '.

This writer does not, however, seem to have been engaged for long on the *Chronicle*. We soon have a return to the plain impersonal narrative style of the earlier entries. Under the year 1100 there is a similar sketch of the character of Rufus, but it is not nearly so vivid. Another author whom it seems possible to distinguish appears to have been at work between the years 1105 and 1118 ; most, if not all, of the annals between those dates seem to be the work of one man. He is as impersonal as usual and when, telling of the appearance of a wonderful star in 1106, he adds ' but we cannot write more openly about it for we ourselves saw it not ', the personal touch is felt as a surprise. The annals become shorter and the author seems to be interested more in astronomical phenomena, which he reports at length, than in national happenings. The weather, too, receives a certain amount of attention, and he rarely omits a descriptive note concerning it at the end of each annal. The first copyist of the manuscript ended his work with the annal for 1122 ; in the remaining part of the *Chronicle* the changes of hand give some indication of the change of authorship.

It seems to have been continued by four different authors as far as the annal for 1132, though, were it not for the difference in writing, the difference in authorship would probably escape us. The same impersonal straightforward style is common to all. But the character of the *Chronicle* is beginning to change. Though the entries become longer the former national outlook is vanishing, and interest is mainly concentrated on local and ecclesiastical happenings. Though more rarely now, an occasional vivid touch lightens the narrative, as in the description of the fire at Gloucester which started ' whilst the monks were singing their mass, and the deacon had just begun the gospel '.

With 1132 the last continuator begins his work. After that date it appears to have been laid aside for a time—probably the unsettled conditions of Stephen's reign were not conducive to historical writing. With the appearance of quieter conditions in 1155 it was taken up again and brought up to date by the insertion of half a dozen annals scattered between the two dates.[1] Naturally enough most of the intervening events are only dated approximately. Only two of the entries are of any length, the remaining ones being short and concerned mainly with local and ecclesiastical affairs and the obits of important people. But those two annals reveal a writer of some skill and considerable descriptive power, one of them being the well-known annal for 1137 describing the misery and wretchedness of the country during the anarchy, whilst the other, under the year 1140, gives the main events in the war between Stephen and the Empress. The *Chronicle* comes to an end in the middle of the annal for 1154, telling of the appointment of a new abbot to Peterborough. Though the last page is defaced and mutilated it is improbable that much has been lost.

[1] The best edition of these last entries is by J. Hall, *Selections from Early Middle English* (Oxford 1920), i. 5–11.

And so, almost a century after the death of the last Saxon king, the historical record commenced under Alfred at last comes to an end, and three hundred years pass before historical writings in English prose again appear. A prose had been developed which had proved capable of great things and its end was not ignoble. In the twelfth-century entries the language shows signs of change and, when the last writer is at work, the West Saxon literary dialect has been forgotten. The old spelling tradition has broken down ; the language is no longer Old but Middle English, and a new spelling system based on the actual spoken speech is being evolved. Working under these handicaps, with a prose tradition only half remembered and a confused syntax, the later annals are not unworthy of the record which told of the triumphs of Alfred and the disasters of Ethelred. A faint undertone of querulousness cannot mar the vividness of the description of the state of the country during the anarchy :

When the castles were built, they filled them with devils and evil men. Then they seized all whom they thought to have any goods, both by night and day, men and women, and thrust them into prison for gold and silver. They tortured them with indescribable torments, for never were martyrs used as cruelly as they. . . . Many thousands they killed with hunger. I know not nor can I tell of all the miseries nor of all the woes which they inflicted on the wretched people in this land, and it lasted during the nineteen years whilst Stephen was king, and ever it became worse and worse. They collected blackmail from the villages at regular intervals and called it protection money. When the wretched people had no more to give, then they plundered and burned all the villages, so that one could travel a whole day's journey and never find a village inhabited or land cultivated. Then corn, meat, cheese and butter were dear, for there was none in the land. Poor people died from hunger ; some lived on charity who had formerly been powerful men, some fled from the land. Never before had there been such misery in the country, for the heathen had never acted worse than these. Contrary to custom they spared neither church nor churchyard, but seized all the goods which were there, and then burned the church and everything together. They spared neither bishop's land, nor abbot's, nor priest's, but plundered monks and ecclesiastics, and every man his neighbour whenever he could. If two or three men rode up to a village all the inhabitants fled from them ; they thought that they were robbers. Bishops and clergy cursed them continually, but they cared nothing for it for they were already accursed, forsworn and damned. Wherever the earth was tilled it grew no corn, for the land was all destroyed by such evil deeds ; and they said openly that Christ and his apostles were asleep. Such things, and more than we can tell, we endured for nineteen years because of our sins.

We are apt to forget that some of the best passages in the *Chronicle*, usually treated as an essentially Old English production, were written long after the Conquest. It does, of course, belong to the Old English literary tradition, and the continuation after the Conquest is simply a carrying on of that tradition. But to treat it as an entirely Old English work is to create an artificial gulf between pre- and post-Conquest vernacular prose and to obscure the essential continuity of English literature. Linguistically, too, it is a record of immense importance. We can see the early West Saxon of Alfred's reign developing into the literary language of the tenth and eleventh centuries. After the Conquest there is a gradual change in this language until, in the last entries, it has disappeared and a new Middle English is in use.

It must not be imagined that Peterborough was the only place where the tradition of historical writing in the vernacular was kept up. By some happy chance it was the only manuscript of the *Chronicle* which was being written at this date that has been preserved. Other manuscripts have been lost but proof of their existence is not wanting. The Peterborough manuscript itself was copied in 1121 from a lost south-eastern original. There must have been, then, at least one place in the south-east where the tradition was kept up until 1121. It may have been continued even later ; since the manuscript has been completely lost we are unable to say how late it may have been carried on. The theory of the descent of the extant manuscripts presumes other intermediate copies, too, which have since disappeared. Best of all a single page of one such manuscript has accidentally been preserved. This, usually lettered H, contains annals for the years 1113 and 1114, and seems to be quite unconnected with the extant E manuscript or with any of the lost manuscripts presumed in our theory of its descent. The material contained in it is not of much importance ; it is concerned chiefly with the movements of the king and with ecclesiastical matters. Its place of origin is not certain, though some of the phrasing suggests that it may have come from Winchester. The main significance of this fragment lies in the fact that it is written in an exceptionally pure West Saxon, much purer than that in which the contemporary parts of the Peterborough manuscript are written. Apparently at some place or other in the south—maybe Winchester—the tradition of historical writing in the vernacular was still strong at the beginning of the twelfth century, but only the accident which has preserved this odd page of the manuscript allows us to recognize the fact. Here again we have no means of knowing how late this particular manuscript may have been continued.

The various manuscripts of the *Chronicle* are the only examples of historical writing in the vernacular which have survived. There is, however, some evidence of a different type of historical writing, no examples of which have been preserved. The importance in the history of English literature of the episcopacy of Wulfstan of Worcester is pointed out below. To such an extent did the tradition of the composition of literature in the vernacular survive in the west that, after the death of Wulfstan, his life was written in English by his chaplain and chancellor Coleman. This is, of course, an exceptional type of literature to find in the vernacular at this date. Biographies of great men, especially of great churchmen, had been written before, but they had been written in Latin and not in the vernacular. Such biographies still remain, those for example of Dunstan, of Æthelwold and of Oswald; we even have the biography of a layman, Asser's *Life of Alfred the Great*. The only parallel to Coleman's writings is an English *Life of St Dunstan* which was used by Osbern and Eadmer. These have all long since disappeared. The English *Life of St Dunstan* is known only from the use made of it by Eadmer and Osbern; Coleman's *Life of Wulfstan* is extant only in the Latin translation of William of Malmesbury, and not even a Latin rendering is available of Coleman's similar *Life of St Gregory*. Such writings in the vernacular were unparalleled in the rest of Western Europe. Only in Iceland was Ari the Wise, a younger contemporary of Coleman, laying the foundations of Icelandic historical writing, but whereas Ari had his successors Coleman had none. Not until the appearance of the *Lives of More* by Roper and Harpsfield in Tudor times do we find biographies again written in English.[1] After Wulfstan Thomas Becket was the next to have his life written in the vernacular but, significantly enough, it was written in French verse and not in English prose.

There can be little doubt that the decay of English historical writing in the middle of the twelfth century is due

---

[1] Though we should not forget the remarkably interesting and significant autobiography of Margery Kempe, written during the first half of the fifteenth century. At present it is available only in a modernized version by W. Butler-Bowdon, *The Book of Margery Kempe* (London 1936), but the Middle English text is being edited by Miss H. E. Allen and Professor S. B. Meech for the Early English Text Society.

in great measure to the increasing influence of Latin. For at least two generations after the Conquest the *Chronicle* is kept up by writers interested in national affairs, who have probably themselves taken some part in them. After the Conquest Latin increasingly becomes the language of record and of administration, and is naturally used by clerics trained in the reformed Norman church. The *Chronicle* then falls into the hands of less learned men, knowing comparatively little of national affairs and interested chiefly in local and ecclesiastical matters, until eventually it falls into complete disuse. This increasing use of Latin is very well illustrated in the extant manuscript of the *Chronicle* usually known as the F manuscript. It was copied some time towards the end of the eleventh century and is at first written entirely in English, but the later entries are in a curious bilingual form, in English and Latin. It illustrates remarkably the transition from the vernacular history of Anglo-Saxon England to the Latin history of Norman and Angevin England. Similar evidence is provided by a series of brief annals which were apparently kept up at Christ Church, Canterbury.[1] As late as 1110 they are written entirely in English, but after that date we find occasional entries in Latin. These become gradually more numerous, and the last entry in English appears under the date 1130. After this the annals are continued entirely in Latin.

Moreover, by the middle of the twelfth century, Anglo-French is beginning to appear as a literary language. It is significant that, just about the time when the *Chronicle* is failing, we find it being translated into French verse by Geoffrey Gaimar. Monastic historians such as William of Malmesbury and Henry of Huntingdon are writing in Latin; others such as Gaimar and Wace, writing more especially for the aristocracy, are writing in Anglo-French. Historical

---

[1] Ed. F. Liebermann, *Ungedruckte Anglo-Normannische Geschichtsquellen* (Strassburg 1879), pp. 1–8.

prose, too, is exposed to an even more insidious attack. When English is again used in historical writings, we find that the authors are under French influence and are using French rather than English models. Robert Mannyng of Brunne, translating the rhyming Anglo-French chronicle of Peter of Langtoft, naturally writes in English verse. But Robert of Gloucester, compiling his more or less original chronicle, also uses verse. English historical prose is, in the first place, displaced by Latin. When English again appears in historical literature the influence of French models decides that it shall be written in verse and not in prose. Not until the time of Capgrave do we again find English prose being used in historical writings.[1]

---

[1] In addition to the *Life of St Dunstan* there is some evidence for the existence of other English lives of the saints, apart from the *Martyrologies*, though the English versions have long since been lost. William of St Albans translated his Latin *Life of St Alban* from an English original [*Acta Sanctorum*, June v, 129]. The *Passio Sancti Indracti*, ascribed to William of Malmesbury, is said to have been translated from English [R. R. Darlington, *Vita Wulfstani*, p. ix]. Jocelyn of Furness, in his *Life of St Helena*, used an English life of the saint [MS. Bodley 240, p. 801a, and cf. MS. C.C.C.C. 252, f. 156], a reference which I owe to the kindness of Mr. R. H. Hunt.

V

THE CONTINUITY OF THE HOMILETIC TRADITION

IN homiletic literature the West Saxon literary dialect continues in use for some time after the Conquest. It is still being used in homilies copied after the middle of the twelfth century, though it is not easy to be certain that it is still in actual use as a language of composition. From what we know of mediæval scribal habits there would be nothing surprising in the fact that pre-Conquest writings in the West Saxon literary dialect should continue to be copied only slightly, if at all, modernized in language. Consequently the continued use of this dialect in such works does not necessarily mean that it is still a living literary dialect. It is very possible that the appearance of twelfth-century texts, written in West Saxon, for which no pre-Conquest original can be cited, is due to the later loss of those originals rather than to the fact that they were actually composed in the twelfth century. Take, for example, the case of MS Bodley 343, which was copied some time during the third quarter of the twelfth century. Most of the contents of this manuscript are late copies of the works of Ælfric ; and in addition there are fourteen homilies for which no Old English source has as yet been discovered. These are in the same late West Saxon as the pieces by Ælfric, and are in the true Old English homiletic tradition. There is no claim to originality ; they are simple, straight-forward expositions of the Biblical story, their early date indicated by the almost complete absence of any of the later popular *exempla*. In the same manuscript and dialect is a prose version of the legend of the Holy Rood, a legend which seems to have been fairly well known in mediæval times and of which later Middle English versions also exist. The legend tells of the discovery by Moses of three twigs growing in the ground. They are carried with him on his wanderings and finally planted in the Promised Land. There they are later discovered as trees by David, by him enclosed in a garden, and trained into a single tree. From this tree a beam is cut to help in the building of the Temple, but its use is made impossible by constant fluctuation in size. Consequently it remains stored and forgotten in the Temple until the Crucifixion, when a part of it is made into the cross on which Christ suffered. Later the whereabouts of the cross is revealed to Helena, the mother of Constantine, by a certain Judas, who also gives to her the nails used in the Crucifixion. The cross is then carried to Jerusalem and the nails forged into a bit for the bridle of Constantine's horse.

The first part of the legend is treated very diffusely, with full descriptions of the various miracles, but the author seems to have grown tired of his work and he deals very briefly with the Passion and the succeeding events. Perhaps the chief interest of the work is the evidence which it provides for the early appearance of oriental ideas and subjects in English literature. It is obviously connected with such late Old English productions as the *Letter of Alexander to Aristotle* and the *Wonders of the East*, and it seems quite possible that the extant text is merely a late copy of a work originally composed at about the same time as these. Certainly the homilies themselves, whatever may be the date of their composition, were written by someone in close touch with the Old English homiletic tradition.

The West Saxon literary prose is used in other similar

collections, as for example that contained in MS Cotton Vespasian D. xv, a mixture of homilies, legends and weather prognostications. Even when the old literary dialect has been lost the homiletic prose continues ; though the medium changes there is no break in the tradition itself. Throughout the tenth century the West Saxon was gradually becoming the literary and official language of the country, and other dialects appear less and less frequently in literature. Nevertheless it is probable that some of them retained a tradition of vernacular composition and that, during the last age of Anglo-Saxon England, whilst the greater part of the literature was written in the West Saxon dialect, there may have been a certain amount—more especially of the homiletic literature—still being produced in other dialects. In most departments of literature the predominance of West Saxon followed naturally from the political supremacy of Wessex. Only in the literature intended for the instruction of the common people would other dialects be able to retain something of their former position. Moreover the very fact that they had been largely superseded by West Saxon would be one of the reasons for their continued vitality in post-Conquest times. The later loss of the literary dialect was largely due to the fact that in orthography and spelling it had become traditional, with but slight connexion with the actual spoken speech of the people. Consequently it is entirely dependent on a written tradition, and when, because of the increased use of Latin in the post-Conquest church, the tradition is lost it can never be re-established, and a new language must be used based on the actual spoken language of the people. Other dialects, because of their almost complete disappearance from literature, had never had the chance of developing a traditional spelling, and so had kept much more closely to the actual pronunciation. In post-Conquest times homiletic teaching in their own language was still necessary to the common people, and, when the traditions of the old literary dialect were broken, the work is carried on by dialects which have retained, however slightly, some tradition of composition in the vernacular.

The result is that, when the West Saxon literary dialect loses its position towards the middle of the twelfth century, the Old English homiletic prose tradition is carried on in some of the Southern and Western dialects. Throughout the Old English period there is a fairly continuous stream of homiletic literature in the Kentish dialect. This continues in post-Conquest times and is represented in the twelfth century by two groups of homilies known respectively as the *Cotton Vespasian* and the *Trinity Homilies*. The former, contained in the MS Cotton Vespasian A xxii, consists of three homilies and the beginning of a fourth. One of them is an expansion and modernization of Ælfric's homily *De Initio Creaturae* and, although no early originals have been found for the others, the occurrence of archaic inflexions and constructions in them suggests that they too may be modernizations of earlier compositions. Nothing is known of their provenance, apart from the fact that they contain numerous south-eastern dialectal characteristics. The presence in the same manuscript of matter connected with the monastery at Rochester suggests that the extant copy of them, at any rate, may have been made there.

The *Trinity Homilies* form a much larger and more important group. The manuscript contains thirty-four homilies, dealing with the various festivals and sacraments of the church, and was apparently written some time during the last quarter of the twelfth century. Since five of the homilies in this collection correspond with five which are found in the Lambeth manuscript, and since the homilies in both manuscripts are followed by a text of the *Poema Morale*, it seems probable that the two compilers had access to the same collection of homilies, one which has since been lost. Apart from these, however, the two collections, from a literary as well as from a linguistic standpoint, have little in common. The Trinity collection seems to represent a weakening of the Old English homiletic tradition ; there is little method or general plan in the group and many of the pieces are equally rambling and incoherent. We find, too, a certain amount of subtle and thin-drawn symbolic interpretation from which twelfth-century homilies are usually free. As we should expect they contain no *exempla*, though they include a certain number of illustrations drawn mainly from the Bestiary literature, and a good deal of popular etymology. Many are probably modernizations of earlier material and numerous archaic words and forms still survive. Yet the south-east was in too close touch with the Continent to have any chance of escaping the influence of the contemporary French homiletic literature. The late thirteenth-century Kentish sermons, which have been preserved in MS Laud Miscellaneous 412, are translations from the French, and have been influenced by the language and constructions of their originals. The evidence available seems to indicate that, though the Old English homiletic tradition continued to exist in the south-east more or less vigorously until the beginning of the thirteenth century, it was then completely lost and the Old English models replaced by French.

In the west, however, the old traditions retain more of their vigour and French influence encounters a stronger resistance. In that district a Middle English homiletic prose is developed, drawing its inspiration and style from the West Saxon models of the Late Old English period, but using a western dialect which seems to have behind it a long tradition of literary use. This western dialect first appears in literature in the glosses of the *Vespasian Psalter and Hymns*, and is found also in some of the ninth-century charters. It is probable, too, that its influence is to be discerned in the pseudo-Alfredian translation of Bede's *Ecclesiastical History* and in the Old English version of the *Martyrology*. The non-West Saxon elements in these texts are usually assumed to be Mercian, and in that case, considering the state of the country at the time of their composition during the reign of Alfred, the probability is that they were written in West Mercia. Presumably these two texts show the increasing influence of the West Saxon literary dialect and, if we are to judge from the surviving literature, it would appear that during the tenth century this western vernacular was almost completely displaced. Though displaced it was never wholly forgotten and, with the breakdown of the West Saxon literary dialect during the twelfth century, it once more emerges and takes its place as a literary language. It must be admitted that there is little evidence for such a literary language in the west during most of the Old English period, but the loss of much of the earlier literature and the later supremacy of the West Saxon dialect are enough to explain this. In any case the appearance in post-Conquest times of a literary prose in the West, which must have years of use behind it, seems to demand some such explanation. It is in this dialect that the Old English homiletic prose, as well as the alliterative poetry, are carried on, little influenced by continental models, until they culminate in the prose of the *Ancren Riwle* and the alliterative revival of the fourteenth century.

Special reasons for the vigorous survival of Old English traditions in the West are not far to seek. West Mercia, of all the Old English kingdoms, was the one which was the most closely connected with, and the most deeply influenced by, Wessex. It is probable that the kingdom of the Hwicce, which later became the south-western part of Mercia, was originally settled by West Saxons. During the Danish invasions of the ninth century West Mercia, as an English kingdom, survived only because of a close alliance with Wessex. Under Edward the Elder it became part of the West Saxon realm, and ever since that time the two countries had remained closely connected. Nor, despite a certain Danish element introduced apparently under Canute, had it ever been so completely Scandin-avianized as the east and the north. The connexion of the two kingdoms during Old English times is shown by the similarity of the later Middle English dialects. In the dialectal characteristics due to early changes it agrees as a rule with the East Midlands, in those due to later changes the agreement is with the south-west. It is not surprising, then, that Old English literary traditions should have struck a deep root in the West, and later conditions continued to favour their growth. Wessex and the East were settled comparatively thickly by the Normans,[1] they were particu-larly vulnerable to continental influences and so would the more easily lose the old literary traditions. The north, hardly recovered from the ravages of the Danes, had been even more cruelly ravaged by the Normans. It was even more immune from continental influence than the west, but the Old English literary traditions had had little chance of growth, and it is not surprising that a written literature in the north hardly exists before the fourteenth century. The west seems to have been less Normanized than the south and east, and it had never been systematically ravaged like the north.

There can, however, be no doubt that the main reason for the strength and continuity of the old traditions in the west is to be found in the long episcopacy of Wulfstan of Worcester. As the Old English bishops died or were deposed their places were taken by foreigners, and the chief town of the diocese became the centre of French in-fluence. Wulfstan, despite the attacks of Archbishop

[1] In connexion with this note the number of Anglo-French writings which were composed in Lincolnshire.

Thomas of York, retained his see until his death in 1095. The result was that at Worcester the old traditions continued to be encouraged for a generation longer than elsewhere, and that a generation was trained in them which had never known an Anglo-Saxon England. Wulfstan himself was no scholar, as witness the persistent legend that he was saved from deposition for illiteracy only by the miraculous intervention of Edward the Confessor. Nevertheless, even amongst the forceful Norman prelates, he enjoyed a reputation for sanctity, and he is described by a contemporary chronicler as ' unus et solus de antiquis Anglorum patribus, vir in omni religione conspicuus et antiquarum Angliae consuetudinum scientia apprime imbutus '.[1] He was fond of books, and is said to have encouraged the copying and illumination of them whilst he was prior of the monastery at Worcester. The chronicle of Marianus was copied and enlarged at his monastery and at his command, and many tales are told of his close friendship with the learned Norman Robert of Hereford. William of Malmesbury tells us that Wulfstan was an indefatigable preacher in the vernacular and, in view of his rigid adherence to Old English customs, it may be assumed that the copying of books in English would be continued in his diocese. It was due to Wulfstan that Heming, the sub-prior of Worcester, compiled his famous chartulary, a work which vies in authority and importance with the *Textus Roffensis*, indispensable for our knowledge of Old English law.

Moreover the vitality of the vernacular traditions at Worcester is shown by the fact that, after the death of that bishop, his biography was written in English by Coleman, a monk of Worcester.[2] Unfortunately this English

---

[1] Eadmer, *Historia Novorum in Anglia* (Rolls Series 81), p. 46.
[2] Incidentally Coleman also wrote, in English, the life of Gregory the Great. This too was translated into Latin by William of Malmesbury, but in this case both English and Latin have been lost.

life of Wulfstan is no longer extant, and is known only from the translation of it into Latin which was made by William of Malmesbury. At the beginning of the thirteenth century, when negotiations for the canonization of Wulfstan were going on, the bishop and convent sent off to the pope an authentic record of the life of Wulfstan ' written in the English tongue a hundred years before '. This can only have been the Old English life by Coleman, and presumably it never returned from Rome. In any case the significance of such a work at that time is obvious. Even during the Old English period the lives of the great bishops had been written in Latin, but at Worcester, more than a generation after the Conquest, English prose is adapting itself to new subjects and evidently still full of vitality.[1] The evidence, such as it is, does seem to point to the continuity of the old traditions in the west. Obviously under Wulfstan there must have been a tradition of composition in the vernacular at Worcester ; a tradition, moreover, which continued to be carried on after his death. Many of the extant manuscripts of Old English works were copied at Worcester in post-Conquest times [2], and it is probable, too, that others of the great western monasteries played a part in the survival of the old traditions. Evesham, for example, may have played a considerable part, though direct evidence is wanting. Its prior, Æthelwig, was one of the most powerful and trusted of the English clerics under the Conqueror, and the monastery seems to be responsible for a number of forged charters which would show in-

---

[1] Prose was not the only medium in which the old traditions were being kept up in the west. In figure sculpture the Anglo-Saxons were far ahead of the Normans and, after the Conquest, the specific Old English traditions are said to have continued more especially in the West ; see A. W. Clapham, *English Romanesque Architecture after the Conquest*, p. 141.

[2] See W. Keller, *Die litterarischen Bestrebungen von Worcester in angelsächsischer Zeit* (Quellen und Forschungen 1900).

terest of a sort in, and some knowledge of, the old traditions.

A good part of the extant twelfth-century vernacular literature seems to have been copied, and much of it was possibly composed, either in this western dialect, or in some slight variation of it. Here, however, we are concerned only with the homiletic literature. The earliest post-Conquest work still surviving, and written in this dialect, is a twelfth-century homily on the life of St Chad, the apostle of Mercia.[1] From a literary point of view it is not very important ; in matter and style there is nothing to differentiate it from the usual homiletic literature of the period. It gives, mainly from Bede, the few known facts concerning the life and death of the saint, but is, as usual, far more interested in the numerous miraculous happenings connected with him. Linguistically, however, the work is most interesting. There can be little doubt that the dialect in which it is written is a direct descendant of the dialect used in the *Vespasian Psalter*, and the ancestor of that used later in the *Katherine Group* and the *Ancrene Wisse*. This is the earliest appearance of the Old English homiletic prose in a dialect other than West Saxon, and it forms a definite link in the chain connecting that prose with the later homiletic prose of the west.

More important from a literary point of view are the *Lambeth Homilies*,[2] a group of some twenty homilies, the extant manuscript of which was copied somewhere about 1180. Their provenance is doubtful, some scholars assign-

[1] Ed. A. S. Napier, ' Ein altenglisches Leben des heiligen Chad ' (*Anglia* x. 131 ff).

[2] Ed. R. Morris, *Old English Homilies, Series I* (Early English Text Society 1867–8) ; on the provenance see Miss B. A. Mackenzie, *The Early London Dialect* (Oxford 1928), and compare R. M. Wilson ' The Provenance of the Lambeth Homilies ' (*Leeds Studies in English* iv. 24 ff).

ing them to Middlesex, others to the West Midland area. There is certainly considerable similarity between the dialect in which they are written and that of the *Katherine Group*, which most scholars agree in assigning to the west, and the only evidence for a localization in Middlesex is provided by the forms of the place-names of that county. It is difficult to decide how much reliance can be placed on the sole evidence of place-names, nor is it at all certain that in this case, even if reliable, it is necessarily favourable to the localization proposed. Certainly, if accepted, it would follow that the dialect of Middlesex and that of the West Midlands must have been remarkably similar, an assumption for which there is otherwise no evidence and which is, in any case, very improbable. The homilies themselves are of varying origin ; at least two of them are modernizations of homilies by Ælfric, and others are identical with homilies preserved in the Trinity manuscript. Probably most of them are adaptations of earlier material, though the originals cannot always be identified and may long since have been lost. One of them—an exposition in rhyme of the *Creed*—is certainly, and others probably, of post-Conquest composition. But, whatever their origin, they are strictly in the Old English homiletic tradition ; plain straightforward expositions of the Scriptural texts with little elaboration and an almost complete absence of *exempla*.

Except as evidence for the strength of the Old English tradition, the twelfth-century homiletic literature in this western dialect is of comparatively little interest. Much of it consists of the adaptation of earlier material. Even when it seems to be of post-Conquest composition it depends so closely on the earlier literature that, in the absence of the originals, certainty is not always possible. The earliest texts which are undoubtedly of post-Conquest composition are those usually classed together under the title of the

Katherine Group. All of them usually appear in the same manuscripts and are obviously connected together in subject as well as in style and dialect. The group includes the legends of the three saints Katherine,[1] Margaret,[2] and Juliana,[3] a homiletic treatise on virginity—*Hali Meiðhad*—and a prose homily—*Sawles Warde*. The three saints, whose martyrdoms are described here, were all popular in mediæval times, and later English versions of the legends are to be found. It was a type of literature of which the Middle Ages was remarkably fond, combining as it did the wonder and excitement of romance with the virtue of pious reading. Today its fascination has disappeared ; there are so many lives of the saints and they tend to be so discouragingly monotonous. The material was worked over so often that, long before the end of the Middle Ages, the matter had become conventionalized. The only possible variation was the transference of miracles from one saint to another, the introduction of still more fantastic and incredible torments, and the grotesque elaboration of devils and evil spirits who attempt, undeterred by their inevitable failure, to undermine the faith of the future saint. Only in the hands of poets such as Chaucer and Lydgate do the old legends retain or regain something of their earlier simplicity and charm.

The freedom of the legends in the *Katherine Group* from most of the later failings, is sufficient evidence for the comparatively early date of their composition. Nevertheless conventionalization is already beginning to appear. As so often happens in such literature the heroines are far from

[1] Ed. E. Einenkel, *The Early English Life of St Katherine* (Early English Text Society 1884).

[2] Ed. F. M. Mack, *Seinte Marharete* (Early English Text Society 1934).

[3] Ed. S. T. R. O. d'Ardenne, *The Liflade ant te Passiun of Seinte Iuliene* (Liège 1936).

sympathetic. They address their persecutors in studiously offensive language, and seem intent on securing the crown of martyrdom at whatever cost of courtesy or good manners. In their prayers and their orations the martyr, however tender in age, sums up the whole matter of the gospels and the fathers. Certain specific torments are appropriated to the different saints, as for example the fiery wheel of St Katherine, but a conventional course of torture, always fruitless, is usually included in addition. Many of the defects to be found in the Middle English legends are due to the influence of their originals since, strictly speaking, the three lives are all derived from previous Latin versions. But the English author uses his originals so freely that his works are rather adaptations than translations. Although he owes his material, and no doubt whatever virtues of formal arrangement he may possess, to the Latin, most of the vivifying touches are due to the English adaptor. This freedom is made possible by the fact that he is using a prose which has behind it a long literary history. He is no innovator self-consciously using a new medium for the edification of the ignorant, but the inheritor of a prose tradition which goes back to pre-Conquest times. Because of this he is freed from the close dependency on his originals so common in vernacular religious literature. The Middle English lives of these saints have all the ease and sureness of original compositions, in which the ability of the author is seen more especially in his remarkably vivid descriptive power, as in his description of the devil in the *Seinte Marherete* :

There came out of a corner, hastening towards her, a devil from hell in the likeness of a dragon, so horrible that it terrified all who saw it. That hateful one glittered as if he were covered with gold. His hair and his long beard shone with gold, and his horrible teeth seemed to be made of black iron. His two eyes, big as basins, in his horned head on either side of his hooked nose, shone brighter than the stars or than ten jewels. Fire glinted from his horrible mouth, and a suffocating smoke, foul to the taste, poured from his nostrils. He thrust out his tongue, so far that he twisted it round his neck and it seemed as though a sharp sword came out of his mouth, glittering like light and blazing with fire. The place was full of a foul and deadly stench, and everything shone and glittered because of the shadow of this devil.

The picture of hell in *Sawles Warde* and, in a somewhat different style, the apostrophe to hell in the same work is a similar masterpiece of gruesome description :

O Hell ! the house of death, dwelling of want, of terror and of misery ; habitation of hate and terrible home of every danger ; city of bale and abode of every bitterness. Thou most hateful of all lands, thou dark place full of every weariness ; I tremble with terror and fear, and every bone quakes and every hair rises up at the memory of you, for there is no sound amongst the damned but ' woe is me ', woe to me and woe to ye, ah woe to ye. Woe they cry and woe they have ; nor shall any woe be wanting to all who earn such an abode for any transitory bliss here in this world.

Such descriptions owe little to the original and bear witness to the power of the Middle English author, or authors. Some attempt is also made to soften the characters of the heroines and to make them more sympathetic ; but in this case the influence of the Latin has proved too strong and they still remain somewhat repugnant figures to the modern reader.

Sawles Warde [1] is an allegorical homily on the text : ' If the householder knew at what time the thief would come he would watch and would not suffer his house to be robbed '. It provides the earliest example in English of the struggle between Wit and Will, a popular theme in later literature and one which maintained its popularity as late as Elizabethan times. The mind of man is represented as a house of which Wit is the Master, with Will as the

[1] Ed. R. Morris, *op.cit.* pp. 245–67 ; R. M. Wilson (Leeds 1939).

foolish mistress. Within the house is the soul, the precious treasure of God, guarded by Wit and by the four daughters of God, Prudence, Spiritual Strength, Moderation and Righteousness, who have been lent for that purpose. Without the house is beset by vices and within threatened by the wilfulness of the mistress. A special post is assigned to each of the Virtues, according to their special qualifications ; Prudence is the doorkeeper, Strength stands near by, ready to help Prudence, Moderation keeps watch over the servants—the different senses—and Righteousness is the judge. In order to keep them watchful Prudence sends in a visitor who announces himself as Fear, the messenger of Death, and describes to them the torments and the pains of hell. His tidings fill them with dread and a discussion on the best means of avoiding hell follows. In order to encourage them again Prudence admits into the house Love of Eternal Life who tells them of heaven and the joys of the blessed. Fear is then cast out of the house, and Will and the rest of the household agree henceforth to act according to the advice of Wit and his helpers.

The homily is not an original work, but an adaptation of some chapters of a treatise, *De Anima*, which has been ascribed to Hugh of St Victor. Nevertheless it has all the characteristics of an original work, to an even greater extent than the lives of the saints. The episode has been given a life and a dramatic quality such as is not to be found in the Latin, and the English author has expanded and altered his original to suit his own particular purpose. The description of hell, a common enough theme in mediæval literature, is less conventional than usual, the bare account of the original having been considerably elaborated. In the description of heaven, which follows, the author keeps much more closely to the Latin, but it may be significant that that part of it dealing with the position of the monks in heaven has been suppressed and the part dealing with the

virgins expanded. Throughout the homily the personification is excellent, and its dramatic quality has been increased
by the inclusion of a considerable amount of direct discourse.
The artistry is consistent and the execution forceful. Both
in matter and style it is probably the most interesting and
artistic of all the Middle English homilies. How much it
owes to the Middle English adaptor and how little to the
Latin is shown by a comparison with the work of Dan
Michael, who, in the fourteenth century, translated the
same chapters from the Latin as an appendix to his *Ayenbite
of Inwyt*. He had apparently no knowledge of the earlier
English version, and produces only an unimaginative literal
translation which cannot compare with the artistry of the
earlier work.

Hali Meiðhad [1] is the only member of the *Katherine Group*
for which no Latin original is to be found. It is a treatise
on the discomforts of marriage and the advantages of a
life of cloistered seclusion. For some thirty pages the
author deals with the hardships and miseries of married
life, the perils of childbirth, the troubles of bringing up
children, and the praise of perpetual virginity. Although the
emphasis is perhaps too often on the merely temporal advantages of virginity the author never forgets that it is only one
of the virtues, for ' many a mild wife or meek widow is
better than a proud maiden '. The work is not particularly
pleasant reading, but there is no reason for the deprecating
air with which it has too often been approached. No doubt
the realistic frankness may occasionally appear embarrassing
to the modern reader, but there is no justification for
supposing that the author's contemporaries would have found
it particularly objectionable. It is obviously propaganda for
the various nunneries and so necessarily prejudiced; for
all that we have no reason to suppose that his pictures of

[1] Ed. F. J. Furnivall, *Hali Meidenhad* (Early English Text
Society, reprinted 1922).

mediæval love in a cottage are at all exaggerated. The treatise provides a very necessary corrective to the ideas as to the position and importance of women in mediæval Europe, which one would gather from the romances. To the mediæval mind there was no necessary connexion between theory and practice, and the fine phrases of chivalry should not blind us to the fact that those who sung its virtues most loudly would have been very much offended by any suggestion that their theories should become a reality in their treatment of their women or their inferiors. Naturally, considering his object, the author has little to say of happy married life, but the touches of homely observation in some of his descriptions provide a realistic contrast to the idealism of romantic love :

It may happen that riches are plentiful ; you may possess mansions proud and full of wealth, and have numerous servants under you in the hall. Yet if it should happen that your husband becomes angry with you, and is hateful so that you quarrel continually, what joy can worldly wealth bring to you. When he is absent you await his homecoming in sorrow, grief and dread. When he is at home all the extent of the house seems too small for you. When he looks at you you tremble. His hateful mirth and his rough behaviour fill you with terror. He scolds and nags at you, and insults you shamefully. He behaves to you with contempt, as a lecher treats his mistress. He beats and thrashes you as if you were his bought thrall or his born slave. Your bones ache, your flesh smarts, your heart swells within you with injured rage, and your face burns with vexation. . . . What is the wife to do, who, when she comes into the house, hears her child screaming, sees the cat at the bacon and the dog at the meat ? Her cakes are burning in the oven, the calf is drinking the milk, the pot is boiling over into the fire, and her husband is scolding her. This may sound foolish, but it ought to deter a maiden from marriage, for it doesn't seem so foolish to anyone who has experienced it.

Attempts have been made by some scholars to prove that the works in this group were written, not in prose, but in a loose kind of alliterative verse. There can be no doubt of the rhythm and alliteration in many of the passages, but there can be even less doubt that other passages are in prose. On the whole it seems clear enough that we must regard the *Katherine Group* as having been written, not in a rough alliterative verse, but in a rhythmical prose, much like the rhythmical alliterative prose used by Ælfric. Stylistically there is some variation between the different members of the group, the legends of the saints contrasting with *Sawles Warde* and *Hali Meiðhad* in the use which is made of rhythm and alliteration.[1] In the former the rhythm is much more regular, and there is a more consistent use of alliteration for the binding together of clauses and sentences. There is some alliteration in *Hali Meiðhad*, and still more in *Sawles Warde*, but in neither of these texts is it regularly used, as it is in the others, to give emphasis to a consistently maintained rhythm, and it adds nothing to the poetic quality of the prose. The basis of the style is apparently the ordinary homiletic prose, and the legends of the saints seem to have been influenced by the style of Ælfric's works on similar subjects. The rhythm and movement of the Old English works is parallel to that which we find in the Middle English texts. There is the same tendency towards a line with a four-stress beat and an indefinite number of unaccented syllables, and the same dependence on alliteration, an alliteration which, in the *Katherine Group*, sometimes tends to become excessive, especially in *Seinte Marherete*. The only difference is that the Middle English author uses a large number of alliterative tags and formulæ of the type that were used by Ælfric's contemporaries, but not, as a rule, by Ælfric himself, whose use of alliteration is much more artistic and unobtrusive.

[1] See especially D. Bethurum, ' The Connection of the *Katherine Group* with Old English prose ' (*Journal of English and Germanic Philology* xxxiv. 553 ff).

No doubt the slighter use of alliteration in the other works in the group is due mainly to a difference of subject, and the style of the legends provides strong evidence of the continued influence of Ælfric's writings in early Middle English.

Nothing is known of the author of any of the works which comprise the *Katherine Group*, nor is it known whether they were all written by one man or by different authors. Various names have been mentioned in this connexion, but there is not the slightest evidence in favour of any of them and, since there is little likelihood that any will ever be forthcoming, it is fortunate that the question is only one of sentimental interest. The question of the unity of authorship is of more value, and perhaps more capable of being answered. It has already been pointed out that there are stylistic differences within the group, and these differences of style and subject have led to their attribution to different authors. Argument from style can be very subjective, and is notoriously dangerous. Moreover in this case it is possible that a difference in style may be the result of a difference in subject. The various theories have convinced few but the propounders of them and we can only say that the works may possibly, though not perhaps probably, all be by the same author. Verbal and phraseological similarities in the works may be due to unity of authorship, or may be accounted for by the fact that they were certainly all composed at about the same time and in the same district.

Most of the texts of the *Katherine Group* are preserved in three manuscripts, some of them only in two, and the earliest of these, a Bodleian manuscript copied during the first-quarter of the thirteenth century, is written in an extraordinarily consistent dialect. The significance of this will be fully dealt with when we consider the same problem in connexion with the *Ancren Riwle*, but the conclusions to be derived from this fact are, in short, either that the Bodley manuscript must be the author's autograph copy, or else that the original from which it was eventually copied must have been written in the same dialect and at approximately the same time. The first explanation is obviously impossible in the face of a number of mistakes in the Bodley manuscript as compared with the right reading in the later manuscripts, so that the second must apparently be accepted. In that case it would follow that the texts of the *Katherine Group* must have been composed in the West Midland dialect some time about the beginning of the thirteenth century—a conclusion with which most scholars would, in any case, agree. The various attempts which have been made to localize them more accurately must, in the present state of our knowledge of Middle English dialects, be accepted with considerable reserve. Certain scribblings on the margins of the manuscript connect it with Herefordshire and, although these are sixteenth-century in character, it is possible enough that the *Katherine Group* was originally written in that county.

The subjects of four of these works, the legends of the three virgin saints and the treatise on virginity, suggest that they were composed for some convent or group of anchoresses, but again with no clue as to their specific identity. Nevertheless there can be no doubt that the survival of the homiletic prose owes much to this, and to other groups of similar recluses, throughout the mediæval period. Rules and instructions addressed to monks during the early Middle English period are naturally written in Latin. Women recluses, however, were not expected to be familiar with that language, and for them translation into, or composition in, one of the vernaculars was considered necessary. This is shown, throughout the mediæval period, by the care with which bishops furnished them with English translations of injunctions and the like documents. In 1277

Bishop Cantilupe of Hereford writes to the nuns of Lynbrook, and adds that the letter should be expounded to them in English or French, whichever they might know the better.[1] In the fourteenth century Bishop Stapleton of Exeter was so painfully aware of the deficiencies of the nuns of Polslo in this respect that he recommended them, should they have to use Latin, to do so without regard to grammar.[2] From the translation of the *Rule of St Benedict* in Anglo-Saxon times by Æthelwold of Winchester to the works addressed by More and Fisher to Joyeuce Leigh and Elizabeth White there is a continuous stream of devotional literature in the vernacular addressed to pious women, and the debt which modern English prose owes to such works has been well emphasized by Professor Chambers.[3]

Sometimes associated with the *Katherine Group* is *The Wooing of Our Lord*,[4] a short work in lyrical prose with a strongly marked alliteration occasionally suggestive of the lives of the saints in the former. It is found in one of the manuscripts which contains the *Katherine Group* and seems to be of approximately the same date and from the same locality. It has, however, very little in common with the homiletic prose of the group, and, together with two similar works, *An Orison of Our Lord*[5] and *A Lofsong of Our Lord*,[6] it forms a group of its own the affinities of which are rather with lyric than with homiletic literature. All three are short and are addressed to Christ as the heavenly lover. The author seems to have been considerably influenced by the phraseology of the secular love lyrics, as of course has been the case with many of the mediæval

---

[1] *Register*, ed. R. G. Griffiths, Cantilupe Society 1906, p. 202.
[2] *English Monks and the Suppression of the Monasteries*, G. Baskerville, p. 208.
[3] *On the Continuity of English Prose*, pp. xciii, c.
[4] Ed. R. Morris, *op. cit.* 269–87.
[5] *ibid.* 183–9. [6] *ibid.* 209–17.

lyrics addressed to the Virgin. *The Wooing of Our Lord*, in which the qualities and achievements of Christ, the perfected earthly lover, are exalted and his sufferings lamented, is probably the best of the three. In the other two the physical increasingly triumphs over the spiritual. All are frequently hysterical and occasionally erotic. They probably owe their inspiration to the Latin mystical writings, and are the predecessors in England of the mystical poetry of Richard Rolle and his school.

VI

THE *ANCREN RIWLE* [1] AND ITS INFLUENCE

SOME obvious connexions exist between the *Katherine Group* and the *Ancren Riwle*. Like the latter the texts of the former were written as devotional reading for some group of holy women. In both cases the prose style is based on the homiletic prose of the Old English period, though the style of the *Rule* approximates more to the straightforward prose of *Sawles Warde* and *Hali Meiðhad* than to the more rhythmical and elaborated prose of the saints' lives. Whether the resemblances are more than fortuitous it is impossible to say definitely at present. The introduction to the *Rule* tells us something of the circumstances of its composition, though the references are so slight and tantalizing that they have given rise to widely differing theories on the subject. The author tells us that he has been asked to write for the guidance of three maidens of noble birth who have decided to abandon the world and to live as anchoresses. They belong to no regular order: 'to anyone who asks you concerning your order, and whether white or black nuns, say that you are both through the grace of God, and of the order of St James.' If we are to judge from incidental remarks the author does not seem to have felt much enthusiasm for his task. 'Now thanks be to Christ are the two parts completed. Let us proceed to the third with the help of God'; and

[1] Ed. J. Morton, *The Ancren Riwle* (Camden Society 1853).

again at the end, ' God knows I would rather set out for Rome than begin to write it again '. Nevertheless he has produced a work which remained popular for some 300 years.

Much of it consists of the ordinary mediæval religious teaching, the exposition of Scriptural texts and a fondness for allegory which, however popular to mediæval readers, has lost much of its appeal. But there is more than enough to make up for all this. The brilliant descriptive powers of the author have been recognized ever since the first publication of the book, and some of his figures have often been compared, not unjustly, with the better-known Characters of seventeenth-century writers. Here, for example, is his classification of the different kinds of flatterers :

The first, if a man is good, praise him to his face and make him appear better than he is ; and if he speaks or does well, they laud him extravagantly with excessive praise and commendation. The second kind, if a man is evil and says and does so much wickedness that the fault is plain and cannot be altogether denied, nevertheless in the man's own presence they treat his vileness as of little importance. ' It is not,' they say, ' so exceptionally wicked as it is made out to be. You are not the first to do such things and you won't be the last. You have plenty of companions. Don't bother about it, sir. You are not by yourself. Many do much worse.' Then there are the third kind of flatterers, who are the worst, for they praise the wicked and their evil deeds, like a man who says to the knight who robs his poor serfs, ' Ah ! sir, how well you do ! The peasant ought always to be well plucked and shorn, for he is like the willow that sprouts the better the oftener that it is pollarded.'

Even better is his description of the backbiter :

He lowers his head and begins to sigh before he says anything. He pulls a long face and hesitates a long time so that he will be the more readily believed. But when it all comes out, then is it yellow poison.   'Alas and alack,' he says, ' woe is me that he (or she) has such a reputation.   I've tried hard enough but I haven't been able to improve matters.   I've known about it for a long time, but it would never have been made known by me. However, since others have spread it about so widely, I can't deny it.   They say it is bad ; it's even worse.   I'm grieved and sorry to have to say it but it is quite true, and that is a great sorrow to me.   In many other things he (or she) is greatly to be praised, but not in this, and sorry I am to have to say it.'

Similar sketches are to be found when he deals with the seven deadly sins, that invariable, and, to be just, usually lively ingredient of mediæval religious or didactic literature. Here the treatment is still further enlivened by his skilful descriptions of the wrathful man, the miser and the glutton. Whoever the author may have been he certainly had an eye for character, an insight into the mental and moral make-up of his fellows, and the ability to pin it down on paper.

For his time the author seems to have been a man of considerable culture and learning.   As we should expect, quotations from the Fathers and from the great theologians, especially Anselm and St Bernard, are frequent ; we also find some acquaintance with the classics, though possibly only through intermediate compilations.   Probably, too, the contemporary chivalrous romance has left some mark on the work, especially in the description of Christ as the ideal knight, and in the tale of the besieged lady :

There was a lady who was besieged by her foes.   Her land was destroyed and she was left in poverty within an earthen castle. Nevertheless the love of a mighty king was fixed upon her, so excessively that, to woo her, he sent his messengers one after the other, and often many together.   He sent to her jewels, many and beauteous, and food and help from his mighty court to defend her castle.   She received everything like a careless creature who was so hard-hearted that he could never be any the nearer to her love. What more would you ? He came himself at last and showed her his fair face, he the fairest of all men to see, and he spoke so sweetly and with such joyous words that they could have raised the dead from death to life. He wrought many wonders and did many miracles before her eyes, and showed her his power, told her of his kingdom, and offered to make her queen of all that he possessed, but all to no avail.

In the same way the influence of the popular bestiaries and lapidaries is to be seen in the accounts of the pelican, the eagle and the agate, whilst the increasing popularity of the *exemplum* is shown by the number of illustrative stories incorporated in the text.

Much more interesting to modern readers are the numerous glimpses which we get of the social life of the period, for many of the illustrations are taken from the homely incidents familiar to all. The author is as fond of popular proverbs as is the author of the *Owl and the Nightingale* : ' From mill and from market, from smithy and from anchorhold, men bring tidings ' ; ' The cock is brave on his own dunghill ' ; ' He cannot when he will who would not when he could.' We see the habits and happenings of the countryside, the hen cackling over her eggs and the pedlar selling his soap. An anchoress should not be ' like a pig fastened in a sty to fatten and grow big, ready for the blow of the axe ' ; the flesh is fastened to the soul ' in the same way as men tie a clog of wood to the swine that is always wandering and roaming about '. Another simile tells us something of the dangers of travel in those days : ' like a shy horse which is startled at a shadow on the high bridge and falls down into the water from the high bridge ' ; and another homely illustration would hold good, with slight modification, today : ' a man ties a knot in his tunic in order to remind himself of anything '. As we should expect, country sports come in for their mention. There are incidental references to wrestling ; the meaning of a hunting term is expounded, ' a " tristre " is the place where one sits with the greyhounds in order to intercept the game or to prepare the nets for it ' ; mention is made of ball-play, sports in the churchyard—that playground of mediæval Europe—and we even find a snatch from some popular song :

> Ever is the eye to the wood-leye (glade),
> Where is he I love.

a longer version of which is given in one of the manuscripts. The references to children are rather unexpected in a book written presumably by a celibate, and for the use of maidens vowed to lifelong chastity, but in them we find the same understanding and power of vivid description. ' If a child stumbles against something or hurts himself, the object against which he stumbled is beaten, and the child is well-pleased and forgets his hurt and quietens his tears.' The appealing picture of the mother and her child was used again in a devotional work in the fourteenth century :

> Our Lord, when he suffers us to be tempted, plays with us like a mother with her darling ; she runs away from him and hides herself and leaves him sitting alone and looking eagerly about, crying ' mother, mother ', and weeping for a time. Then she runs forward laughing with outspread arms, embraces and kisses him and wipes his eyes.

It is not surprising that such incidental illustrations should prove more interesting to the modern reader than the more serious religious instruction. Much of the latter is such as can be found in almost any mediæval religious manual, and it is only vivified by the wealth of illustration and by the descriptive power of the author. He is concerned not only with the spiritual but also with the physical welfare of the anchoresses, and he has much practical advice to give. The first and last of the eight parts into which the work is divided deal with what the author calls the 'outer rule' as distinct from the 'inner rule' of the other six parts. But, since the intention is to instil the idea and not simply the form of religion, the author constantly emphasizes the fact that, concerning the outer rule, he makes suggestions only, any of which may be altered as necessity shall dictate; it is of little importance as compared with the inner rule. The first part deals with the formal religious duties, the prayers and meditations, of the anchoresses. The variety of subject in the last part is sufficiently indicated by the heading given to it in the list of contents following the introduction :

The eighth part has to do with the outer rule ; first of all concerning food and drink and other things which have to do with them ; thereafter of the things which you may receive, and what you may keep and possess ; then concerning your clothes and such things as have to do with them ; next of the cropping of your hair, your work and your blood-letting ; lastly the rule concerning your maidens and how you ought lovingly to teach them.

Little as was the importance which the author attached to this part, it is the one which will appeal most to the modern reader. In it we find numerous sidelights on the social history of the period. We learn much concerning feminine costume of the time from the elaborate suggestions as to the clothes of the anchoresses which are given, and the directions as to how their health is to be preserved afford a good deal of information on the medical knowledge of the period. The author is always practical, sometimes amusingly so as when he suggests that an anchoress, if she desires a pet, should content herself with a cat, and paints a harrowing picture of the troubles awaiting an anchoress who keeps a cow. Not that this liking for the practical is found only in this last part. We find the same mixture of the spiritual and the practical elsewhere as, for example, in the list of things which are to be confessed :

Pride, ambition, arrogance, envy, wroth, sloth, negligence, idle words, undisciplined thoughts, idle hearing, false rejoicing, grievous mourning, hypocrisy, eating or drinking too much or too little, grumbling, looking miserable, breaking silence, sitting too long at the window, saying the hours badly without serious attention or at the wrong time, lying, swearing, playing, scornful laughter, spilling crumbs or ale, letting things grow mouldy, or rusty, or rotten, clothes unsewn, wet or unwashed, a cup or a dish broken, being careless with anything which is being used, or which ought to be taken care of, cutting or damaging anything through negligence.

Throughout this part, as indeed throughout the book, the main theme of the author is Moderation, 'everything may be overdone, Moderation is always best', and again 'the middle way of Moderation is always golden'. He will have nothing to do with hysterical abandonment, so common in periods of religious excitement. He speaks of the incredible fasts, penances and disciplines which some anchoresses inflict on themselves, and declares that too often they defeat their own object.

Wear no iron, nor haircloth, nor hedgehog skins ; don't beat yourself with them nor with a leaded scourge with leather thongs. Don't make yourself bleed with holly or briars without leave of your confessor ; and don't, at any one time, use too many flagellations.

Again his remarks on the subject of personal cleanliness strike what we are inclined to regard as a modern note : ' Wash yourselves wherever necessary, and your clothes, whenever you wish. Dirt was never dear to God, though poverty and simplicity are pleasing to him.' Throughout the author appears as a kindly, humane and cultured personality, religious but not inexperienced in the ways of the world. He never forgets the needs of the particular limited audience to which he is addressing himself, and he must have proved an excellent adviser to the three anchoresses. He is fortunate, too, in his prose ; a prose which has already a long tradition behind it. In his hands it becomes capable of almost anything, of practical admonition, of simple straightforward exposition, of vivid description and of a mysticism which sometimes approaches that of Rolle and his followers. The *Ancren Riwle* is the first, and by no means the least influential, of those great devotional books in the vernacular, written for the edification of pious women, which have exerted so great an influence on the development of English prose style.

Almost the only question connected with the *Rule* which seems to have been finally settled is that of the language employed by the author. We know that it was written in England since the author thanks God that ' heresy prevails not in England ', but the question of whether the author wrote in English, French or Latin was long disputed. No one of the extant manuscripts can be considered as being the author's autograph copy, and since versions in French and Latin are also extant, it was perhaps inevitable that, before the importance and variety of English religious prose in the early period had been established by Professor Chambers, the English versions should have been taken to be translations from an original *Rule* in French or Latin. The earliest scholars rather naturally took it for granted that the author wrote in Latin. But the first editor of the English text showed, mainly by examples of mistranslation in the Latin due to a misunderstanding of the English,[1] that it was the Latin version which was translated from the

---

[1] e.g. *hore* ' their ' translated as *meretrix* ; *herboruwe* ' lodging ' translated as *herbarium* ; *bode* ' an offer ' translated as *corpus*.

English. Consequently later scholars acce
native and attempted to show that both En
were ultimately derived from the French
Miss Dymes,[1] however, has made it clear t
Rule must have been written in English. I
instances where the two versions disagree i
English which gives the better meaning.
a Latin distich into verse is given in prose
writer, and a snatch of popular song and
on words are to be found in the English wh
agrees closely, though without the rhyme
words. On the whole it seems certain e
extant French version is a translation fro
though it is possible to argue that the Engl
adaptations of a French original which ha
and which has nothing to do with the extant I
However, there is not the slightest evide
view and the probabilities are against it.
of such a French work during the twelfth
have been quite unprecedented. During t
of that century French, as a literary langua
was just beginning to come into promine
notable that the more ambitious writings ar
not in prose which, as yet, is in the expe
English, on the contrary, already had a lo
composition in the vernacular prose. B
Alfred it had become classic in the hand
homilists, Ælfric and Wulfstan, and so firm
it could survive the Conquest.

The exact date of the composition of th
known but it was almost certainly in existen

,[1] D. M. E. Dymes, 'The Original Languag
Riwle' (*Essays and Studies* ix. 31–49). See also R
'Recent research upon the *Ancren Riwle*' (Re
Studies i. 4 ff).

the author appears as a kindly, humane and cultured personality, religious but not inexperienced in the ways of the
world. He never forgets the needs of the particular limited
audience to which he is addressing himself, and he must
have proved an excellent adviser to the three anchoresses.
He is fortunate, too, in his prose ; a prose which has already
a long tradition behind it. In his hands it becomes capable
of almost anything, of practical admonition, of simple
straightforward exposition, of vivid description and of a
mysticism which sometimes approaches that of Rolle and
his followers. The *Ancren Riwle* is the first, and by no
means the least influential, of those great devotional books
in the vernacular, written for the edification of pious women,
which have exerted so great an influence on the development
of English prose style.

Almost the only question connected with the *Rule* which
seems to have been finally settled is that of the language
employed by the author. We know that it was written in
England since the author thanks God that ' heresy prevails
not in England ', but the question of whether the author
wrote in English, French or Latin was long disputed. No
one of the extant manuscripts can be considered as being
the author's autograph copy, and since versions in French
and Latin are also extant, it was perhaps inevitable that,
before the importance and variety of English religious prose
in the early period had been established by Professor
Chambers, the English versions should have been taken
to be translations from an original *Rule* in French or Latin.
The earliest scholars rather naturally took it for granted
that the author wrote in Latin. But the first editor of the
English text showed, mainly by examples of mistranslation
in the Latin due to a misunderstanding of the English,[1]
that it was the Latin version which was translated from the

---

[1] e.g. *hore* ' their ' translated as *meretrix* ; *herboruwe* ' lodging '
translated as *herbarium* ; *bode* ' an offer ' translated as *corpus*.

English. Consequently later scholars accepted the alternative and attempted to show that both English and Latin were ultimately derived from the French. Research by Miss Dymes,[1] however, has made it clear that the original *Rule* must have been written in English. In the occasional instances where the two versions disagree it is usually the English which gives the better meaning. A translation of a Latin distich into verse is given in prose by the French writer, and a snatch of popular song and occasional plays on words are to be found in the English where the French agrees closely, though without the rhyme or the play on words. On the whole it seems certain enough that the extant French version is a translation from the English, though it is possible to argue that the English versions are adaptations of a French original which has not survived and which has nothing to do with the extant French versions. However, there is not the slightest evidence for such a view and the probabilities are against it. The production of such a French work during the twelfth century would have been quite unprecedented. During the second half of that century French, as a literary language in England, was just beginning to come into prominence, but it is notable that the more ambitious writings are in verse and not in prose which, as yet, is in the experimental stage. English, on the contrary, already had a long tradition of composition in the vernacular prose. Beginning with Alfred it had become classic in the hands of the later homilists, Ælfric and Wulfstan, and so firmly rooted that it could survive the Conquest.

The exact date of the composition of the *Rule* is unknown but it was almost certainly in existence by the year

---

, [1] D. M. E. Dymes, ' The Original Language of the *Ancren Riwle* ' (*Essays and Studies* ix. 31–49). See also R. W. Chambers, ' Recent research upon the *Ancren Riwle* ' (*Review of English Studies* i. 4 ff).

1200, at a time when the Old English homilists were still being copied and at which later works, such as the *Katherine Group* and the *Vices and Virtues*, show that the Old English homiletic tradition was still vigorous in different parts of the country. There is no difficulty in supposing that the three noble maidens were able to read English, since the author refers them to their ' English book of St Margaret ' and recommends the reading of ' English or French ' books. Moreover, sometime between 1140 and 1215, a priest Robert was asked by an anchorite Hugh for a rule. Robert replied, ' Diversas sententias de anglicis libris in latinam linguam transferre studui.' [1] The *Ancren Riwle* may perhaps have been one of those rules which he consulted, but in any case the statement does indicate the existence of such writings in English whereas there is no evidence for the existence of similar French works before the following century. Moreover, the language in which the majority of the extant manuscripts is written tends to confirm the theory that the original was in English. As was noted previously the author's autograph copy has not survived ; in fact we have no versions earlier than the thirteenth century. Eight of the fourteen extant manuscripts or fragments of the work are in English, four in Latin and two only in French. Five of the English versions were written during the first half of the thirteenth century ; one of the French versions was written at the end of the thirteenth or the beginning of the fourteenth century ; the other French and two of the Latin versions are from the early part of the fourteenth century ; three in English and one in Latin date from the second half of the fourteenth century, and the fourth Latin manuscript seems to have been copied at the beginning of the sixteenth century. Now during the thirteenth and the first part of the fourteenth centuries there can be no doubt that French, as the language of

[1] *Antonianum* iii. 151 ff, 299 ff.

literature, was more important than English. If the original rule had been written in French it is difficult to believe that, in the following two centuries, it and all the French copies of it should have been lost whilst English versions and French translations of the English should have survived. If, on the other hand, the English were the original this is what we should have expected. The growing importance of French leads to the translation of the rule into that language, but the influence of the English original is enough to ensure that the majority of copies shall be in English. There can be no doubt that the extant French versions are translations from the English. There is not the slightest evidence for a lost French original and the probabilities are against it. Lack of evidence will perhaps prevent us from going further than that, but few who have worked on the *Rule* will have much doubt as to the language in which it was originally written.

The questions of the date and authorship of the *Rule* have not yet been satisfactorily answered. Numerous theories have been brought forward to most of which, if they have not been completely disproved, grave objections can be made, and even the most attractive theory has little direct evidence in its favour and depends mainly on general probabilities. In the Latin version we learn that it was written by Simon of Ghent, Bishop of Salisbury, for his sisters who were nuns at Tarrant Keynston in Dorsetshire. It is probable enough that Simon of Ghent was responsible for the Latin version, but, since he died in 1315, he can have had nothing to do with the English original, manuscripts of which were in existence a hundred years before. The mention of Tarrant in the Latin version has led to the theory that the author may have been an earlier Bishop of Salisbury, Richard Poor, who seems to have been a considerable benefactor to the nunnery there. But there is not the slightest reason for connecting the English version with Tarrant which seems to be the only basis for the theory. Other scholars would see in the author a Dominican friar and are even prepared to give him a name. The difficulty is that the passage indicating Dominican author-ship, a list of prayers said to have been in use in that order, is found only in a single manuscript of the *Rule* and is so inconsistent with the *Rule* as a whole that it seems unlikely to have formed part of the original. Even if we accept Dominican authorship there is not the slightest evidence which would allow us to give a name to the friar. It was perhaps inevitable that Gilbert of Sempringham, the founder of the only English monastic order, should have been suggested. Again there is not the slightest direct evi-dence in favour of the supposition. There are some cases of agreements between the *Ancren Riwle* and the rule which Gilbert certainly wrote, but there are also decided contrasts.

The most attractive theory is that brought forward and developed by Miss Hope Emily Allen.[1] She suggests that the three well-born sisters for whom the rule was compiled may have been identical with the ' tribus puellis, Emmæ videlicet et Gunildæ et Christinæ ', to whom the Abbot and the convent of Westminster granted the hermitage of Kilburn sometime between 1127 and 1135. The numbers of the anchoresses at Kilburn gradually increased, and be-tween 1225 and 1230 we know that a dispute arose between the Abbot of Westminster and the Bishop of London over the jurisdiction of the nunnery, a dispute which was settled by the Pope in favour of the Bishop. Now somewhere about 1230 the rule was revised to make it suitable for the use of a larger community. In that revision there were cer-tain instructions concerning the visitation of a bishop which

[1] H. E. Allen, ' The Origin of the *Ancren Riwle* ' (*Publications of the Modern Language Association of America* xxxiii. 474 ff), and cf also *Modern Language Review* xvi. 316 ff.

appear to have been written by someone who did not altogether approve of the bishop exercising such jurisdiction. It is tempting to connect the general development of Kilburn, the dispute between the Abbot of Westminster and the Bishop of London and the revision of the rule. The circumstances of the foundation of Kilburn would fit in well enough with what we know of the three anchoresses mentioned in the *Rule*, and the later history of Kilburn is consistent with what we know of the later development of the *Rule*. The earliest extant manuscript of the work was written somewhere about 1230, but what we know of contemporary conditions, the numbers of anchoresses and hermits and the lack of nunneries in the twelfth as compared with the opposite in the following century, would indicate a date of composition much earlier than that of the earliest extant manuscript. In addition the moderate opinions expressed by the author of the *Rule* have been connected with the appearance, in the twelfth century, of a body of opinion opposed to the ascetic practices then in vogue.

Nevertheless, despite the attraction of this theory, it must be admitted that, apart from a similarity in the circumstances of foundation and history so far as they are known to us, there is no definite evidence in its favour and a number of objections has been raised. In the first place there is no reason for assuming that the original rule and the revised version were both intended for the same place. Strife between ecclesiastical authorities and monastic foundations is far from unusual throughout the mediæval period and, if the writer of the revised rule were connected with a monastery or a nunnery, hostility to the claims of a bishop is not particularly surprising. Moreover, in the rule as it has come down to us, there are references to the writings of St Ailred of Rievaulx on a similar subject; St Bernard is quoted frequently and the author seems also to have drawn from a work of St Bernard's secretary and biographer, Geoffrey of Auxerre, written after the death of the saint. Taken together these seem to indicate that the *Rule* could hardly have been composed much before 1160. The general impression we get is that the three anchoresses for whom the book was written were still quite youthful, and certainly the anchoresses of Kilburn could hardly have been that in 1160. No doubt it is possible to explain away separately each of these objections. We know that the work was later revised at least three times, and it might be suggested that all the extant copies are to be derived from a similar revision of the original Kilburn Rule made during the second half of the twelfth century. It may be so but, even were there proof of this, in the absence of the original version we have no means of telling how drastic that revision may have been. On the evidence available we are not justified in dating the extant versions of the *Rule* early enough for it to have been composed for the Kilburn foundation. If a rule were indeed composed for those anchoresses it must have been different, and may have been very different, from the extant versions.

In any case Professor Tolkien [1] has shown that, in any enquiry into the date or localization of the *Rule*, there are linguistic aspects of the problem which must be taken into consideration. The earliest and best of the extant manuscripts of the *Rule* is that contained in a manuscript preserved in the library of Corpus Christi College, Cambridge, in which the original version has been revised for the use of a larger community—usually known as the *Ancrene Wisse* in order to distinguish it from the *Ancren Riwle*, as written for the three anchoresses. Since references to the friars appear in this text the revision was apparently carried out about 1230 and this, the only extant version of the revised

---

[1] J. R. R. Tolkien, ' *Ancrene Wisse* and *Hali Meiðhad* ' (*Essays and Studies* xiv. 104 ff).

text, was written at about the same date. This manuscript is textually of considerable importance and probably stands nearer to the original *Rule* than any of the others, but linguistically it is even more significant in that it is written in an extraordinarily consistent and unadulterated dialect expressed by an equally consistent and individual spelling system. The greater number of Middle English texts is written in a mixed language showing the influence of different dialects and containing forms from different linguistic periods. In fact the language of every text is in part the product of its textual history, and the dialectal and orthographic consistency of the *Ancrene Wisse* is equalled only in texts such as the *Orrmulum* and the *Ayenbite of Inwyt* which are known to be the authors' autograph copies. We should expect then that the *Ancrene Wisse* must have had a particularly simple textual history ; the lack of scribal contamination indicates that the scribe, or scribes, must have used naturally the dialect in which their original was written.

Even more significant is the use of the same dialect and the same spelling system in the Bodley manuscript of the *Katherine Group* which also was written somewhere about 1230, but by an entirely different scribe. Such a fact is quite exceptional in Middle English and would suggest that the two manuscripts must be closely connected both in time and place. It is hardly possible that the originals of these two texts can have been written in a different dialect or dialects from that used in the extant manuscripts, and that the present similarity is due to the accurate translation of these originals into this dialect. There is no evidence for such accurate and consistent translation from one dialect into another in Middle English ; nor could there be any reason for it. The object of the scribe is to provide a text which can be read without undue difficulty by his contemporaries ; he is concerned with the matter and not with the manner of his originals. Consequently, whilst he would tend to modernize archaic forms and introduce the more familiar forms from his own dialect, there would be no attempt to do this consistently. In the absence of any standard spelling system many of the orthographical and linguistic details of his original, since they did not obscure the meaning, would be of little importance and so would be left unaltered. Even were a motive present for such accurate and careful translation it is inconceivable that the most painstaking scribe should not have left in his version some accidental trace of his original. The consistency of the language, both in spelling and phonology, which is used in the Bodley manuscript of the *Katherine Group* and in the *Ancrene Wisse* can only be explained if we assume that the vanished originals of the two texts were in the same language, and so belonged to practically the same period and place as the copies which still remain. The texts can hardly have had a long, even if simple, textual history since there is practically no trace in the language of forms from any period sufficiently remote to differ in orthographic or linguistic usage. Since a consistent modernization is as difficult to believe in as a consistent translation from a different dialect, it would appear that the language of the district in which these texts were produced must have changed very little during the interval which has elapsed between the composition of the originals and the copying of the extant manuscripts. It is difficult to say how long an interval in years this would suggest. No doubt the written language has become to some extent traditional ; even so if it differed to any considerable extent from the actual spoken speech of the scribe we should have expected traces of such difference to appear. On the whole it is difficult to believe that the originals of the two manuscripts could have been produced any earlier than the last quarter of the twelfth century, a date it may be noted which would fit in very well with the various allusions found in the *Rule*.

These connexions between the two texts have led to the suggestion that the *Ancren Riwle* and some, or all, of the texts of the *Katherine Group* may have been written by the same author. This is possible enough ; there are verbal and phraseological similarities between the different texts and it seems certain enough that the author of one at least knew the others. The difference in spirit between the author of the *Ancren Riwle* and the author of say *Hali Meiðhad* has been exaggerated by those who do not realize the difference between a book of devotion and edification and a book of practical advice. Nevertheless there is no real evidence for identity of authorship. Most of the verbal and phraseological similarities are no more than we should expect in works produced in the same district, at about the same time, and drawing upon the same homiletic tradition.

Is it possible to localize the dialect in which the originals of the *Ancrene Wisse* and the *Katherine Group* seem to have been written ? It must be admitted that our knowledge of Middle English dialects is far too slight to enable us to localize definitely any text on linguistic evidence alone. Since external evidence does not seem to be forthcoming all that we can say is that the dialect is western in character. Further than that it is unsafe to go on linguistic evidence alone, and attempts to indicate the particular county or district in which the works were produced cannot be held to have succeeded. The two manuscripts are connected with Herefordshire in so far as the Bodley manuscript was there in the sixteenth century, and the *Ancrene Wisse* was apparently at Wigmore Abbey by about 1300. This does not, of course, justify us in assuming that both manuscripts were copied, and hence originally composed, in that county. On the evidence available all that we can say is that the two texts seem to have been composed, towards the end of the twelfth century, somewhere in the West Midland dialectal area. Whether there will ever be sufficient evidence to enable us to name definitely the author, the locality and the date of the *Rule*, and to identify the anchoresses for whom it was written, is more than doubtful. However, the most important manuscripts of the work have not yet been edited in full. It may be that the complete edition of all the texts, Latin, French and English—a long-awaited desideratum of Middle English scholarship—now being undertaken by the Early English Text Society, will throw some light on the various questions.

Whatever may have been the occasion for the composition of the *Rule* there can be no doubt, as has been shown by Miss Hope Emily Allen,[1] that its popularity was immediate and prolonged. About 1230 it was revised for the use of a larger community and, some time later, it was also being translated into French. At about the time when the *Ancrene Wisse* was written the original work was being transcribed again in a text (Cotton Titus D. xviii) which is adapted at points for both sexes ; and in the Caius manuscript, written towards the end of the century, the sisters of the original version have become ' friends '. By 1300 it was so authoritative that Simon of Ghent, Bishop of Salisbury, translated it into Latin for the benefit of his sisters, nuns at Tarrant Keynston in Dorsetshire. Towards the close of the fourteenth century it was being copied into the Vernon manuscript—that great anthology of religious prose and verse—and about the same time it was being revised and rewritten in a manuscript now preserved in the Pepysian collection. Its continued popularity throughout the fourteenth century

---

[1] See especially ' Some Fourteenth Century borrowings from *Ancren Riwle*.' (*Modern Language Review* xviii. 1–8) and ' Further Borrowings from *Ancren Riwle* ' (*Modern Language Review* xxiv. 1–15).

is sufficiently indicated by the fact that more of the extant manuscripts were copied in this than in the preceding century. Possibly some part of its continued favour may have been due to the mystic movement initiated in that century by Rolle and his followers. Certainly its influence on the religious prose of the fourteenth century was considerable. As early as the beginning of the thirteenth century we find that it has been used in the compilation of the *Dublin Rule* —a collection of rules written for the Augustinian canons of Dublin. It has been suggested that Rolle's *Psalter* may show borrowing, either from the *Rule* itself or from some intermediate commonplace book which is quoting it ; the *Cambridge Rule* which is sometimes attributed to him certainly shows borrowings from our work. Its influence is predominant in the popular devotional works of the fourteenth century, it is found to a greater or lesser extent in books such as the *Poor Caitiff*, the *Grace Dieu*, *Adam and Eve* and the *Chastising of God's Children*, the popularity of which is evidenced by their frequent mention in contemporary wills. Moreover, this popularity continues even later. The fifteenth-century manuscript of the *Oxford Rule* may reflect its influence and, towards the middle of the century, the writer of a tract on the Five Senses uses our work so extensively that we have ' what may almost be called another text of Books II and III of the *Ancren Riwle* '. The tract may possibly have been by that prolific preacher Dr William Lichfield who, on his death in 1448, is said to have left behind him, in addition to other material, 3,083 sermons ' written in English with his own hand ', though the evidence for the attribution of this tract to him is not, apparently, conclusive. Even in the sixteenth century the influence of the *Rule* had not altogether vanished, a fact which is less surprising when we remember that one of the extant Latin manuscripts was being transcribed at the beginning of this century. The section on Temptation was inserted in the version of Rolle's *Emendatio Vitæ* which was printed at Paris in 1510 and its influence may appear in the *Reliques of Rome* by that fierce Puritan Thomas Becon (1512–67).

It would be difficult to overemphasize the importance of the *Ancren Riwle* in the history of English literature. Ever since the publication of the first modern edition in the middle of the last century its interest has been apparent, but only comparatively recently has its commanding position in the history of English prose been fully recognized. Composed at a time when the Old English homiletic tradition was still vigorous, it helped to hand on the prose developed by that tradition to the fourteenth and fifteenth centuries. Historical, narrative and didactic prose all succumbed to the increasing preference for rhyme due to the overwhelming influence of French. Homiletic prose alone survived, and some credit for this survival must be given to the *Ancren Riwle* and its amazing popularity during the succeeding centuries. In it a prose style had been developed which was not improved upon for over 300 years. The great names of the text-books, Wyclif, Malory, Pecock and Lord Berners, are novices compared with this unknown twelfth-century author. All are overshadowed by their Latin and French originals and have hardly yet learned to use their unaccustomed English. If we compare the various translations of biblical texts which appear in the *Rule* with Wyclif's English version of the Bible, there is no doubt of the vigour of Wyclif's translation, but time and again we find that the smoother translation is that which appears in the earlier text. Wyclif is still, rather self-consciously, translating for the benefit of the ignorant and unlearned, but the author of the *Ancren Riwle* is the possessor of a prose which, proved by long usage, has no need to humble itself in the presence of Latin. That prose is passed on to the fourteenth-century writers such as Rolle and Hilton ;

it continues in the religious prose of the fifteenth century, the works of More and the religious oratory and pamphleteering of the sixteenth century until it culminates in the prose of the Authorized Version.[1]

[1] Relatively few of the later sermons have been printed, but see the late fourteenth- or early fifteenth-century sermons published by D. M. Grisdale in *Three Worcester Sermons* (Leeds 1939).

VII

THE *OWL AND THE NIGHTINGALE*

'THE most miraculous piece of writing . . . amongst the mediæval English books.' Such a verdict, even when it comes from a scholar so widely read as the late W. P. Ker, may arouse suspicion. Students of mediæval literature are perhaps rather apt to be led away by their enthusiasm, and to hail their own particular favourites as masterpieces. All students of mediæval literature have, however, united in praise of the *Owl and the Nightingale*,[1] a poem whose fame and commanding position is not due simply to its early date, or to the poverty of contemporary literature, but which can bear comparison with the literature of any age. The subject, a debate between an owl and a nightingale, is conventional enough for the twelfth century, and had the poem been in Latin we should have known what to expect. But the author writes in English, and the conventional framework is vitalized by his imagination and sense of humour.

The poet represents himself as accidentally hearing the dispute between the two birds. The nightingale starts the quarrel by commenting acidly and pointedly on the quality of the owl's song. 'Monster,' she says, 'fly away! It's the worse for me when I see you. Because of your harsh noise I often have to stop my song; my heart comes into

---

[1] Ed. by J. E. Wells (Belles Lettres Series, London 1907), by J. W. H. Atkins (Cambridge 1922) and by J. H. G. Grattan and F. H. Sykes (EETS, Extra Series 119, 1935).

my mouth and my tongue falters when you come near.
I'd rather spit than sing because of your vile gurglings.'
When evening comes the owl replies to her accuser. She
claims that she can sing as well as anyone, though admitting
that there are no fancy trills in the song ; complains of the
constant malice of the nightingale, and threatens violence if
she ever has the chance. The nightingale admits the superior
strength of the owl and enumerates her characteristics :

> You are hateful to behold and horrible in many different ways.
> Your body is scraggy, your neck short, and the biggest thing
> about you is the head ; your eyes are coal-black and staring as
> if they had been painted with woad ; you glare as if you wanted
> to bite apart all that you can get your claws into ; your bill is
> strong and sharp and as curved as a flesh-hook. You are always
> clacking with it and that is all there is to your song.

The nightingale goes on to discuss the habits of the owl
and tells the tale of the hawk who, in ignorance, reared an
owl in her nest, but had to cast it out because of its filthy
habits. She then bursts into song but is promptly chal-
lenged to trial by battle by the angry owl. The challenge
is declined and, after some discussion, it is agreed that the
case shall be judged by a certain Nicholas of Guildford.
Before proceeding to judgment the nightingale once more
attacks the song and night-flying propensities of the owl
who, in defence, claims that by her song she gives warning to men, and that it is not cheapened by over-use as is
that of the nightingale ; as for the charge of blindness she
can see all that is necessary. The attack then changes
ground and complaint is made of the mournfulness of the
owl's song, heard only during the winter and never during
the summer when all is gay. The obvious reply is made ;
winter is the very time when people most need cheer and
summer leads only to wantonness, the theme of the nightingale's song. In winter the nightingale flies away whereas
the owl stays and helps people in their misery. The

nightingale tries to interrupt, but is silenced by the owl who proceeds to attack in turn. She emphasizes the uselessness of her adversary and again refutes the charge of uncleanness, flinging back the accusation at the other. After considerable thought the nightingale claims that her single accomplishment, which makes her loved by all men, is better than the many which the owl claims to possess. A fox has any number of tricks and the cat but one, yet the fox loses his skin whilst the cat saves hers. In reply the owl claims that her song leads men to repentance and a better life ; as for the nightingale she sings only of worldly things and, if her song is as wonderful as she says, there are plenty of people in the far north whom she neglects but who need calling to heaven. The owl on the other hand is known everywhere and sings to all men. But, asserts the nightingale, in such lands the people are so barbarous that it would be quite useless to sing to them, so she stays in more favoured lands and there does her duty. Following up the charge of wantonness the owl tells how a lady was seduced by the song of a nightingale. In revenge the bird was seized by the husband and torn asunder by wild horses. The nightingale, however, gives a different version of the tale, tells how the knight was punished for his cruelty, and claims that, because of that punishment, no one now dares to harm her ; the owl, on the other hand, is universally hated and hunted down, rightly so, since in her song she foretells only misfortunes to come. The owl admits this, but claims that the power of foreseeing future events is a virtue which she uses to help mankind. The nightingale pounces on this admission and accuses her of witchcraft, defends herself from the charge of wantonness and tells how she protects maidens from folly. In return the owl claims to help married women and, although realizing that she is disliked by men, even in death helps them by acting as a scarecrow. At this the nightingale claims the victory on the grounds that the owl has boasted of her own disgrace. She sings so loudly that all the song-birds flock to her and join in the triumph. Angrily the owl threatens to summon all the birds of prey against them ; the wren, however, intervenes, reminds them of their agreement to submit to the judgment of Nicholas of Guildford and the disputants fly away in search of him.

It is difficult for us to estimate the exact amount of popularity enjoyed by any one mediæval work. An estimate based on the number of manuscripts of it which are still extant may be misleading. Nevertheless, there are certain indications, for what they are worth, which suggest that the *Owl and the Nightingale* enjoyed in its own day something at least of the popularity which it deserved. It has been preserved in two different manuscripts, the earlier of which was probably written towards the end of the first quarter of the thirteenth century, the later about fifty years afterwards.[1] In addition other manuscripts are known to have existed, though they have long since disappeared. The two extant manuscripts are both copied from the same common original which, it can be shown, could not have been the author's autograph copy. It follows that there must have been once in existence at least two other manuscripts, very probably more. In addition the library of the Premonstratensian canons of Titchfield Abbey in Hampshire seems to have contained a copy of the poem. When the library was catalogued in 1400 an item in one of the volumes was given as ' De conflictu inter philomelam et bubonem in anglicis ', and this must refer to a copy of our poem ; the remaining contents of the volume are sufficient evidence that it was not identical with either of the extant manuscripts. Similarly in the late thirteenth-century

---

[1] i.e. in MS. Cotton Caligula A ix. and MS. Jesus Coll., Oxon., 29. On the date of the manuscripts see J. E. Wells, ' The *Owl and the Nightingale* and MS. Cotton ' (*Modern Language Notes* xlviii. 516).

Anglo-French treatise on the French language by Walter de Bibbesworth we find the following :

> Aloms ore iuer a boys,
> Ou la russinole, *the nithingale*,
> Meuz chante ki houswan (houle) en sale.[1]

This may indicate that vernacular poems concerning the owl and the nightingale were popular, and since this is the only one of which we know it is possibly the one referred to.

The date at which the poem was composed is unknown and the question has proved a fruitful source of dispute.[2] Obviously it must have been written some time before the end of the first quarter of the thirteenth century, the date, on palæographical evidence, of the earlier of the two extant manuscripts. In the poem itself there are three indications which, at first sight, seem to throw some light on the question. The most important of these is a reference to a certain King Henry. The nightingale, when giving his own version of the killing of the nightingale by a jealous knight, tells how the news of it came to the king :

> This came to the ears of King Henry,
> Jesus have mercy on his soul.

This is usually taken to indicate that the King Henry in question must have been dead when the poem was written. The date of the earliest extant manuscript indicates that it is probably Henry II who is referred to and, since the words would have been ambiguous had Henry III actually been reigning at that time, the poem must have been written

---

[1] A. Owen, *Le traité de Walter de Bibbesworth sur la langue française* (Paris 1929), p. 110.

[2] For the extensive, but inconclusive, literature on this and the following questions see J. E. Wells, *A Manual of the Writings in Middle English 1050–1400* and *Supplements*. Possibly the most important single work on the subject is K. Huganir, *The Owl and the Nightingale, Sources, Date, Author* (Philadelphia 1931), though few of her conclusions have as yet been generally accepted

some time after the death of Henry II and before the accession of Henry III. Other scholars have attempted to show that the formula could have been applied to a living man, so that the poem could have been composed during the reign of Henry II. But the point can hardly be said to have been established beyond reasonable doubt, and it still seems more natural to take the formula as referring to a dead rather than to a living person.

Secondly, when the wren, towards the end of the poem, warns the two disputants against breaking the peace :

> What ! will you break this peace,
> And do such shame to the king ?
> Yet is he neither dead nor lame ;
> Harm and shame will come to us
> If you break the peace in his land.

It has been argued that some particular peace is intended here, the peace under Henry II, or that under the justiciar Hubert Walter in the reign of Richard. There is, however, no proof that the reference is particular rather than general, and the exact sense which we give to the passage must depend on our dating of the poem on other evidence.

Finally, the conditions pictured in the nightingale's description of the north have also been used in an attempt to date the poem more definitely. In reply to the taunt of the owl :

> You never sing in Ireland,
> You are not found in Scotland.
> Why don't you go to Norway,
> And sing to the men of Galloway ?

the nightingale describes the conditions of these northern countries :

> That land is neither good nor favourable,
> But wilderness it is, and waste,
> Crags and hills reaching to the heavens,
> Snow and hail are common there.

The land is fearful and unlovely,
The men are fierce and uncanny,
There, there is neither peace nor concord ;
They have no care how they live.
They eat fish and uncooked flesh
Which they tear apart like wolves,
They drink milk and whey as well,
Since they don't know what else to do ;
They have neither wine nor beer,
But live like wild beasts ;
They go clothed in untanned skins,
As if they had just come from hell.

It seems fairly certain that the description here is meant to apply especially to Norway. It is perhaps possible that the outburst was provoked by the expulsion of Archbishop Eysteinn, and that the reference to the barbarous people is meant to apply more especially to the *Birkibeinar* of King Sverrir. There is no need to assume that the description must have come to the author from Eysteinn himself during his stay in England, and that the poem therefore must have been composed before the return of that prelate to Norway in 1183. English and Norwegians were in fairly close touch throughout the twelfth century, and the career of King Sverrir is given in considerable detail by contemporary English chroniclers. In any case earlier sources exist for such a description of Norway and may have been used by the author. The nightingale then continues :

Though a good man visit them,
As one did formerly from Rome,
To teach them good customs,
And to abandon their vices,
He had better stay away
For all his labour will be lost ;
A bear more easily could be taught
To carry well both shield and spear,
Than that those savages could be brought
So that they would hear me sing.

There can be little doubt that some special mission is referred to here, and the two most in favour seem to be those of Cardinal Vivian and of Nicholas Breakspear.[1] Cardinal Vivian visited Scotland in 1176, but it is improbable that the description can refer to that country and Vivian never got as far as Norway; nor did the English, after their experience of him, regard him as a ' good man '. It is possible enough that the mission of Nicholas Breakspear, later Pope Adrian IV, to Norway in 1152–4 is the one actually referred to, but even if this were certain, which is far from being the case, it could only prove that the poem must have been composed some time after his return in 1154. With the evidence at present available, we can only say that the poem was probably written some time during the period between the death of Henry II and the accession of Henry III. Attempts to prove an earlier or a more definite date have so far produced only theories of greater or lesser probability, and convinced few beyond the proposers of those theories.

In neither of the extant manuscripts is any clue given as to the name of the author. The only person mentioned in the poem itself is a certain Nicholas of Guildford. He is the judge agreed on by the birds and, when the wren is telling of his whereabouts, we obtain a probable hint as to the reason for the composition of the poem :

> ' What ! don't you know his home,' she said,
> ' He dwells in Portisham,
> A village in Dorset,
> On an outlet by the sea ;

---

[1] Professor Dickins also points out that Reginald of Durham (*Surtees Society* 1, 108) tells of the despatch of a papal legate in 1163 ' qui Noruuagæ gentis barbariem, prædicandi gratia, convertisse vel correxisse debuerat '.

There he utters righteous judgments,
And composes and writes many wise things,
And because of his words and his deeds
Things are the better in Scotland.
It is an easy thing to find him,
He has only a single dwelling,
And that is a great shame to the bishops,
And all to whom his name
And deeds are known.
Why will they not be wise
And have him often with them,
And grant him revenue in many places,
So that he can always accompany them?'

There can be little doubt that the poem was written with the main object of bringing Nicholas to the notice of his superiors and so obtaining promotion for him. It is natural enough for the reader to suspect that it is Nicholas himself who has adopted this method of drawing attention to his own merits. The different objections which have been brought forward at various times have not proved convincing. It has been suggested, for example, that the references to Nicholas are far too laudatory for them to have been written by himself. It has not yet been demonstrated, however, that modesty is an inherent virtue in every author. Such an argument, if allowed, would be fatal to many well-established attributions ; Giraldus Cambrensis, for example, could hardly have written a word of the works attributed to him. Moreover, we must keep in mind the probable reason for the composition of the poem. If Nicholas did indeed write it in order to commend himself to the notice of his superiors undue modesty would have defeated his own object. The fact that, at the end of the poem, the birds fly away to Portisham has also been used as an argument against the authorship of Nicholas. If Nicholas were the poet who overheard the dispute, it is said, why did he not appear to the birds and give judgment instead of allowing them to fly away to Portisham. Such a proceeding would, of course, have made known to everyone that he was the author. In view of the reason for the composition it was obviously better not to declare that fact too loudly. In any case the delivery of the verdict was no part of the convention of these debate poems.

The only other name which has been suggested for the authorship is that of John of Guildford. In the later of the two manuscripts a seventeenth-century owner has noted that ' on part of à broken leaf of this MS. I found these verses written, whereby the Author may be guesst at (viz) :

> ' Master John greets you from Guildford then,
> And sends to tell you he will sing no more.
> Now in this way he will end his song :
> Lord God of Heaven be with us all.'

Almost the only argument in favour of this theory is that it would give us a possible fellow-townsman of Nicholas who may have been anxious to obtain promotion for him. The broken leaf is no longer extant, though there is no reason to doubt its existence in the seventeenth century. There are gaps in the manuscript which it may have filled at one time, but it is improbable that it was ever tacked on at the end of the *Owl and the Nightingale* ; there is no gap in the manuscript at that point and the metre is dif- ferent. We may accept John of Guildford as the author of one or more of the other poems in the manuscript, but there is no reason for supposing that he also wrote the *Owl and the Nightingale*, and there are several arguments against such an attribution. On the whole, if we must have an author, Nicholas of Guildford is as probable as anyone. There is, however, little real evidence and unless more should come to light—which is unlikely—there can be no certainty. Attempts which have been made to identify this Nicholas are so far quite unconvincing. Nor, since little is known beyond the name of any of the twelfth-century Nicholases who have been identified with Nicholas of Guildford, would any identification, even if proved, be of much value. What we know of the date and author, such as it is, is supported by what can be deduced from the linguistic evidence. As extant the poem is written in a western, probably south-western, dialect, but many of the rhymes can only be explained on the assumption that original south-eastern forms have later been westernized. So far as we can tell from the two versions in the extant manuscripts the original must have been written in some border dialect in which south-western and south-eastern forms might be found side by side, and where dialectal variants would be available for rhyme ; such a dialect, for example, as the place-names show to have been in use round Guildford during the twelfth century.

The poem is written in the form of a debate, a form with a long history and one which was widely popular during the twelfth and thirteenth centuries. It was known by different names, *altercatio, debat, estrif*, but was essentially a contest in verse in which rival views of two or more disputants were expounded. The literary type had been popular in Carolingian times and probably goes back ultimately to the pastoral eclogues of Theocritus and Virgil. Such debates were common during the earlier mediæval period and reached the height of their popularity in the twelfth century, when they are said to have owed something to the interest in dialectics aroused by the appearance of the *Sic et Non* of Abaelard. A wide variety of subject is represented in the extant debates, those between Summer and Winter, Wine and Water, the Soul and the Body, being amongst the most popular. Not that such stock subjects were invariable ; contemporary questions were also debated and the form was used by the Goliards in their satires. According to the pattern conventionalized by the Latin

examples such poems consisted of a short descriptive introduction, followed by a spirited discussion with more or less
dramatic incident ; the final judgment might or might not
be pronounced. Within this framework, however, a large
amount of variation was both possible and usual. The
Owl and the Nightingale retains the conventional framework,
but the dialogue has been enlivened by the introduction of
considerable narrative detail, and the classical references of
the models are replaced by popular proverbs.

Probably the most characteristic feature of the poem is
its legal background. A vague legal flavour was characteristic of most of the vernacular debates but it does not, as
a rule, go beyond that. The dispute in the *Owl and the
Nightingale*, however, is modelled on the form of a twelfth-
century law-suit, and the author consistently uses legal
terminology. The nightingale, as plaintiff, begins by stat-
ing the charge against the owl, bringing forward as con-
firmatory evidence certain proverbs ascribed to Alfred. As
required by contemporary legal custom the owl denies the
charge and declares her willingness to accept trial by battle.
Since this is not accepted she continues and also cites the
proverbs of Alfred in her defence, and also claims the right
of showing cause why the action should proceed no further
by charging the nightingale with various misdemeanours.
The plaintiff defends herself against these charges and the
case tends to degenerate into a mere exchange of abuse,
and is probably no further from realism on that account.
Each attempts, by angering the other, to trap her into a
mistake in pleading. The owl tries to show that the whole
charge is due to malice and so cannot legally stand, whilst
the nightingale claims that the owl, by boasting of her own
disgrace, has lost the case. This claim seems to be endorsed
by the other birds and the dispute then ends.

Obviously the dispute between the two birds is allegorical,
but the exact significance of the allegory is more difficult

to determine. Is it the old conflict between pleasure and asceticism, between an active and a contemplative life, between a monastic and a secular life, or between art and philosophy ? Possibly they all enter into it, though if any single formula must be applied the suggestion that the contest is between the older didactic and religious poetry and the newer lyric is probably the best. The owl, representing the former, claims to sing to men for their good and to warn them of the coming judgment. She sees in the song of the nightingale only frivolity and an incitement to wantonness—a criticism frequently levelled at secular literature during the Middle Ages. The nightingale, as the representative and defender of the new lyric poetry, jeers at the mournfulness of the owl, which only arouses dislike and suspicion, and proclaims that the mission of poetry is to express beauty and to give pleasure. The claim that she also sings in church is probably a reference to the way in which the phraseology and diction of the secular lyrics was borrowed by the church and reproduced in the religious lyrics.

Whether it was popular in its own day or not, the poem certainly possessed all the ingredients necessary and likely to appeal to the twelfth-century reader. It was written in the debate form which had become fashionable. Its title and characters would attract a public which enjoyed the contemporary fables and beast tales. Apart from the allegory, which, no doubt, would interest the cultivated reader, it contained something of interest for everyone. The extracts from natural history and patristic learning would be far from repellent to an audience accustomed to but a thin veneer of entertainment over the solid foundation of didactic material. The reminiscences of the contemporary French lyric would attract the reader to whom English was, as a rule, but a barbarous tongue, and all would welcome the inclusion of popular proverbs and the number of illustrative stories. Moreover at a time before the rise of a professional legal class, when some knowledge of law and legal procedure was essential to all, the background, the legal allusions and terminology, would arouse interest by their very familiarity.

Much mediæval literature suffers from an almost complete lack of form. This is especially true of many of the romances, which are too often only a disjointed collection of incidents from various sources; the end is due only to the weariness of the narrator and not to the inevitability of the tale. In comparison with such productions the *Owl and the Nightingale* comes as a welcome relief. A clear-cut scheme has been worked out steadily, and all the various episodes and illustrative tales are strictly relevant to the different arguments. There is little of that interpolation of extraneous matter for the sake of displaying an ostentatious learning or of rousing a possibly flagging interest. Every speech by the disputants carries the argument a stage further forward. No doubt much of the firmness of outline is due to the Latin models which the poet, consciously or unconsciously, is following : moreover the legal framework which he has adopted has helped greatly in giving a unity to his conception. Nevertheless, obvious as has been the influence of his models on the form of the poem, the work is far removed from the conventional insipidity of most of the Latin debates, with their carefully balanced arguments in speeches of exactly the same length. In the English poem vividness and reality have been gained by giving the disputants speeches of different length, making them interrupt each other, and by the occasional evasion rather than refutation of the charges brought against them. The narrative element, usually cut down to a minimum in the Latin models, has been skilfully worked in. The dispute is the sole reason for the poem, but the preceding events are so told that the debate arises naturally out of

them. The succeeding events help to characterize the disputants and to emphasize the steps in the argument, but
they are never allowed to attain such importance that attention is distracted from the dispute to the narrative. The
events at the end are treated so skilfully that, when the
birds finally fly away to lay their dispute before Master
Nicholas, we hardly appreciate the fact that after all we are
not to hear the judgment.

In an allegorical poem there is always the danger that
the allegorical or the narrative element shall be disproportionate, so that eventually it becomes a lifeless abstraction
or a simple romance. The perfect balance between the
two elements is so difficult that it is perhaps rarely achieved
in mediæval literature. The *Owl and the Nightingale* is one
of the few works in which this balance has been attained.
The allegory is obvious and consistent ; since the purpose
of the author is primarily to interest and entertain and only
secondarily to instruct, allegory has not been allowed to
overbalance the narrative elements. Indeed, it might be
argued that the allegory is on the whole too slight for a
perfect balance. We recognize that it is there, but the
number of different explanations which have been suggested
indicates its vagueness. The two disputants are no care-
lessly drawn allegorical figures but real birds which have
been vivified by the descriptive power of the author. The
little touches, the owl on her ivy-covered stump and the
nightingale in the leafy branches, help to bring them to
life. Moreover they are consistently birds ; the author is
never so carried away by his subject that he forgets to make
them speak in character. Naturally they are endowed with
a human personality, and act and speak as birds would be
expected to act and speak were they known to possess
human ideas and feelings. This was necessary if any tale
at all was to be told. The individual character of the birds
is allowed to develop during the debate itself. We see

them hiding their pain at a shrewd thrust, seizing joyfully on an imagined advantage and, when beaten in argument, taking refuge in abuse. No doubt the nightingale is the more likeable character, but there is no denying the shrewd-ness and tenacity of the owl. Although the author holds the scales evenly balanced between the two the owl seems, on the whole, to get the better of the argument, though the quicker wit of the nightingale is able to seize on a technical mis-pleading and to claim the victory. An especially human touch is the way in which the two birds are made to appear particularly sensitive on their weak points. The owl wishes to be considered broad-minded and the nightingale is anxious not to appear a mere worldling.

There is no need to suppose, as some scholars have done, that the author was anything of a naturalist. The descrip-tion of the two birds, the owl as given above, and the nightingale :

> You are an accursed thing ;
> Good for nothing but chattering.
> You are dark and ugly in colour,
> You look like a muddy ball.
> You are neither fair nor strong,
> Neither well-built nor tall ;
> You are lacking in any beauty,
> And your value is small,

are vivid enough, but all the details could have come from books accessible to the author. Details in other descrip-tions, the fox chased by the hounds, or the way in which the hare eludes his pursuers, suggest a country-bred poet, but we must remember that in the Middle Ages, and for some considerable time after, urban life was still rural to an extent we can hardly conceive today.

There are no purple passages in the poem ; subject and treatment alike forbid this. Nevertheless, by creating a new style, the poet has achieved something which, so far as we know, no previous English poet had even attempted. He has dispensed with the help of an artificial poetic language and achieved a completely new style by using in his poetry the ordinary daily speech of the time. This conversational style never, it is true, rises to great heights, but on the other hand it never sinks below poetry. Moreover the colloquial effect is heightened by the number of homely similes and illustrations which are used. To the owl the song of the nightingale is like the chattering of an Irish priest, whilst the song of the owl reminds the nightingale of the squawking of a hen lost in the snow. The defeat of the owl rouses an excitement likened to that which follows the overthrow of a gambler. Vivid sketches are given of the common scenes of the time ; we see the horse standing patiently before the mill-door, the hawk baited by carrion crows, and the owl hanging as a scarecrow in the corn. Incidental allusions to country sports and to the religious life of the period all help to provide a realistic historical background. Occasionally, indeed, it may become too realistic. Some of the proverbial sayings quoted by the poet are as frank as most popular sayings, and the abuse occasionally descends to the type which it is usual to treat as non-existent.

So far as we know the author seems to have been one of the earliest English poets to use the octosyllabic couplet, but there is no suspicion of the novice in his employment of the form. No doubt he learnt much from foreign models and he has succeeded in acclimatizing in English a verse which was to become the favourite medium for metrical romance, and which supplies a smooth uninterrupted form for narrative poetry. It has of course its dangers, notably a tendency towards monotony and carelessness in rhyme. The former of these has been skilfully and successfully overcome by the poet. The normal iambic rhythm, with the sense complete in the couplets, has been competently varied by the omission of syllables, either at the beginning or in the middle of the line, and by the use of enjambment. We might have expected some unskilfulness in the handling of the numerous rhymes required by the metre, a tendency to repetition or the use of approximate rhymes. On the whole, however, the rhyming is wonderfully correct, and though it occasionally breaks down and we find self-rhyming words and even assonances allowed, such lapses are infrequent. In any case the former of these devices is in use, even amongst the best poets, throughout the Middle English period. Living as he did in an area of mixed dialect he has appreciated the value of variant and dialectal forms in eking out his stock of rhymes. Variety is obtained, too, by the use of both masculine and feminine rhymes though, naturally enough considering the inflexional character of the language, the latter type predominates.

Probably the greatest achievement of the author is the way in which he has succeeded in blending the English and French elements in his poem. In a work written towards the end of the Middle English period, when the two literatures had existed side by side in the same country for centuries, this would have caused little surprise. When we find it in *Sir Gawain and the Green Knight*, for example, we hardly notice it. But here, at the very beginning of the period, we find a poet capable of appropriating and using the best of both literatures, mingling them inextricably, and producing a work to which the very mingling gives a modern air. He uses a form and convention, that of the debate poem, which he has borrowed from French and Latin models. In it we find reminiscences of other French literary types, the beast tale, the *fabliau* and the Provençal lyric. He writes in rhyme, a poetic ornament borrowed into England from France, and in one of the commonest French metres. Moreover the whole outlook and atmosphere of the poem is French. Not before Chaucer

do we find another English poet capable of writing successfully this whimsical type of poetry, with no sign of the
amateur or obvious imitator. The author of the *Owl and
the Nightingale* has made his own the light ironic and humorous style which most mediæval English poets, more at home
in the epic or the elegy, found so difficult to imitate. For
all that it is essentially an English poem. It is written in
English, and though French loans are fairly frequent it is
probable that no more are used than were actually current
in the spoken English of the time. The author has not
found it necessary to borrow wholesale in order to present
the atmosphere of his originals ; he shows that the style
can be achieved quite as well in contemporary English.
The influence exerted by native alliterative metre is shown
by fondness for alliteration, especially for alliterative tags,
and by the richness of synonym. Above all the whole
background of the poem is English. The scene is laid in
an English valley, the characters are English and the illustrations are drawn from the life of the English countryside.
The progress of the debate is closely modelled on the procedure of a twelfth-century English law-court and the legal
vocabulary is almost entirely English, many of the technical
legal terms being derived from the pre-Conquest legal
vocabulary. With the possible exception of some of the
lyrics such a successful mingling of the two literatures is
not found again in English before the time of Chaucer and
the *Gawain* poet. The appearance of such a poem in the
twelfth century is enough to overthrow all our theories of
the development of English literature ; had it been lost
we could never have deduced the existence of any such
poem from the extant literature of the twelfth century.

In all probability we shall never know definitely whether
the *Owl and the Nightingale* had any predecessors in English. The maturity of art which we find in the poem would
incline us to believe that it had ; if so they have long been

lost. On the whole it is most probable that there was none, and that the very novelty of the poem is the greatest achievement of the author. However, there were successors and two of them come within our period. The first of these, the *Thrush and the Nightingale*, was written towards the close of the thirteenth century and is extant in two manuscripts, though less than half of the poem is to be found in the later of the two.[1] The subject of the debate has nothing of the personal quality which we find in the earlier poem ; women in general are attacked by the thrush in the usual mediæval way, and defended by the nightingale. Abuse soon takes the place of argument, but when the nightingale cites the Virgin Mary as the type of perfect womanhood the thrush confesses herself vanquished. The poem is written in twelve-line stanzas in which a four-stress couplet is followed by a three-stress line rhyming with the following three-stress lines. The speeches are occasionally dramatic, but there is no connecting narrative. The fact that all the speeches except one are complete in the stanza recalls the formalism characteristic of the Latin models and so skilfully avoided by the author of the *Owl and the Nightingale*. The later poem is said to have been influenced by the earlier, but the only likeness discernible lies in the fact that the disputants are birds in both cases. The atmosphere and the workmanship of the two poems are very different and no comparison is possible, though it is not improbable that the earlier poem may have provided the inspiration for the *Thrush and the Nightingale*. The opening stanza is reminiscent of the well-known lyric ' Lenten is come with love to town ' and the poem is, in fact, a compromise between the debate and the lyric. Its affinities are with such poems as *The Nut-Brown Maid* and

---

[1] The earlier of the two texts has been edited by Carleton Brown, *English Lyrics of the XIIIth Century* (Oxford 1932), pp. 101 ff., and the later by H. Varnhagen, *Anglia* iv. 208 ff.

Debate between the Clerk and the Maiden rather than with the *Owl and the Nightingale.*

The original English of the second of these debates is no longer extant. It is known only from the Anglo-French version, *La Geste de Blancheflour e de Florence*, preserved in a thirteenth-century manuscript. The subject is the oft-debated topic of whether a knight or a clerk is to be preferred as a lover. The last stanza tells us all we know of the circumstances of its composition :

> Banastre en englois le fist,
> E Brykhulle cest escrit
> En franceois translata.[1]

The Banastre in question may be identical with the William Banastre mentioned in the *Scalachronicon*, side by side with Thomas of Erceldoun, in words which suggest that, like Thomas, he was an English poet. Further identification is impossible, nor do we know anything of the Brykhulle who is said to have been responsible for the translation of Banastre's English poem into French. Since we have no means of knowing how far the extant French version represents the English original, nor which of its qualities are due to the French translator rather than the English poet, nothing can be said of it here beyond the mention of its one-time existence.

[1] P. Meyer, ' Notice du MS. 25970 de la Bibliothèque Phillipps ' (*Romania* xxxvii. 209 ff).

VIII

RELIGIOUS AND DIDACTIC LITERATURE

WHEN we consider the conditions of survival of mediæval literature it seems natural enough that an undue proportion of the extant works should be either religious or didactic. The proportion is greatest during the earlier period since, in the later, a class of secular readers is beginning to grow up, a class which, in the earlier period, depended more on the oral than on the written word for entertainment.

The earlier didactic and religious literature carries on, to a greater or lesser extent, the literary traditions of the Old English period. This is true especially of the homiletic tradition in the West; it is true also of other writings which are not in this direct line of descent, such as the *Worcester Fragments* and the *Vices and Virtues*. The former of these consists of the remnants of a manuscript, parts of some sixty-six folios in all, which had been cut up and pasted together to form covers for a book in Worcester Cathedral library.[1] Most of the fragments contain portions of a copy of Ælfric's *Grammar* and *Glossary*, interesting as giving some indication of the continued popularity of the classical Old English writings, since the fragment from which these

---

[1] Ed. T. Phillipps, *Fragment of Ælfric's Grammar, etc.* (London 1838); the short poem and parts of the Debate between the Body and the Soul are to be found in J. Hall, *op. cit.* I. 1–4; II. 223–40.

fragments come seems to have been written somewhere about 1180. At the end of the *Glossary* there has been added a short poem by some English patriot calling to mind how the great saints of the Anglo-Saxon period taught the people in English. Now their place has been taken by foreigners ignorant of the language, and people and teachers together are lost. This is followed by seven fragments containing parts of a debate between the Body and the Soul, a favourite subject throughout the mediæval period. In addition to the Old English poems in the Exeter and Vercelli manuscripts the subject is found also in four of the homilies ; in Middle English it is found in the *Worcester Fragments*, in later poems and in a twelfth-century homily. So far as we can tell the version in the *Worcester Fragments* is not closely connected with any of the others, though its affinities seem to lie rather with some of the Middle English than with the Old English versions. It is of the usual type in which the Soul blames the Body for its former wicked life, and some of the descriptions are characterized by consider-able vigour and power ; compare, for example, the descrip-tion of old age in the first of the fragments and the horror of man's former friends for his corpse in the second. ' Now you are hateful and despised by all your friends ; it seems to them too long that you lie near them before you are brought to the place where you must go, into the deep pit, into the doorless house, where the worms possess all that was dearest to you.' It is unfortunate that the fragmentary state of preservation denies to us a proper appreciation of what must have been a powerful, if gloomy, work, though it is possibly less vigorous and more diffuse than the Old English poems on the same subject. The form of the two poems is interesting. They are written in the alliterative line, but in a type of line which differs considerably from that used in the classical Old English poetry. It seems rather to be derived from the popular poetry, an earlier example of the verse used by Laȝamon. Apart from the metre they have little connexion with Old English poetry, little of the poetic vocabulary is to be found in them, and in vocabulary and spirit they seem rather to have been influenced by the rhythmic homiletic prose. They appear to have been written in a West Midland dialect, possibly at or near Worcester, but otherwise nothing is known of their author or provenance.

The *Vices and Virtues* [1] is extant in a unique manuscript, copied about 1200, of which the beginning is lost. It is written in prose and in debate form, and begins in the middle of the confession of a formidable array of sins by the Soul to Reason. At the end the Soul asks for help from Reason, who, in return, urges various Christian virtues and dilates on their qualities. The Body then protests, but Reason shows how both Body and Soul should work together, and passes on to discourse of other Christian virtues, concluding with a recommendation that the Soul should practise its counsels and praise God. The subject is not particularly interesting, but the work is written in a clear straightforward prose and the author probably makes the best of it by throwing it into debate form. He is fond of allegory and uses it not unskilfully, as in the description of the Ship of the Church and in the episode where Mercy and Truth debate concerning the fall of man and Mercy, accompanied by Pity and Peace, is sent to plead for man before God. There is probably little that is original in the work ; the author owes much to the Latin religious writers and much to the older English homiletic literature. In style, vocabulary and spirit he carries on that tradition, as it was being carried on also in the West at about this date. Linguistically the work is interesting since it provides a lengthy specimen of the Essex dialect, in which area it was probably composed.

[1] Ed. F. Holthausen, *Vices and Virtues* (EETS 1888–1921).

Apart from the homiletic literature in the West the *Worcester Fragments* and the *Vices and Virtues* are almost the only literary works in which the influence of the Old English homiletic tradition can still be perceived. Most of the didactic and religious works which follow them have been influenced considerably by French models—in some cases, indeed, they are translations from that language. One of the earliest, however, the *Orrmulum*,[1] is an exception to this ; it is completely isolated in style, with no predecessors and no followers. It is a homiletic work, extant in a unique manuscript, and containing some 10,000 lines. Its name, as the author tells us, is due to the fact that Orrm made it. The intention of the author, as he explains in the introduction, is to give an English version of the Gospels in the Mass book for the whole year, followed by an interpretation and application. The introduction is followed by a table of contents in Latin listing 242 homilies. Then, after a short preface, we have the first thirty-two of these homilies, consisting of a translation of the Gospel for the day with its interpretation and application. Evidently the extant 10,000 lines are only about an eighth of the complete work envisaged by the author ; the remainder may have been accidentally lost or, more probably, it may never have been written.

Metrically the *Orrmulum* is an experiment, and an experiment which has not succeeded. Orrm uses neither rhyme nor alliteration but, almost alone amongst English poets, depends on a strict syllabic regularity. His metre is based on the Latin septenarius, a purely syllabic metre of seven feet, with or without end-rhyme, the first section of the line having four stresses with a masculine, the second three with a feminine, ending. An anacrusis is allowable before either or both of the half-lines and is used regularly by Orrm who has an invariable line of fifteen syllables. Un-

[1] Ed. R. M. White and R. Holt (Oxford 1878).

fortunately invariable is the correct word ; every line has fifteen syllables, neither more nor less, with a feminine ending and a cæsura after the eighth syllable. The rhythm is always iambic, the natural word-stress usually corresponding with the rhythm, though for the sake of uniformity the stress occasionally falls on an unaccented syllable—especially at the beginning of the line. The only freedom which he allows himself is the elision of a final -*e* before an initial vowel or *h*, but this is so regular that it ceases to be a freedom. A single line is sufficient illustration of his metrical system :

þiss boc iss nemmnedd *Orrmulum* ; forrþi þatt Orrm itt wrohhte.

This agrees exactly with every single one of his extant 10,000 lines with the result that the metre soon becomes intolerably monotonous. There is never the slightest variation to relieve the reader, and highly interesting material would have been necessary to make endurable the deadly monotony of the rhythm.

The line quoted above reveals another of Orrm's peculiarities—his use of a special spelling system. The most noticeable part of this system is that all consonants are doubled after a short vowel, except when that vowel is in an open syllable. Various theories have been suggested, the earliest being that Orrm by this method is intending to mark the length of the vowels. It was noted, however, that short vowels were occasionally marked with a short sign and some of the long vowels with an accent, and it was argued that on such a theory these markings would be redundant. This led to the suggestion that he was really concerned with the length of the consonants. The next stage was a compromise of the two earlier theories by which it was suggested that the observation of the varying length of the consonants first led Orrm to adopt his system, though in the result it came to indicate the quantity of the vowels.

But it is difficult to see why Orrm should have been interested in the length of consonants. Moreover it must be remembered that it is not the difference between a short and a long consonant which he is supposed to be representing, but the length of a consonant when following a short vowel as compared with the length of the same consonant when following a long vowel. It is difficult to believe that Orrm was any more conscious of such subtle phonetic differences than are most modern educated people and, even if he were, it would be difficult to suggest a reason why he should need to express it in his writing. On the contrary, since he was a practical man who composed his homilies with a definite end in view, the probability is, as Mr Sisam has pointed out,[1] that he had a similar practical reason for his sp lling system. His work, when complete, was intended as a course of sermons to be read in church to the common people. Complaints of the way in which mediæval preachers mumbled and stumbled when reading the sermon are frequent enough for an earnest author, such as Orrm, to wish to give them every help in the reading of his work. The first thing is to provide a consistent spelling system and to mark clearly the divisions of the words. In reading aloud the length of the vowel is bound to be important, so it is made clear by doubling the consonant after a short vowel in closed syllables. In open syllables such a device may lead to confusion and so is abandoned ; instead a short sign is sometimes added above the vowel. Since Latin vowels before a final -t are usually short, English words with a long vowel in such a position would present difficulties to preachers trained in the reading of Latin. Consequently Orrm helps them by placing double or treble accents over syllables containing a long vowel followed by -t in the same syllable. In the same way the confusion

---

[1] In *Review of English Studies* ix. 4 ff., where also is given a convenient summary of previous theories on the subject.

which might arise from the fact that, in Middle English, *g* was used as a spelling for three different sounds is avoided by using a different shape of the letter for each different sound. The suggestion that these various orthographical devices are simply intended to help preachers in reading aloud to the congregation is far more plausible, and in accordance with what we know of mediæval scribal habits, than any suggestion that we have to deal here with a rigorous phonetician or a spelling crank.

From a linguistic point of view the *Orrmulum* is one of the most important of Middle English texts. In the first place we seem to have the author's autograph copy so that, in any consideration of the dialect, there is no need to allow for scribal corruption. In addition the care and consistency in the spelling make any variations significant, whereas as a rule in Middle English it is often difficult to tell whether a change in spelling is merely orthographical or represents a definite change in sound. The spelling system, too, gives us a clear picture of the vowel quantity in this particular dialect at this time. But from a literary point of view the case is very different, and the editor's suggestion that the loss of the greater part of the work is due to the jealousy of Orrm's contemporaries must be adjudged somewhat optimistic. In that part which has remained there is little to make us regret the loss of the rest; on the contrary, most people would probably suggest, rather ungratefully, that the extant 10,000 lines are far too many. No doubt the work contains much of the best mediæval religious teaching—though even this seems to be somewhat old-fashioned—drawn from such authors as Bede, Isidore, and also perhaps from Old Norse sources, but every other virtue has been sacrificed to clarity. Orrm is so determined that there shall be nothing obscure or unexplained that he constantly repeats himself, and the result is an intolerably diffuse and tedious work. In homilies written to be read aloud some repetition was necessary in order to drive home the sense, but in Orrm this is carried to excess. Taken in conjunction with the monotonous regularity of the metre it makes it impossible to read the work today except in short extracts ; only the earnest phonologist can find pleasure in it, and even to him it must often be a weariness of the flesh. Orrm asks that any scribe who copies the work should be careful to retain his special spelling system, but there is no evidence that any scribe ever found the courage to attempt it ; certainly the work seems to have exerted no influence at all on succeeding literature.

Nothing is known of the author, who calls himself indifferently Orrm and Orrmin, beyond what we learn from his work. In this he tells us that he was an Augustinian canon and that he wrote at the request of his brother Walter, a canon of the same order. Further information is completely lacking, nor is anything known definitely of the date or provenance of his work. On palæographical grounds it has been dated as *c.* 1210, but twelfth- and fourteenth-century dates have also been assigned to it. It must be admitted that too little material is available during the early Middle English period for any dating, on purely palæographical grounds, to be unassailable. In the absence of external evidence we can perhaps hardly say more than that an early thirteenth-century date has the support of the majority of scholars. The work is usually accepted as having been written in the East Midland dialect, and it has been suggested that Orrm may have been an inmate of Elsham Priory in North Lincolnshire. It has, however, been pointed out that a certain Walter, grandson of Gospatrick, was Prior of the Augustinian canons of St Mary at Carlisle between the years 1150 and 1170. He had a brother Orm who may, for all we know, also have been an Augustinian canon, and the suggestion is that this was the author of the *Orrmulum* and that Prior Walter was the brother at whose instigation he wrote. There is no evidence for either identification, nor is any supplied by the dialect in which the work was written. So far as we can tell it is the kind of dialect which would have been spoken in North Lincolnshire *c.* 1200. On the other hand, we can hardly say that the dialect used is definitely not northern since practically nothing is known of the northern dialect before the fourteenth century, due to the lack of texts. At present, whilst either identification is possible, neither is very probable, but most scholars are inclined to believe that the work was written somewhere in the northern part of the East Midland dialectal area.

The French fashion for rhyme very soon affected the homiletic literature, and versified sermons begin to appear towards the end of the twelfth century. One of the most popular of these seems to have been the *Poema Morale*,[1] or *Moral Ode*, containing 400 lines and extant in seven manuscripts. The verse used is that employed by Orrm but fitted with end-rhyme and with variation allowed so that the monotonous regularity of the former is avoided. On the whole, despite its undoubted popularity, it is not a very distinguished or interesting production. A lament for lost opportunities and a disquisition on the transitoriness of earthly things emphasized by the usual mediæval descriptions of heaven and hell. It is full of the usual platitudes of such literature and is saved only by the simplicity and earnestness of the author. In addition a certain personal and subjective quality is in pleasant contrast to most of such Middle English verse. So far as we know it seems to be an original work, but nothing is known of its provenance, except that it appears to have been written originally in a southern dialect and the mention in some of the manuscripts of ' neither Avon stream nor Stour ' as

---

[1] Ed. J. Hall, *op. cit.* I. 30–53 ; II. 312–54.

being able to quench the flames of hell suggests a central southern localization.

More interesting is *A Lutel Soth Sermun*,[1] a poem of a hundred short lines extant in two thirteenth-century manuscripts. It begins with the fall of Adam and goes on to indicate those who are certain to go to hell, backbiters, robbers, thieves, lechers, false merchants, bakers and brewers who give false measure, priests' wives and young men and maidens who think only of each other.

At church and at market when they meet they whisper together and speak of secret love. When they come to church on holy days everyone wishes to see her sweetheart if possible. She smiles at Watkin and forgets her pater noster. She cares nothing for masses or matins ; her mind is full of Willekin and Watkin. Robin takes Giloth to the tavern where they sit and talk together. He pays for her ale and she doesn't think it shameful to walk with him in the evening. Her father and mother threaten to beat her, but she won't give up Robin for all their threats.

It is not, of course, poetry but simply a versified attack on the evils of the time. Nevertheless, it is more amusing than many much better poems and furnishes a pleasant sidelight on the social conditions of the period.

A similar piece, written before 1250, is *Hwon Holy Churche is under uote*,[2] which laments the waning power and increasing corruption of the church.

Those who ought to defend the church are her foes. Under the early Popes it was not in bondage, but now people seek to overthrow it with gold and silver. St Thomas suffered death for it. Archbishop Stephen defended it and St Edmund held it in honour. But now all strive against it ; even the Pope is guilty of corruption.

Again the poetic value is almost negligible, and the main

[1] Ed. R. Morris, *An Old English Miscellany* (EETS 1872), pp. 186–191.
[2] *op. cit.* p. 89.

interest of the piece lies in the early appearance of views often expressed in later Middle English literature.

Translations and paraphrases of parts of the Bible continue to be made throughout the Middle English period. The earliest of these is a poem, containing just over 4,000 four-stress verses, to which the title *Genesis and Exodus* [1] has been given. It appears to have been written by one author, about the middle of the thirteenth century, and probably somewhere in the southern part of the.East Midland dialectal area. In the introduction the author tells us that it is translated from the Latin, but in the main it seems to follow the popular *Historia Scholastica* of Peter Comestor, with other less important and subsidiary sources, rather than the Bible itself. Since the purpose is narrative most of the moralizings and learned disquisitions of the original are omitted, and the work is simply a paraphrase of the principal events in *Genesis* and *Exodus*, the story of Moses and the wanderings of the Israelites being completed by the inclusion of extracts from *Numbers* and *Deuteronomy*. The style is simple and straightforward, and no doubt the author succeeds in his design, but it is never more than a mere paraphrase. The freedom which we find in similar Old English works, their vigour and occasionally epic treatment, is completely absent. The epic has given way to the verse chronicle. The octosyllabic verse is managed competently and a considerable use is made of alliteration. But it must be admitted that all its competence of execution does not make it an interesting work. Linguistically the very length, which detracts from its literary value, makes it important, but it is not a work that can be read with any great enthusiasm.

A shorter and much more interesting poem on practically the same subject is *Iacob and Iosep*,[2] written about the

---

[1] Ed. R. Morris, *Genesis and Exodus* (EETS 1865).
[2] Ed. A. S. Napier, *Iacob and Iosep* (Oxford 1916).

middle of the thirteenth century and preserved in a single manuscript. It tells the story of Joseph in some 500 lines —not counting a missing page in the manuscript—of mixed septenaries and alexandrines. The story differs in slight details from that told in the Bible, but the additions are probably not original since they are found also in contemporary French translations and in the episode as told in the *Cursor Mundi*. Nothing is known of the author, who seems to have written in some central southern or south-western dialect. Taking the well-known biblical story as a basis he has succeeded in producing a vigorous and interesting narrative. He picks out the most moving and picturesque incidents of the Old Testament history and gives to them life and movement. The background has been completely mediævalized, a fact which no doubt helps to explain his success. Knights, minstrels and mediæval castles complete with drawbridge are common ; Jacob is represented as a lord who ' sits in hall ' and Pharaoh goes hunting with ' bowe ybent '. The poem is full of action and direct speech ; the author may not have been a great poet but he has an effective vigour and simplicity. No doubt, like the author of the *Genesis and Exodus*, he is writing for the edification of the ignorant, but the didacticism is never obtruded. He writes as though he enjoyed the story, not as one conscientiously fulfilling a somewhat weary task.

Subjects from the New Testament proper are not represented by paraphrases or translations in this early period, but the legendary part is to be found in a version of the *Harrowing of Hell*. As a rule this and the *Acta Pilati* combined to form the *Gospel of Nicodemus*, which had a tremendous influence on mediæval faith and drama. The two parts seem to have originated independently and at different times, the *Descensus Christi ad inferos* probably being developed during the second and third centuries, the *Acta Pilati* probably not before the fifth century. The two seem to have been combined during the fifth century, and after that time all the prominent theologians show an intimate knowledge of it in their writings. A prose translation of the *Gospel* is extant in Old English, and its influence is to be found in some of the poetry and homilies of the Old English period. In Middle English there are a strophic version and several prose versions, but all are contained in manuscripts written after 1300. The only representative in our period is a metrical paraphrase of the *Descensus*, composed before 1250 and extant in three manuscripts, containing some 250 lines of four-stress verse. After a narrative introduction it proceeds as drama by speeches assigned to Christ, Satan, a doorkeeper and other persons in Hell. It is probably this which has led to the assumption that the poem was written for actual dramatic performance ; this remains a pure assumption for which there is no evidence whatever. From a literary point of view its interest lies more in the fact that it is the first appearance in Middle English of a theme which exerted considerable influence on mediæval literature than on any outstanding performance by its author. In addition there are poems on such themes as ' The Fifteen Signs before Judgment ' or ' The Eleven Pains of Hell ', both subjects which are treated independently and are also found frequently in homilies and in longer works. Some of the independent versions, all in rhyme and varying to a certain extent amongst themselves, were written before 1300, but they are of comparatively little literary interest.

Already during the Old English period saints' lives had proved a popular subject in poetry, and as the cult of the saints increased during the Middle English period so also did the habit of writing down the legends of the different saints. The versions in the *Katherine Group* are not the only individual ones which have survived from the earlier period, though they are by far the most interesting. There is in addition another version of the martyrdom of St Margaret, written in monorhymed quatrains possibly during the first half of the thirteenth century, with the title of *Meidan Maregrete*. It is distinguished by an imaginative treatment of the subject and seems to have become widely popular. A version of the legend of St Eustace, written in tail-rhyme stanza, is also extant. In addition there were probably others which have since been lost, such as the life of St Kenelm, the supposed son of Coenwulf of Mercia, who died in 821. Many of the twelfth-century Latin chroniclers tell how the youthful saint—he was only seven years old at the time of his father's death—was murdered soon afterwards by the contrivance of his wicked sister Cwenthryth, abbess of Winchcombe. Moreover, most of them record a vernacular distich concerning the saint which, with slight emendation, would give two reasonably good alliterative lines :

> In clento cou bathe Kenelm kynebearn
> lith under (haȝe)thorn hævedes bereaved.[1]

It is possible enough that these two lines are all that has remained of some life of the saint in alliterative verse current during the early Middle English, or perhaps even the Old English, period. No doubt this is not the only one which has been lost, and probably many of those which are extant only in later copies were current also during the earlier period. But with the increase, both in popularity and number, of festivals of the saints there was an increased demand for legends of their lives available for reading aloud either in place of, or in addition to, the sermon. The result was that collections of these legends began to be made, the best known of which is, of course, the *Legenda Aurea* of Jacobus a Varagine. At about the same time, when this was being

[1] Found, for example, in Roger of Wendover, *Flores Historiarum* (Rolls Series 95, I. 412).

written, but independently of it, there was also being prepared in England the collection of legends of the saints
known as the *South English Legendary*.[1] The earliest extant
manuscript, written towards the end of the thirteenth century, shows the scheme in an early stage of development.
The first seven pieces have been lost and the manuscript,
as extant, commences with a fragment on the Life and
Passion of Christ, followed by a poem on the Infancy of
the Saviour. After these come the legends of some sixty
saints, together with homilies for various other festivals,
the Invention and Exaltation of the Cross, New Year's Day,
Twelfth Day, All Hallows and All Souls, and an excursus
on the Purgatory of St Patrick. These are given in any
kind of order, but in later manuscripts the festivals are
arranged according to date and a large amount of new
material is incorporated. The numerous manuscripts in
which the *Legendary* is found, dating from the thirteenth
to the sixteenth century, fall into various groups and show
different stages of development. The final scheme com-
prises a synopsis of the more important Old and New
Testament material, apocryphal matter from the fall of
Jerusalem, lives of most of the important saints and of
some of the Popes, and homily cycles for the Advent, the
Passion and Easter. We are, however, not concerned here
with the completed scheme, which seems to have been the
result of a long stage of development, but only with the
beginning of it as shown in the earliest extant manuscript.

So far as we can tell the work seems to be the result of
the collaboration of a number of different writers, perhaps
even of different groups of writers, in different places.
Little is known of the provenance, but the dialect in which
it is written is southern, and the fact that passages from it
are incorporated in the chronicle of Robert of Gloucester

---

[1] Ed. C. Horstmann, *The Early South English Legendary* (EETS.
1887).

suggests that it possibly had its origin in the same district, maybe amongst the monks of Gloucester. All the various legends are written in the same metre, rhyming septenaries, though in some of the later manuscripts these have mostly been modified into alexandrines. Occasionally older poems seem to have been worked over and included in the scheme ; the account of St Mary Magdalene, for example, seems to be derived from an original poem in four-stress verses and mid-rhymes still remain in the septenaries.

It is easy enough to criticize the work adversely. The collaboration seems to have crushed out all individuality, and as a rule the different works present a dead level of narrative with few high lights. Perhaps naturally, considering the subject and length of the work, there is a tendency to monotony which is avoided all too infrequently. All the saints tend to undergo similar torments and to work the same kind of miracles, the comparative lateness of date being shown by the increasing number of miracles and fantastic marvels which are included. The metre is irregular and the narrative plain and unpolished. Nevertheless, there are compensations and exceptions. The legends are derived from all kinds of sources, and some curious and interesting information is sometimes the result. More especially the connoisseur of mediæval demons and strange animals will find much of interest in the compilation. The lives of the English saints are probably the most interesting, and of them the life of St Thomas Becket is treated at considerable length, the story of his murder being told with vigour and dramatic power. Nor are the legends of the saints the only subjects which are dealt with ; the account of St Patrick's Purgatory is the first appearance in English of one of the most influential of the mediæval visions. It tells how heaven and hell were visited by Sir Owen, a Welsh knight, and of the sights which he saw there, details which are continually reproduced in similar later descriptions.

The information is not always religious ; the influence of other types of literature has made itself felt. In the account of the parents of Thomas Becket the influence of the crusading romance is very evident ; the whole tale, in fact, is a romance in miniature. Some of the secular instruction, the geographic and scientific disquisitions, are not only interesting in themselves but valuable for the incidental light which they throw on mediæval life and beliefs. The legend of St Michael includes an account of the fall of the angels, a good deal of information on angels and devils, the situation of heaven, earth, hell, the heavenly bodies, and an excursus on celestial distances.

> The distance between heaven and earth is great. If a man could travel forty miles or more a day he would not reach the highest heaven where the stars are, which you see during the day, for eight thousand years. If Adam, our first father, had begun immediately he was made and travelled towards heaven, and had gone forty miles every day, he would still be a thousand miles or more from heaven.

Natural phenomena, thunder, lightning, etc., are discussed, and a good deal of information on natural history is given. The legend of St Kenelm includes a brief account of the geography of England, the bishoprics and the extent of the Old English kingdoms. Many of these accounts, by the way, are found also independently in later manuscripts. The voyage of St Brendan introduces eastern tales from the Sindbad cycle, and we are given a pleasant description of the Happy Isles. In short, despite its lack of many of the literary graces, there is much more interest in the *Legendary* than anyone acquainted with the usual mediæval collections would have expected.

Apparently at about the time when the *Southern Legendary* was being put into shape a collection of homilies for the church year, to which was later added a legendary, was also being compiled in the north, possibly at Durham.

This, the *Northern Passion*, is a much more poetic and literary production than the *Southern Legendary*, but since the earliest extant manuscripts were apparently not written until after 1300 it cannot be dealt with here.

One of the most popular types of didactic literature during the mediæval period was the *Bestiary*.[1] Its origin seems to have been a compilation called *Physiologus*, or *The Naturalist*, which was put together, probably in Egypt during the fourth century, in some community of monks. It consists of some forty chapters in each of which some valuable moral or religious lesson is drawn from the usually fabulous habits or characteristics of an animal. Written originally in Greek, it soon became immensely popular and was translated into many of the eastern languages. More important it was also translated into Latin, probably as early as the fifth century, and from there made its way into most of the Western European languages. Sections dealing with the Panther, the Whale, and possibly the Partridge appear already in Old English, though, so far as we can tell, there is no connexion with the later Middle English version, which is based on the popular metrical Latin version of a certain Thetbaldus.

The Middle English work is extant in a single manuscript written towards the end of the thirteenth century. It has passed through the hands of so many copyists that we can say no more of the original than that it was probably composed somewhere in the East Midlands during the first half of the century. In his version Thetbaldus uses a variety of metres and the English adaptor does the same, even improving on his model by mixing the different kinds of verse in the description of the same animal. He uses most frequently the octosyllabic couplet, the alliterative long line —with or without rhyme—and a verse of three measures, but he also employs Common Metre, the septenary and a

[1] Ed. J. Hall, *op. cit.* I. 176–96 ; II. 579–626.

verse of two measures. All are, on the whole, managed quite competently though scribal corruption has done much to injure the original rhymes. In some 700 lines of this varying metre the author deals with the lion, eagle, adder, ant, hart, fox, spider, whale, mermaid, elephant, turtle-dove and panther of his original and also adds a further section on the dove. For once it is the matter rather than the manner which is the most interesting part of this work. Its general characteristics may be gathered from the accounts of the Lion and the Whale. The Lion has three peculiarities; he baffles the hunter by dragging dust after him with his tail and so obliterating his footsteps, when born he lies still for three days and is then roused by the roaring of his father, when he sleeps he never closes his eyelids. The first characteristic signifies how Christ eluded the devil and became man, the second and third that He was three days in the grave and watches over us as a shepherd over his sheep. The Whale, when hungry, opens his mouth widely and from it there comes a sweet smell. This attracts other fish who swim into his mouth; when his mouth is full the Whale closes his jaws and so traps them. During stormy weather the Whale can no longer remain on the sea bottom, but rises to the top and there floats. Sailors mistake it for an island, land on his back and build a fire. As soon as the whale feels the heat of the fire it dives to the depths of the sea and so drowns all the sailors. The Whale naturally signifies the Devil, who attracts men to him only to their destruction. The *Bestiary* is full of such unnatural natural history, and its importance lies in the fact that the legends continue to appear in literature long after the *Bestiaries* have ceased to be copied and the natural history has been corrected. It is from this type of literature, too, that many of the animals of heraldry, the gryphon, the unicorn and the phœnix, are derived. Its popularity is not surprising; it provided the mediæval reader with the marvels and monsters in which he delighted, whilst at the same time the allegorical interpretation gave to it a religious and didactic twist which would appeal to many.

Proverbial writings were not uncommon in the Old English period, and numerous proverbs are scattered about in some of the Middle English works, for example in the *Owl and the Nightingale*, the *Ancren Riwle*, the *Brut* and *Havelok*. About a score in Latin and French, with parallel versions of most of them in English, are to be found in an early thirteenth-century manuscript, but the earliest important collection is that which is known as the *Proverbs of Alured*.[1] More or less complete versions of this work are extant in three thirteenth-century manuscripts, and another version, of which transcripts still remain, was contained in one of the burnt Cottonian manuscripts. No doubt all go back to a lost twelfth-century original, and their ascription to Alfred rests merely on the memory of his wisdom. It is a type of work which would lend itself readily to addition or editing so that the variation in the contents of the extant manuscripts is natural enough. Most of the proverbs which are ascribed to Alfred in the *Owl and the Nightingale* do not appear in the collection, but this does not necessarily indicate a lost expanded version ; the presence of such a collection would naturally lead to a similar ascription of isolated proverbs which never formed part of it. The dialect of the various texts differs slightly and, though it is possible, as the latest editor believes, that the original was written somewhere on the borders of the South-Western and the Midland dialect, the evidence is too slight for any definite localization. They are written in a mixture of the alliterative long line, with or without rhyme, and rhyming couplets, though here again scribal corruption has gone far to disguise the original scheme. There are few proverbs in the modern sense of the word. At the beginning Alfred

[1] See H. P. South, *The Proverbs of Alfred* (New York 1931).

is represented as sitting in council with his thanes ; most of the following irregular sections into which the work is divided open with the words ' Thus quoth Alfred ', and then follow lines of homely advice and conventional moralization. The chief emphasis is on the uncertainty of life and the transitoriness and vanity of worldly things, conventional mediæval themes which, through constant emphasis, have lost much of their interest. Only when the equally conventional mediæval misogynistic attitude finds utterance do they become interesting, ' Many a man sings when he brings a wife home, if he knew what he brought he would rather weep.' Equally amusing is the advice never to chose as a companion a small, a tall, or a red-haired man, advice which would seem to leave little choice. The small man is too fierce, the tall man too weak and helpless, whilst the red-haired man is thoroughly wicked and will lead one to destruction.

Another collection of proverbs is that which goes under the name of the *Proverbs of Hendyng*.[1] Nothing is known and little can be guessed as to the identity of this Hendyng. In one of the manuscripts, he is said to be the son of Marcolf, known as the opponent of Saturn in one of the Old English dialogues. This Marcolf again may be the same as the Mearchealf who is mentioned in *Widsith* as the ruler of the Hundingas, but it would be rash to argue from this that there is any connexion between these Hundingas and Hendyng. The proverbs are extant in four manuscripts of thirteenth- and fourteenth-century date. The length and arrangement of the work varies in the different manuscripts but, taken together, they give a composite piece of fifty-one stanzas. The original seems to have been written in some Midland dialect, probably about the middle of the thirteenth century. Material is found in the work which is as old

[1] Ed. R. Morris and W. W. Skeat, *Specimens of Early English* (Oxford 1873), pp. 35 ff.

as that contained in the *Proverbs of Alured*, but it has been remodelled under the influence of similar French collections. Instead of alliterative verse a six-lined stanza, aabccb, is used followed by the proverb and the words ' Quoth Hendyng '. The general character of the compilation can be gathered from the following : ' Never tell your enemy your shame or grief, care or woe ; for he will try, if he can, by night and by day, to increase it. Never tell your foe that your foot aches,' Quoth Hendyng. Modern proverbs are represented in the collection, ' A good beginning makes a good ending ', ' As many nations, so many customs ', ' A fool's bolt is soon shot ', and others are included which occur incidentally in other mediæval works. They are much less religious in tone than the *Proverbs of Alured* ; the latter seems to be the production of some priest, the former is simply an elaboration of the sayings of the common people.

Two medical works, dating from the twelfth century, are still extant ; the *Perididaxeon*, a collection of medical recipes, and the *Medicina de Quadrupedibus*, a compilation giving information on the medical use of such animals as the badger, fox and hare. Both are written rather in Old than in Middle English, the latter being extant in earlier manuscripts, and they belong rather to the history of Old English literature. Of a more popular type of medical literature there is a twelfth-century charm beginning ' Wenne, wenne, wenchichenne ', which seems however to be simply a more or less modernized copy of an Old English original. Also extant is a poem on the *Names of the Hare* [1] in a manuscript written towards the end of the thirteenth century. This curious work, consisting of some sixty-four lines of rude octosyllabic verse with occasional shorter lines, and a

[1] Ed. A. S. C. Ross, ' The Middle English Poem on the Names of a Hare ' (*Proceedings of the Leeds Philosophical and Literary Society, Lit. and Hist. Section*, iii. 347 ff.).

rhyme-scheme varying from the couplet to larger groups, is of considerable interest. The first ten lines tell of the ritual to be adopted on meeting a hare, and then follow forty-four lines containing seventy-seven terms, mostly of abuse, which are to be applied to the animal. The extant copy seems to have been written somewhere in the West, possibly in Shropshire, a localization made more probable by the signs of Welsh influence to be found in the work, which, in addition, has affinities with similar Welsh poems. Naturally enough it is of much greater interest to the lexicographer and the student of folk-lore than to the literary historian.

There are also a number of miscellaneous documents in English, a poem on the characteristics of the various counties ; a description of the shires and hundreds, and a proclamation of Henry III to the citizens of London in 1258, are of some interest. Most of the other legal documents, charters, wills, etc., which are in English were written soon after the Conquest and mainly carry on the Old English traditions[1].

[1] Henry II's writ to Canterbury, preserved as Lambeth Palace MS. 873, is perhaps the latest of such documents.

IX

ROMANCE

AFTER the Conquest there is a complete change in the manner and style of current narrative poetry. The heroic poetry of the earlier period gives way to romance, though we should beware of being influenced by the modern meaning of the word. There is no evidence that the romance was felt to be romantic by the contemporary audience ; on the contrary one of its greatest attractions seems to have been its modernity. Whatever the subject the setting was invariably mediæval ; whether they tell of the Siege of Troy, of Alexander or of King Arthur there is little beyond the names to indicate the period in which the action is supposed to take place. The heroes have become mediæval knights, speaking and acting like the author's contemporaries. Naturally enough it is an idealized modernity which is described. The chivalry of the romances was perhaps rare in real life, the feasts are more splendid, the clothes and jewels more wonderful, the battles and adventures more fantastic. But all the time the background and the adventures, though idealized and exaggerated, are essentially mediæval.

A number of fairly obvious differences exists between the earlier and the later types of narrative poetry. In the heroic literature interest is usually concentrated on character. The old familiar legends are retold in such a way that the character of the hero is unfolded by means of the different incidents. Since character is shown best of all by adversity most of the heroic poems end in the inevitable death of the hero, a tragedy usually brought about by the merits and defects of his own character. In romance the old themes have ceased to stir the imagination; incident, a means to an end in the heroic poetry, has become the end itself. Often enough an idealized theory of character is presented, as, for example, the ideal of chivalry, but we never see the development of that character and the author relies for interest on a mass of extraneous incident. The simplicity and naturalness of the earlier poetry is, to a large extent, replaced by fantasy and exaggeration, as is seen more especially in the different attitudes towards warfare. In heroic poetry the characters have no illusions on the subject; they recognize the danger of warfare and avoid it whenever possible. The hero always had some good reason for fighting, even if it were only a devotion to some code of loyalty or kinship. The warfare, too, is realistic. Unless by some favourable accident of position the hero must always fail against impossible odds and may be hard-pressed by even a single opponent. In romance, on the other hand, the hero may or may not have a good reason for fighting. The reason is unimportant, the stress is always on the fighting itself. Moreover the warfare has become fantastic, due partly to the fact that in real life the increased use of armour has made its wearer almost invulnerable so that battle has changed from a hazard to a sport. No mediæval hero would fight against a single opponent, unless he were a giant or one of the most important of his fellow knights. More often he fights against incredible odds and always with the same self-confidence and monotonous success. Of course such invariable success soon defeats its own object; an invincible hero arouses less interest and so the adventures must become even more fantastic and far-fetched. The abundant supply of the marvellous and the baldness of its treatment results in the atrophy of the reader's sense of wonder and dulls his interest. Another important difference between the two types of poetry lies in the different position occupied in the plot by women. In heroic poetry woman is man's equal and may, because of a clash of loyalties, play a considerable part in the plot. But in such cases the interest is aroused by the clash of loyalties and not by the sex of the character; the fact that she is a woman is quite incidental. In romance, and especially in Arthurian romance, the case is very different. The audience has changed; heroic poetry was composed for the chieftain's hall, romance for the ladies' bower. The result is the increased importance of women in the plot and the development of the ideas of courtly love. She has become a superior being to be wooed artificially and won according to conventional rules[1].

Naturally enough these differences are not to be found in all romances, they are merely characteristic of the majority. Individually they differ considerably according as to when, by whom and for whom they were written. For example, it is not before the twelfth century that the ideas of courtly love become prominent. The earlier romances, especially the French romances dealing with the Charlemagne legend, approximate much more closely to the heroic poetry than do the later ones, and the *Chanson de Roland*, the earliest and most famous of them, has few of the characteristics of romance. In England romances of this type are not to be found; the English translations of the Charlemagne legends usually having been made from the later and more romantic French versions. Consequently the intermediate stage in the development from heroic poetry to romance is absent, except that some of the characteristics of later romance,

---

[1] On mediæval romance in general see A. B. Taylor, *An Introduction to Medieval Romance* (London 1930); many of the romances are edited by W. H. French and C. B. Hale, *Middle English Metrical Romances* (New York 1930).

as, for example, the stress on sentiment as opposed to action, are not to be found in the earlier tales of the ' Matter of England '. The sudden transition in English narrative poetry is presumably due to the Conquest, though, in the absence of early texts, it is difficult to tell whether the gap is more apparent than real. It was inevitable that narrative should have been one of the earliest types of literature to feel the effects of the Conquest. The older heroic poetry was essentially aristocratic in tone ; it may have appealed also to the common people, but only as aristocratic literature had it any chance of a written existence. This was the class which felt the fullest effects of the Conquest,. and which was mainly replaced by Normans with but little interest in the literature of the conquered. We have no reason to suppose that heroic poetry ceased to be composed, but it certainly ceased to be written down, and when narrative poetry was again written in English it had been greatly influenced by contemporary French fashions. Even when the old subjects were still used they had been completely remodelled and the result was romance and not heroic poetry.

Presumably the change would have taken place whether the Conquest had intervened or not. In the later Middle Ages the attraction of French romance was too great to have been resisted even by an Anglo-Saxon England. Already in late Old English there are signs of the coming change ; the prose version of *Apollonius of Tyre*, a translation of the spurious *Letter from Alexander to Aristotle*, and a work on the *Wonders of the East*, are all examples of a type of literature which was later to become popular. It is impossible to tell whether these three works were isolated examples, or whether they really indicate a change in taste, but it must be remembered that the change from heroic poetry to romance is one of style and not necessarily one of subject. Of course, the chief subjects of mediæval romance, Charlemagne, Arthur, or the Siege of Troy, do not appear before the mediæval period ; naturally enough, since the various legends were not elaborated before the twelfth century. At the same time there is evidence that the characters of the heroic age are still being celebrated, and a whole class of English romance deals with the heroes and subjects of Old English history. These latter must have already been celebrated during the Old English period, presumably in some kind of popular heroic poetry or less probably in prose, but we know them today only from the romances of the Middle English period.

Many of the heroes of the older epic poetry must also have retained their popularity. Not a single romance dealing with them has survived, but the frequent references in other literature indicate that the stories must have been quite familiar. The legend of Offa, who ruled over the Angles during the fourth century, is mentioned twice in extant Old English heroic poetry. His fame, reinforced by memories of the historic Offa of Mercia, was still remembered as late as 1200 when a distorted account of the legend was written down in Latin by a monk of St Albans.[1] It will be remembered how, in Chaucer's *Troilus and Criseyde*, Pandarus 'tolde tale of Wade', and elsewhere Chaucer makes mention of the boat of Wade.[2] He was a famous Germanic hero who is mentioned incidentally in the extant fragments of Old English heroic poetry. No work dealing exclusively with him has been preserved, but numerous references in Middle English bear witness to his popularity. Walter Map gives a Latin version of one of his adventures, a fragment of a Middle English tale of Wade has been

[1] *Vitae duorum Offarum* printed by W. Wats in his edition of Matthew Paris, *Chronica Majora* (London 1640).
[2] *Troilus and Criseyde* iii, 614, and *Marchantes Tale* 179 :
'And eek thise olde widwes, god it woot,
They conne so muchel craft on Wades boot.'

discovered in a Latin sermon,[1] and references to him are found in some of the romances. As late as the reign of Henry VIII Leland found that vague memories of him still remained amongst the common people. Similarly Weland the Smith remains popular in Middle English, and mention is made of him in Geoffrey of Monmouth, Laȝamon, *King Horn* and *Torrent of Portugal*. Other references indicate that such Germanic heroes as Unwen, Wudga, Hama, Hrothwulf, Hunlaf, Attila, Hengist and Horsa, were all remembered long after the Conquest.[2] None of the works celebrating these heroes have survived ; in all probability many of the legends depended entirely on oral tradition and were never written down. Nevertheless their one-time existence is as clear as anything can be for which no direct evidence is available, and such tales must have helped to fill in the apparent gap between the earlier and the later types of narrative poetry.

Jean Bodel, one of the earliest of the French romancers, in the course of a poem celebrating Charlemagne's wars against the Saxons, classified the subjects available to a writer of romance as ' the Matter of France ', ' the Matter of Britain ', and ' the Matter of Rome the Great '. This classification became conventional, the ' Matter of France ' containing

---

[1] ' Ita quod dicere possunt cum Wade :
    Summe sende ylues
    and summe sende nadderes :
    Summe sende nikeres
    the bi den watere wunien
    Nister man nenne
    bute Ildebrand onne.'

Discovered in a thirteenth-century Latin sermon on Humility and published by M. R. James. Reproduced by R. W. Chambers, *Widsith* (Cambridge 1912), p. 98.

[2] The Middle English references to these Germanic heroes have been collected by the author in his ' Lost Literature in Old and Middle English ' (*Leeds Studies in English* ii. 15, 16).

the romances dealing with Charlemagne, the 'Matter of Britain' those to do with the Arthurian legend, whilst in the 'Matter of Rome the Great' are included the romances whose subjects are derived from classical history or legend. No doubt the classification was comprehensive enough when it was made during the twelfth century, but during the following 200 years a great number of new romance themes were introduced, mainly from the east. These would not, of course, fit into the scheme devised by Bodel and they are usually somewhat negligently grouped together as 'Miscellaneous Romances'. This is rather misleading since many of them became remarkably popular, and were quite as important as some of the romances of the conventional matters. In addition there grew up in England a class of romance peculiar to the country and based, though often very remotely, on the earlier history of England. In imitation of Bodel's classification these are usually grouped together under the title of the 'Matter of England'.

The 'Matter of France' [1] was the earliest of the romance cycles to be developed—it was the song of Roland from which Taillefer is said to have sung as he led the Norman advance at Hastings. It was the nearest in spirit to the earlier heroic poetry, and in the romances of this group the stress is still on the fighting rather than on the sentimentalities of the later romances. The theme of the *Chanson de Roland*, like that of much of the heroic poetry, is a desperate defence against overwhelming odds, ending in the death of the hero. There is no reason to suppose that the 'Matter of France' owes anything to the growth of genuine tradition. Almost certainly legend was soon busy with Charlemagne and popular tales grew up round his name, but, according to what is probably the most

[1] On the origins of the *chansons de gestes* see J. Bédier, *Les légendes épiques* (3rd ed. Paris 1926–9).

plausible theory of their origin, the growth of the extant romances seems to be due to a purely literary development. In this theory they are usually divided into four different groups, according to the subjects, and it is thought to be possible to indicate the probable source of each of these groups. The first, dealing with religious warfare against the Saracens, partly historical but mainly fictitious, seems to owe its inspiration to the propagandist efforts of the various monasteries on the pilgrimage routes and their attempts to attract patronage by the claim of a famous founder or benefactor. The second group, dealing with the struggles of rebellious vassals against the tyranny of the Emperor, were probably produced by poets under the patronage of the great nobles, at a time when royal authority had become weakened. When any hero of romance became popular it was usual for authors to draw upon that popularity and to tell of the adventures of his ancestors or relatives. This tendency leads to the appearance of the third group containing narratives of the supposed relatives of Charlemagne. Finally any folk-tale or unattached legend is apt to be connected with some popular hero ; consequently the fourth group consists of tales of adventure attached with little or no reason to his name.

On the whole the ' Matter of France ' is of comparatively little importance during our period. A number of romances on the subject, all translated from French originals, though the original is not in every case extant, exists in Middle English. But the extant manuscripts of these romances were all written during the fourteenth and fifteenth centuries and, although it is possible enough that some of these are only later copies of works composed at a much earlier period, there is not enough evidence to justify the inclusion of any of them here. Nevertheless there is some evidence for the popularity of the Charlemagne legend in England during the twelfth and thirteenth centuries. The best and one of the earliest manuscripts of the *Chanson de Roland* was written and is still preserved in England. Walter Map laments that ' only the triflings of mimes in vulgar rhymes celebrate the godlike nobility of Charlemagne or of Pepin ', though whether he refers to English or to French versions of the Charlemagne romances it is impossible to say—probably to both. However, we do know definitely of at least one English romance which existed in a written form before the end of the thirteenth century. In 1286 Baron Bjarni Erlingsson of Bjarkey, one of the great Norwegian magnates, was in Scotland looking after the interests of the Maid of Norway. On his return to Norway in the following year he took with him a romance in English, which he later had translated into Norse. The English original has long since been lost, but the Norse version is still preserved as part of the *Karlamagnussaga*, with the title *Af Frú Olif ok Landres Syni Hennar*. It is the introduction to this which tells us how the tale became known in Norway.[1] Judging from the Norse version we need not greatly regret the disappearance of the English original. It is a dull work on the old folk-lore theme of the calumniated wife and the cruel mother-in-law, and is a member of the fourth group of Charlemagne romances—those attached with little or no reason to his name. Its only importance is that it is the sole romance on the ' Matter of France ' which we can prove to have been extant in England during the thirteenth century.

There are various theories as to the origins of the Arthurian legend.[2] Some scholars see in it the development of

[1] C. R. Unger, *Karlamagnussaga ok Kappa Hans* (Christiania 1860), p. 50 ; see also H. G. Leach, *Angevin Britain and Scandinavia* (Harvard 1921), p. 241.

[2] Of the voluminous literature dealing with the origin and development of the Arthurian legend the following works may be noted : J. D. Bruce, *The Evolution of Arthurian Romance* (2nd ed. Göttingen 1928) ; E. Faral, *La Légende arthurienne* (Paris 1929) ; E. K. Chambers, *Arthur of Britain* (London 1927).

an originally Celtic myth ; others look for a historical Arthur ; whilst others again attempt to combine the two theories and believe that the growth of the legend was due to the gathering of folk-lore material round an actual historical character. On the whole there can be little doubt of the actual existence of Arthur, though the historical Arthur had little in common with the later hero of romance. His name, Artorius, suggests that he may have belonged to one of the noble Romano-British families, and he certainly came to the fore in the wars against the Saxons which took place towards the end of the fifth century. Our nearest contemporary source, the *De Excidio* of Gildas, probably has no mention of Arthur, whose name first appears in the early ninth-century *Historia Brittonum* of a certain Nennius, or Nemnus. It is quite clear, however, that Gildas was writing a lament, not a chronicle, and in any case he seems to have had little knowledge of the past history of the country. Both Nennius and Gildas tell how the Britons fought twelve great battles against the Saxons in the last of which, the famous battle of Mons Badonis variously dated somewhere round about the year 500, the Saxons suffered such a crushing defeat that the Britons had peace for forty years. There can be little doubt as to the historicity of the events described in these two independent sources, and Nennius further ascribes the victories to Arthur, and tells how, in the last great battle, 960 men fell before the ' sole onslaught of Arthur '. From Nennius, too, we obtain some indication of the exact position of Arthur. Whatever later legend may say he was never a king but simply *dux bellorum*, an independent military commander who co-operated with the various British kings against the Saxons. It has been suggested [1] that he may have been a Romano-Briton who

---

[1] By R. G. Collingwood in R. G. Collingwood and J. N. L. Myres, *Roman Britain and the English Settlements* (Oxford 1936), pp. 320–4.

raised a retinue of mailed horsemen of the type which formed the backbone of the contemporary Roman armies. Against the Saxon invaders, consisting as they did only of infantry with little or no body armour, such cavalry would prove almost invincible. The slaughter ascribed to Arthur in the battle of Mons Badonis would suggest that on that occasion he and his retinue had been caught unsupported by any of the local levies. Twenty-one years later was fought the battle of Camlan in which Arthur was killed. His slayer Medraut is said to have been one of his knights, and this may imply that internal dissension had broken out and the force was destroyed in a last great battle of one party against the other. It is an attractive theory which would fit in well enough with most of the few facts known to us, but one for which there is not, and probably never can be, any definite proof.

Whatever may have been the exact course of events the memory of the victorious leader would be cherished by the Britons during the forty years of peace and the disastrous wars which followed. Any unattached legends would tend to be attracted to his name, though, since the early development would be oral, we naturally know little about it. There are some references in early Welsh literature, but that literature is too scanty and the references are too brief to be of much value. The only detailed pictures of the Arthur of Welsh tradition which we possess, untouched by French influence, are to be found in the comparatively late tales, *Kulhwch and Olwen* preserved in the *Red Book of Hergest* (*c.* 1360), and *The Dream of Rhonabwy* in the *White Book* compiled towards the end of the thirteenth century. The legendary, as distinct from the historical or pseudo-historical, Arthur appears first in literature in various of the Latin lives of the Celtic saints, dating from the eleventh and from the early twelfth century, as, for example, in the *Vita Cadoci*, the *Vita Carantoci*, and the *Vita Iltuti*.

Herman of Tournai in his *De Miraculis Sanctae Mariae Laudunensis*, describing the visit of some of the monks of Laon to Cornwall in 1113, tells how the scepticism of their servants over the question of whether Arthur was still alive led to a riot with the men of Bodmin. The earliest allusions by an English writer to the traditions which had grown up round the name of the historical Arthur are to be found in the Chronicle written *c.* 1125 by William of Malmesbury. Arthur is mentioned only incidentally—' It is of this Arthur that the Britons tell so many fables, even to the present day ; a man worthy to be celebrated, not by idle fictions, but by authentic history.' But the first complete and connected account of Arthur was that which was given to Western Europe in the *Historia Regum Britanniae* of Geoffrey of Monmouth, written somewhere about the year 1137. Geoffrey apparently intended his book to be a complete history of the Britons, from the conquest of the island by Brutus to their final subjugation by the Saxons. He devotes considerable space to Arthur and evidently regarded him as the greatest of the British kings. He claims to have based his work on a certain British book, lent to him by Archdeacon Walter of Oxford, but the claim is regarded with a considerable amount of scepticism. It is possible enough that he may have obtained some Latin—hardly British—chronicle or other from the Archdeacon, but the probability is that that part of the Arthurian material which is not sheer invention is drawn from the oral traditions of the Welsh with which he was no doubt familiar.

As we should expect, Geoffrey represents Arthur as a Norman king ambitious of conquest and military fame. His court is modelled on the court of the Norman kings and the whole background is mediæval. Not content with defeating most of the northern nations he overruns Gaul and conquers Rome itself. At the last he is mortally wounded by Mordred at the battle of Camlan, and departs to the isle of Avallon to be healed of his wounds. The outline of the story as it was known to the later Middle Ages is already to be found in Geoffrey, though the details are yet to be filled in. Arthur and his court are still the centre of interest, they have not yet become merely a background for the adventures of the individual knights, and the various knightly adventures of Arthur himself show that he has not yet become the mere figurehead of the later romances. Some of the characters later to become famous are already there. Guinevere appears, though no attempt is made to characterize her, and there too are Gawain, Bedevere and Kay. Much, however, is still missing—Lancelot, Tristram and the minor knights are absent; there is no fellowship of the Round Table and no Quest of the Holy Grail.

Whatever may have been its merits as history there can be no doubt of the immediate popularity of Geoffrey's work. Ailred of Rievaulx, writing in 1142, tells how a novice confessed to him that he had often been wont to shed tears over the sorrows of a certain Arthur, and Alfred of Beverley, c. 1143, says that the hearing of tales of Arthur led him to borrow Geoffrey's work and to write his own Chronicle. These legends may have been derived from the *Historia Regum Britanniae*, or Geoffrey may have taken advantage of an interest already aroused. Certainly the number of extant manuscripts bears witness to its popularity, and it was translated into French verse about 1150 by the Anglo-Norman Geoffrey Gaimar. This translation has since disappeared, probably because within about five years it was superseded by a newer translation by Wace, and it was the latter which formed the basis of the version into alliterative English verse by Laȝamon.[1] We know

[1] The only complete edition is by F. Madden, *The Brut* (London 1847), but selections have been edited by J. Hall, *Layamon's Brut* (Oxford 1924).

nothing of this author except for what he tells us at the beginning of his work :

There was a priest amongst the people, Laȝamon was his name ; he was the son of Leovenoth—may God be gracious to him. He lived at Ernleye (Arley Kings in Worcestershire), at a noble church, on the banks of the Severn—pleasant it seemed to him there— near by Redstone ; there he studied books.

Then it came into his mind that he would tell of the deeds of the English and of those who first possessed the land. As a result he produces a work containing some 16,000 long alliterative lines telling the history of Britain from the landing of Brutus to the death of Cadwallader.

There is little justification, except for the sake of con- venience, for describing Laȝamon's *Brut* in a chapter on romance. He conceived himself to be writing history, and based his work on what he considered to be good historical sources. He tells us what these were : first of all an English translation of Bede's *Ecclesiastical History*, another book which seems to have been the Latin original of the same work, and the Norman-French metrical trans- lation of Geoffrey's work by Wace. The last is indeed his chief source and he seems to have used Bede hardly at all, but his version is an adaptation rather than a translation. He treats his original very freely, expanding it and adding numerous vivifying touches. Whole episodes are occasion- ally introduced, and it has been supposed that he drew on a fund of independent oral tradition, especially in his addi- tions to the Arthurian legend. This is possible enough ; living as he did on the Welsh border he must have been in the middle of the living Arthurian traditions, but most of his additions can be found in contemporary French or Breton sources and there is little evidence for a Welsh origin. His changes are not entirely additions ; when it suits his purpose he omits episodes and even at times contradicts his source.

The *Brut* is preserved in two manuscripts, the earlier of which seems to have been written somewhere about 1205, probably not long after the completion of the poem, and, so far as we can tell, in approximately the same dialect as that which we should expect to have been used by the author. It was copied again some fifty years later in a version of extraordinary interest to students of the language. The second scribe was not content with a mechanical copying of his original; he abbreviated and altered it considerably. The agreement between the two texts indicates that they were probably based on the same original, or the later may even have been based on the earlier. In both cases the vocabulary is remarkably archaic and in many respects seems to preserve the poetic traditions of the Old English poetry. This is, however, much truer of the earlier than of the later version. The later scribe often substitutes a less archaic word or phrase, occasionally uses a commoner instead of the specifically poetic word, and sometimes uses a French loan in place of the English word in his original. The result is that a comparison of the two texts throws considerable light on the changes of vocabulary which have taken place during the fifty years which separate them. We see the gradual disappearance of the poetic Old English vocabulary and the influx of an increasing number of French loan-words.[1]

Though Laȝamon uses the alliterative line there are a number of obvious differences between his use of it and that in Old English. Probably the most characteristic feature of his style is the profusion of epic formulæ and the constant use of them in the summing up of a situation or an emotion. The use of such formulæ is, as a rule,

---

[1] On the differences between the two texts, see especially H. C· Wyld, ' Studies in the Diction of Laȝamon's *Brut* ' (*Language* vi· 1 ; ix. 47, 171 ; x. 149) ; and compare the differences in vocabulary between the two texts of the *Owl and the Nightingale*.

common to early epic poetry but seems to have been avoided by the Old English poets. Allied to this is his use of the simile—many of them being contained in the epic formulæ —though, in addition to the numerous short similes, we find some which are long and elaborate in the Virgilian style, the best known being that in which Arthur compares the flight of· Childeric to a fox pursued by the hounds. Even short similes are rare in Old English poetry. In addition to the development of these new features he has dropped many of those characteristic of the older poetry. The common Old English use of understatement is no feature of his style, and when it does occur it is by way of comment or ironical forecast rather than in the regular course of things. The kenning, a decorative phrase used instead of or in apposition to a noun or pronoun, sometimes metaphorical and imaginative, sometimes merely descriptive, has almost entirely disappeared and there are only about a dozen in the *Brut*. There is little too of the former repetition and parallelism, and parenthetical clauses are merely occasional as in modern poetry. Enjambment is usually avoided ; indeed the chief function of the shorter epic formulæ is to fill up the line, so that the second half-line is apt to contain more rhythm and less meaning than in Old English. In the verse the chief differences which we find in the *Brut* are the greater length of the line, the frequent use of rhyme or assonance, greater licence in the alliteration, and the occurrence of lines with both rhyme and alliteration or with neither. On the whole the affinities of Laȝamon's verse seem to be rather with the popular poetry of the Old and Early Middle English period than with the strict classical line. This looser type of poetry may have been produced by the disintegration of the classical style, but it seems more possible that the classical poetry is a purely literary development. Alongside there existed the popular type which still retained its hold on the common people long after the literary poetry, along with the class for whom and by whom it was developed, had been destroyed by the Conquest.[1]

The fact that Laȝamon considered himself to be writing history is probably the reason for most of the faults to be found in the poem. There are lists of unimportant kings and an unavoidable monotony of event, invasion followed by invasion and battle by battle, which the most skilful variation of detail cannot avoid. Yet on occasion he does show himself capable of presenting a great amount of material and of handling it effectively. The numerous characters are brought to life by vivid touches of descriptive detail, and some of the great stories of English literature, Lear and Cordelia, Brennus and Belinus, the passing of Arthur, appear in English, not unworthily, for the first time. Natural descriptions are frequent and are skilfully used to diversify the narrative. Occasionally it is the bleak and hostile scenery common to the older poetry as in the description of Loch Lomond, a description reminiscent of the haunted pool in *Beowulf* : ' That is a wonderful lake, placed amid fens and reeds, with broad waters, fish and water fowl and terrible creatures. Broad is the lake, sea monsters bathe in it ; there is the sport of elves in the terrible pool.' More frequently he describes the softer and gentler scenery of the Christian poems, the beauty of summer or the freshness of spring, so common a theme in the Middle English lyric.

References to hunting and to animals are frequent in the *Brut*. Easily the best is the description of a fox-hunt, but it is by no means the only one :

Along the hillside men approach him with horns, with hounds, with loud voices ; huntsmen call there, hounds give tongue, over

[1] For Laȝamon's verse see especially J. P. Tatlock, ' Laȝamon's Poetic Style ' (*J. M. Manly Anniversary Studies* (Chicago 1923), pp. 3 ff.

hill and dale they hunt the fox. He flees to the forest and seeks his refuge, he goes to earth in the nearest place. Then is the bold fox deprived of all his joy ; men dig towards him from every side. There is most unhappy the proudest of all animals.

Such references are found often in his more elaborate similes, and some scholars have seen in their frequency a typically English characteristic. It must be remembered, however, that such interests were common in mediæval times ; even fox-hunting does not become typically English until comparatively late. Laȝamon shows little of the interest in dress and ceremonial which is to be found in his original, and he shares this indifference with the later English romancers. On the other hand long and detailed descriptions of the numerous feasts are frequent ; many of his hall scenes are reminiscent of similar scenes in *Beowulf* or the poems of Cynewulf. Similarly reminiscent of Germanic models is the emphasis on the bonds of kinship and loyalty and its occasional significance in the plot.

Mention of the sea could usually bring to life even the dullest of Old English poems and this liking has been inherited by Laȝamon. Occasional references to the sea are frequent and even appear when not demanded by the narrative. Not that there is reason to ascribe any special knowledge to the author. Wace seems to know more of actual nautical procedure than Laȝamon, but by the use of simple detail Laȝamon usually succeeds in presenting a fuller, more vivid and more effective picture. He is at his best in describing voyages, whether pleasant or stormy, the following being one of the best of his storm descriptions :

The wind sprang up on the left, it grew dark beneath the sun with black clouds, hail and rain fell terrifying all who saw ; waves moved like burning towns, planks were smashed, women wept ; the ships ran before the storm, twelve were lost there. The others were driven apart and hurried on by the sea. There was no steersman who could know what to do ; nor had the man been born of whatever country, however brave a warrior or however hard-hearted, if he heard this weeping and this terrible noise and the calling to the saints with loud voices, whose heart would not, be grieved because of the great sorrows.

In the same way Laȝamon's delight in arms, armour and the scenes of battle goes back to his Old English models. References to arms and armour are numerous throughout the poem, the most striking being the two full-length descriptions of the arming of Arthur, one of which, in the names given to the different weapons, is strongly reminiscent of the arming of Beowulf:

Then he put on his mail coat, woven of steel, which an elvish smith wrought with noble craft; it was called Wygar and Witege made it. His legs he covered with steel greaves. By his side he hung the sword Caliburn, fashioned in Avallon by magic craft. He set a helmet, lofty with steel, on his head. On it were many gems set in gold; it belonged to the noble king Uther and was called Goswhit and was unlike all others. Across his shoulder he slung a precious shield called in British Pridwen; therein was engraved with tracings of red gold a precious image of the Mother of God. In his hand he grasped his spear whose name was Ron.

His subject gives him plenty of battle scenes and he avails himself of his opportunities to the full. Working from conventional models monotony is avoided by the use of graphic detail. They are made more vivid by accounting for stroke after stroke where the original uses only general terms. His faculty for visualization and keen sense of the dramatic are given free rein, and remarkably picturesque scenes are the result in which the alliterative measure emphasizes every detail of the battle. Equally reminiscent of Old English models is the insistence on the part played by Fate. Nevertheless, in spite of his skill, monotony is not always avoided. Essentially the battles are all the same, the hosts advance together, the leader exhorts his men, there is the clash of onset, arrows fly, helmets resound and the doomed fall. Not that all his battles are of this epic type ; there is an excellent and vigorous description of a wrestling match between Corrineus and Geomagog.

Laȝamon follows his authorities in giving a disproportionate amount of space to the reign of Arthur. The outline remains the same but many fresh details have been incorporated. More especially most of the marvellous elements in the account are due to Laȝamon himself, and he casts over his hero a poetic glamour not to be found in the more straightforward and prosaic version of Wace. Amongst these additions are the appearance of the elves at the birth of Arthur, the marvellous properties of the Round Table, Arthur's dream foreshadowing the treachery of Mordred, and the glamour and mystery which he casts round the departure of Arthur for Avallon :

Arthur was mortally wounded and there came to him a youth of his own kindred, he was the son of Cador, earl of Cornwall, Constantine was his name and he was dear to the king. Arthur gazed on him as he lay on the earth, and with a sorrowful heart said these words : ' Constantine, son of Cador, you are welcome. I entrust my kingdom to you ; ever watch over my Britons with your own life, and preserve the laws which have been in my day, and all the good laws which were established in the days of Uther. And I will to Avallon to the fairest of all maidens, to Argante the queen, most beautiful of fairies, and she shall heal my wounds and refresh me with healing draughts. And afterwards I will return to my kingdom and dwell among the Britons with great joy.' Even as he spake there came from the sea a small boat, urged on by the waves. Two maidens were in it wondrously arrayed ; they took Arthur and carried him aboard ; gently they laid him down and bore him away hence.

The character of Arthur, too, has undergone change. In the somewhat blurred portrait of Wace he is a Norman king, a leader in battle and, to a limited extent, a knight errant. In Laȝamon his characteristics have been so developed as to make him a figure of individual and striking personality, and he has taken on many of the attributes of the race against whom he is represented as fighting so fiercely.   The knight of chivalry has become the Germanic hero.

There can be little doubt that the *Brut* is one of the most significant of Middle English poems.   In spirit, in vocabulary and in metre it is a continuation of the Old English alliterative tradition.   The more specifically English characteristics have been emphasized, especially by Professor Wyld,[1] but Laȝamon has also been influenced, though to a lesser extent, by the contemporary French romance.   The fact that he writes a history in verse instead of prose is due to the influence of his French source, and many of his characters, despite their links with the old Germanic heroes, are beginning to show the influence of the French romances of chivalry.   At first sight the length of the poem is discouraging and naturally enough the excellence of the best parts is not uniform.   Nevertheless the variety of interest, the vigour and the poetic imagination which we find in the great scenes make it one of the best of the Middle English poems.

On the whole, however, Geoffrey of Monmouth and his successors exerted comparatively little direct influence on the later English Arthurian romances.   Most of them are derived from French sources, and there is evidence that Arthurian legends were widespread in France long before the appearance of Geoffrey's *History*.   The names of Arthur and of Gawain are found in use in Lombardy by the beginning of the twelfth century.   Alanus de Insulis, writing in the same century, recorded the widespread belief amongst the Britons of the return of Arthur, and the denial of it by a servant of some monks of Laon led to a riot at Bodmin.

---

[1] In ' Laȝamon as an English Poet ' (*Review of English Studies* vi. 1–30), but see also F. P. Gillespy, *Laȝamon's Brut, a Comparative Study in Narrative Art* (University of California Publications in Modern Philology iii, (1916), no. 4) and R. S. Loomis, ' Notes on Laȝamon ' (*Review of English Studies*, x. 78 ff.).

Such firm beliefs must have been old and Geoffrey seems to have owed more to them than they did to Geoffrey. His *History* exerted a great influence on the later chronicles ; and probably much of the Merlin episode and the death of Arthur is derived from it, though the whole significance of the latter is changed by the appearance of Lancelot and his share in the dissolution of the Round Table. But on the whole the later romances ignored the chronicles and seem to have been based rather on legends, either in prose or verse, ultimately derived from Brittany. These formed the basis of French poems on the same subjects, and from these poems, with the incorporation of elements from other sources, were composed the long verse romances. Other romances then arose offering different versions of the same theme, due partly to variations in the oral traditions, and partly to the variant traditions which had arisen in the different localities. Here again extraneous matter may be incorporated and Arthur introduced into originally unrelated stories in order to enhance their interest. The next stage saw the composition of the long prose romances in which the careers of the various knights were dealt with and, by the help of the chroniclers, a composite narrative of Arthur's life composed. In these romances adventures have become more fantastic and marvel succeeds marvel until the basic conceptions are almost completely lost. In the last stage of all the theme is revived by writers such as Malory, Spenser and Tennyson, each preserving what was best in the mediæval romances, but adapting their subjects to suit their own particular aim.

The only part of the Arthurian romance which was extant in English during our period seems to have been a version of the Tristram legend, probably the most important part, after the Arthurian material proper, of the ' Matter of Britain '. The story, obviously of Celtic origin, was originally quite unconnected with the Arthurian legend, and, in fact, though Tristram later became one of the knights of the Round Table, the connexion between the two always remained slight with Arthur and his court as a mere background. The exact provenance of the legend is still in dispute. According to some it may have originated amongst the Picts and travelled thence, via Wales, Cornwall and Brittany, to France, whilst others see in it a reflection of the Viking kingdom of Dublin. In any case it was certainly known in France by the middle of the twelfth century. There are references to it in the poems of the famous troubadour, Bernart de Ventadorn, and Chrestien de Troyes tells us that he had written *Del roi Marc et d'Iseut la blonde*, though his poem has long since disappeared. The earliest surviving forms of the legend, the versions of Thomas, of Béroul, the prose *Tristan* of the thirteenth century, all seem to go back to a lost version written in French about the middle of the twelfth century. There is evidence for the existence of some version, or versions, of the Tristram story in English during the early Middle English period. The author of the Anglo-French *Waldef* tells us that both Waldef and Tristan were famous heroes, beloved by the English both high and low, in words which seem to indicate that, translating as he is from an English original, he knew also of English poems on Tristram. However, it is certain that such poems, if they ever existed, have long since vanished, and the only extant romance on the subject in English is the fourteenth-century *Sir Tristrem* of Thomas of Erceldoun.

The Charlemagne and Arthurian romances, as they have survived in English, were almost without exception translated from earlier French sources. But heroes and subjects from English history naturally survived and were not despised by Anglo-French authors. Five of these romances have been preserved in English, *King Horn, Havelok the Dane, Athelston, Bevis of Hampton* and *Guy of Warwick*, of which the two former were written down during our period. No doubt versions of the others also existed, though the extant manuscripts are all of a later date, and in any case these five are only the accidental survivors of a much larger group. It is difficult to say whether accident is a sufficient explanation of why they survived when so many perished. No doubt they were amongst the most popular, but the existence of earlier French versions of them may be another reason for their survival. Most of the romances on English subjects seem to have depended mainly on oral transmission, and were committed to writing only when they fell into the hands of Anglo-French romancers. The English writers of romance seem to have been dependent on French originals; only when they came across French versions of the English tales would they write them down, though then they might prefer to give the current English version rather than translate the French. This dependence of English romancers on French originals may explain why, in the ' Matter of England ', only those romances of which earlier French versions are extant have been written down in English.

There is evidence enough for the existence of other romances, oral or written, drawing their material from early English history and still popular in the centuries following the Conquest, but since lost. William of Malmesbury and Henry of Huntingdon tell us that much of their material was taken from the songs of the country people. Such were the tales of Athelstan, those telling of Edgar's love for a low-born maiden, the legends which gathered round the marriage of Gunhilda, the sister of Canute, to the German emperor, and of how Alfred's ghost walked after his death. Legends, too, of Offa and his wicked queen Cynethryth seem to have been long remembered. Most of the twelfth-century chroniclers tell of the single combat between Canute and Edmund Ironside for the possession of England, and Walter Map tells us that the details of the fight were still remembered when he was writing ; the same author tells of the romance which had grown up round Earl Godwine. The Norman Conquest also had its heroes. In the forests of the West Eadric the Wild for long kept up the struggle with the Conqueror ; already in Map he has become a legendary hero, and tales with which he had originally no connexion have gathered round his name, whilst details of his mythical struggle with Ralf de Mortimer were known to Dugdale. Probably most of these tales were never written down at all, but we know of others which were. The romance of *Waldef* is extant only in an Anglo-French version, which the author explicitly tells us was translated from English at the instance of a lady who did not understand that language. The deeds of Hereward the Wake were written down in English by his chaplain Leofric, but are extant only in a Latin version, the author of which tells us that Hereward was still celebrated in the songs of the country people. Incidentally he also mentions a certain Godwine, the son of Guthlac, celebrated in the songs of the ancients, though the very memory of his deeds has long since disappeared. Robert Mannyng of Brunne knew of a work by a certain Master Edmund, probably in French, and another by Thomas of Kendal dealing with the exploits of Engle and telling of the foundation of Scarborough and Flamborough by two of his followers, Scarthe and Flayn.

The English versions of these legends, whether written or oral, have long since been lost and we know of them only from casual references. Yet if we are to have a true picture of mediæval romance we must remember that the Matters of France and Britain were not so overwhelmingly popular in England as they sometimes seem to be. Throughout the period purely English legends continued popular and their importance cannot be judged by the comparatively small number which happen to have been preserved. Even post-Conquest history continued to produce subjects for romance, sometimes still extant as in the romance of *Richard the Lion-heart*, sometimes known only from a brief allusion like the rhymes of Randolph Earl of Chester which Langland knew.

King Horn,[1] the earliest of the extant romances in the ' Matter of England ', is found in three manuscripts of the late thirteenth and early fourteenth centuries. They differ slightly in length and in detail but tell essentially the same story. The king of a country called Sudene is attacked and slain by pirates who capture his son Horn and set him adrift with his companions. The latter come ashore in Westerness and are welcomed and taken into the king's household. Rimenhild, the daughter of the king, falls in love with Horn and after some difficulty succeeds in making known her love to him. Horn, however, refuses to plight troth until he shall have been knighted, and, when Rimenhild has persuaded her father to knight Horn and his companions, again refuses until he shall have proved his knighthood. Rimenhild gives to him a gold ring and he sets out to seek adventures. He meets a pirate ship by the seashore, slays the crew and returns to show the proof of his prowess to the king. Later Horn and Rimenhild are surprised together by the king and Horn is exiled. Taking refuge in Ireland he slays a giant and rescues the country from the Saracens, but, remembering his vows to Rimenhild, refuses the hand of the princess. In the meantime Rimenhild, being wooed by another prince, contrives to send word to Horn who arrives in Westerness in time for the wedding feast. He enters the hall in the guise of a palmer, and when Rimenhild offers him wine shows the ring which she had given to him. On being questioned he declares that Horn is dead,

---

[1] Ed. J. Hall, *King Horn* (Oxford 1901), and also in W. H. French and C. B. Hale, *op. cit.* pp. 25–70.

but when she attempts to kill herself he is convinced of her faithfulness and makes himself known. The rival wooer is slain and Horn and his companions set out to recover his heritage. This is soon done, and Horn is reunited with his mother who had been living in a cave by the sea. He is warned in a dream that Rimenhild is again being pursued by an unwelcome wooer and has been imprisoned in a castle. He arrives there before the wedding has taken place, succeeds in entering in the disguise of a minstrel, slays the traitor and is at last wedded to his betrothed.

Other versions of the tale are extant, the earliest being a thirteenth-century Anglo-French version with the title *Horn et Rimel*, and it was also rewritten in English during the fourteenth century as *Horn Childe*. These different versions seem to be independent of each other and are probably based on some oral legend, the variations in names and localities being due to the different minstrels through whose hands the tale has passed. It is possible enough that the tale is based on actual happenings which took place maybe during the English conquest but more probably during the Viking raids. There is little point in attempting to localize the events recorded in the romance. Sudene has been identified with the Isle of Man, Surrey and the Scottish border, but it is futile to expect to find exact geographical detail in a story which, for some five centuries and possibly more, has been carried on by oral tradition. What basis of fact there may have been in the original story has been overlaid by a mass of folk-tale. Only Horn and Rimenhild retain the same name in all three versions, and this is natural enough in an oral tradition. The hero and heroine remain, but the names of the less important characters are forgotten and they are renamed afresh by almost every minstrel through whose hands the story passes. The same is true of the geography ; it will be modified or deliberately changed to suit local conditions, and there is no reason to suppose that the indications in the extant versions can tell us anything of the locality in which the original happenings took place.

The Anglo-French *Horn et Rimel* was apparently written by a certain Mestre Thomas who alludes to a previous work of his telling of the death of Aaluf, the father of Horn, and promises that his son Gillimot will treat of the deeds of Horn's son Hadermod. Nothing further is known of Mestre Thomas nor have the other romances survived, if indeed they were ever composed. Not even a name can be given to the author of the English *King Horn*, nor do we know where the original of the three extant manuscripts of it was composed. The original dialect, as far as it can be deduced from the rhymes, seems to have shown south-eastern influence, and it is possible that the poem may have been composed somewhere in the southern part of the East Midland dialectal area.

The metre in which the poem is written is interesting and seems to be a development of the native alliterative line, strongly influenced by the newer French fashions. The two parts of the original four-stress line have been separated and end-rhyme added to turn them into couplets, a change which is beginning to appear already in Laȝamon who, in the course of his poem, grows progressively fonder of rhyme, either with or in place of alliteration. Examples of the regular two-stress line developed in this way are still to be found in *King Horn*, but more usually the lines have three or four stresses with an irregular number of unstressed syllables, though the alternation of stressed and unstressed syllables is becoming regular. The metre is almost as strongly recitative as Old English poetry and the poem was obviously meant to be spoken rather than read.

As a fast-moving story in which simplicity and energy of expression are the chief merits *King Horn* has much to recommend it. Apart from that its literary value is small.

Naturally enough no colouring of the original Viking story remains and the background has been completely mediæval-ized. Horn is dubbed knight and, in approved crusader fashion, fights against the Saracens. There is little attempt at descriptive writing; the author was interested mainly in fighting and adventure, and the love element is merely there to provide the conventional happy ending. Rhyming tags and the use of words in a forced sense are too common, and it is difficult to believe that even a mediæval audience could receive with equanimity the statement that Horn was 'fairer by a ribbe Than any man that libbe'. Even as a purely narrative poem objection is possible. Already, in the double rescue of Rimenhild from unwelcome wooers we see the appearance of that duplication of incident which was to prove a godsend to the later writers of romance and a weariness of the flesh to the modern reader. There can be little doubt that the poem was written for an audience who demanded adventure and incident and little more.

Havelok the Dane [1] is a more interesting work in every way. Written sometime towards the end of the thirteenth century in the usual octosyllabic couplets of romance it seems, like *King Horn*, to be based on events of the Viking period, but events which have been overlaid by a mass of folk-tale material. King Athelwold of England, when on his death-bed, appoints Earl Godrich as guardian to his infant daughter Goldeboru. The wicked earl seizes power and imprisons his ward in Dover castle. The scene then moves to Denmark where a similar act is being played out. King Birkebayn has appointed Earl Godard as guardian to his son Havelok and his two daughters. Godard seizes the kingdom, kills the two daughters, but spares the son. But soon afterwards Havelok is handed over to a fisherman,

[1] Ed. W. W. Skeat and K. Sisam, *The Lay of Havelok the Dane* (Oxford 1923), also in W. H. French and C. B. Hale, *op.cit.*, pp. 71–176.

Grim, with orders that he is to be drowned. The sight of a mysterious flame issuing from the mouth of the sleeping child convinces Grim of his royal birth, whereupon he and his wife adopt the child and set sail for England where he founds the town of Grimsby. Havelok, brought up as one of the family, works as a fisherman until a famine causes him to secure the place of scullion to the cook of Earl Godrich, and he wins all hearts by his beauty, strength and skill at games. Godrich, to make sure of the throne, has determined to wed Goldeboru to a low-born husband and he compels her to marry Havelok. The pair return to Grimsby where the miraculous light informs Goldeboru of Havelok's royal birth and, as the result of a dream, they leave for Denmark accompanied by the sons of Grim. There they are befriended by Earl Ubbe but attacked by a gang of thieves whom they defeat and slay. As a result of this they are taken into the house of Ubbe and the light shows Havelok to be the rightful heir. Ubbe does homage and raises the country against Godard who is defeated and hanged. Having been crowned as king, Havelok sails with a large army to England. Godrich is defeated, captured and burned, and the story ends with the wholesale marriage of the minor characters.

The tale is extant in earlier Anglo-French versions, with which the English version seems to have no connexion. It was inserted by Gaimar into his *Estoire des Engleis*, and an unknown author of the same century rewrote it in the form of a Breton *lai*. Both these Anglo-French versions seem to have been derived from some common original, now lost. Another English version is known. Robert Mannying of Brunne, in his translation of the *Chronicle* of Peter of Langtoft, refers to the legend, and in one of the manuscripts of his work the reference has been omitted and replaced by a different version of the story, the *Lambeth Interpolation*. References are found in other minor sources and, as late as the sixteenth century, Camden and Gervase Holles apparently knew of it. The *Lambeth Interpolation* seems to have been drawn from the same lost original as the French versions, but nothing is known of the previous history of the version with which we are concerned and which is extant in a single manuscript.

There are some indications of an originally historical basis for the legend. In the French versions Havelok is given the name of Cuaran, and it has been pointed out that Havelok is the English form of the Irish Abloc, a name often substituted for the Old Norse Óláfr. During the tenth century there was a famous Viking, Óláfr Cuaran, who fought at Brunanburh against Athelstan and had a long and adventurous life. It is certain, however, that none of the incidents in the English poem can be connected with anything which we know of the life of Óláfr Cuaran. The story seems rather to contain vague references to the union of England and Denmark under Swegen and Canute during the following century. Another possible historical reference is the name Birkebayn given to the father of Havelok. This seems to be taken from the Old Norse *Birkibeinar*, the name given to the followers of King Sverrir of Norway, who fought his way to the throne in 1184. However, the tale, as a whole, certainly has nothing to do with history. It is simply a folk-tale of a common type which has become attached to the name of a famous hero, and uses historical material and names to increase the interest. A good story and a well-known hero would interest an audience who would not trouble whether the hero fitted the story historically or not. The author of the Anglo-French *lai*, for example, has even attached it vaguely to the Arthurian legend. In the extant versions the story has become localized in Lincolnshire. It provides an eponymous founder for Grimsby, and much of the action centres round that town and Lincoln. Whether it has always been a purely local story is a more difficult question. Possibly not, though in the earliest extant version, that by Gaimar, whose patroness was perhaps significantly a Lincolnshire lady, the story is already connected with Grimsby, and by the reign of Edward I it had become firmly established—the seal of the town, dating from that period, showing representations of Havelok, Grim and Goldeboru. The English version of the story has passed through the hands of a number of different scribes but, so far as can be judged from the dialect, it seems to have been written in the neighbourhood of Grimsby.

There is no pretentiousness about *Havelok* ; it sets out to be an exciting tale of adventure and succeeds. The whole emphasis is on incident and fighting, but there are few of the marvellous and fantastic adventures of later romance, though the miraculous flame and the slaughter of the sixty thieves by Havelok and his three companions are perhaps signs of what was to come. The poet takes little interest in Goldeboru and none at all in the sentimental possibilities in which the French authors of the Arthurian romances revelled. This predilection for fighting and adventure is usually referred to as being characteristic of English romance, but it is found too in the earlier French Charlemagne romances and is, in fact, rather a characteristic of early romance. Later on the increasing importance of women as the patrons of romance, and the general softening of manners due to the influence of the ideals of chivalry, lead to the elaboration of the sentimental aspects ; but in England the pure romance of adventure always remained in favour, especially amongst the lower classes. There can be no doubt that this was the class for which *Havelok* was written. The author addresses his audience familiarly throughout, he is fond of interpolating popular proverbs, emphasizes Havelok's position as a scullion and gives a vivid description of the sports of the common people. The whole background, in fact, is the lower-class life of thirteenth-century England. Nobles are necessary for the sake of the plot, but little interest is shown in their way of life. Only when we come to the lower-class aspects, the work of Grim the fisherman, Havelok as a seller of fish and the scene in Lincoln market, do we find the vivid descriptions which add greatly to the interest of the plot. Throughout the tale there is a curious duplication of incident ; both Havelok and Goldeboru are left to the care of wicked guardians, twice is the life of Havelok spared, and the conquest of Denmark is followed by that of England. But this duplication is relieved by a variation of detail so that it never becomes too obvious. The octo-syllabic couplet is managed competently, the rhymed coup-lets being varied by occasional larger groups of verses rhyming together and by variation of masculine and feminine rhymes, whilst the accentuation is varied in the usual ways. Alliteration is infrequent, except for occasional common phrases, and the usual use of conventional tags is not frequent enough to be specially objectionable. On the whole the author, taking perhaps a historical name or two, adding vague historical reminiscences and a mass of popular folk-tale material, has produced a good, straightforward tale of adventure, one of the best of its type in Middle English literature.

Subjects drawn from classical legend and ancient history were amongst the most popular themes of mediæval romance. The siege of Troy and the conquests of Alexander were popular throughout the period, though it was rarely that the romances bore much resemblance to the actual or classical events, comparatively historical sources usually being ignored in favour of more attractive, if less trust-worthy, accounts. The Troy tale, for example, was based not on Homer or Virgil, but on the late forgeries ascribed to Dictys Cretensis and Dares Phrygius who claimed to have been present at the siege, the former on the Grecian, the latter on the Trojan side. In the same way the Alexander legend was based on an account which purported to have been written by Alexander's secretary, Callisthenes. Parts of the Alexander legend are already found in Old English, in which language has been preserved a translation of the *Letter of Alexander to Aristotle* and a description of the *Wonders of the East*, both of which formed part of the Alexander Legend as it was later elaborated. The French versions of these legends, from which most of the English were ultimately derived, appeared during the twelfth century in the *Roman de Troie* of Benoit de Sainte-More and the *Roman d'Alexandre* of Lambert le Tort and Alexandre de Bernai, but the extant English romances were all written after 1300. It is possible enough that earlier versions existed in English before that date, but if so all trace of them has been lost.

In addition to the four great matters there were, during the Middle English period, numerous unrelated subjects of romance. More especially the influence of the Crusades was seen by the adaptation of numerous plots from eastern sources. Some of these became more or less loosely attached to the heroes of one of the conventional matters but most of them retained their separate identities. The only one of which manuscripts written before 1300 still exist is *Floris and Blancheflour*.[1] The story tells how a young French widow, one of a band of pilgrims, is captured by a Saracen king and carried off to Spain. There she gives birth to a daughter, Blancheflour, and on the same day the queen gives birth to a son, Floris. The two children are brought up together and fall in love. Various attempts to cure Floris of his infatuation fail, and as a last resort Blancheflour, during his temporary absence, is sold to a slave

[1] Ed. A. B. Taylor, *Floris and Blancheflour* (Oxford 1927), also in W. H. French and C. B. Hale, *op.cit.*, pp. 823–55.

merchant. When Floris returns he is told that she is dead and an empty tomb inscribed with her name is shown to him. Thereupon he attempts to kill himself, but his parents relent, tell him the true fate of Blancheflour, and promise to help him to regain her. He follows her in disguise and eventually discovers that she has been taken to Babylon to the harem of the Emir. On his arrival there he bribes the porter and succeeds in making his way into the harem where he is reunited with Blancheflour. The lovers are, however, discovered by the Emir and condemned to death. One of his nobles suggests that if Floris is pardoned it will be possible to discover how he obtained access to the harem, when any recurrence of such a happening can be prevented. Floris tells his story, and the Emir is so touched that he not only forgives the lovers but has them married, though he had intended Blancheflour for his own wife. Soon afterwards Floris hears of the death of his father, returns home, is crowned king and becomes a Christian.

The plot is very similar to that used in a far better known French romance, *Aucassin and Nicolette*, of which no Middle English version exists. Its origin is unknown, but fairly close parallels are found in Arabic stories, and it probably reached the west either orally through pilgrims or crusaders, or in an oral or written form via Constantinople. The original Middle English version, possibly written somewhere in the south-east Midlands, was adapted from the French about the middle of the thirteenth century and is represented by four extant manuscripts, two of them dating from the latter half of the thirteenth century, one from the second quarter of the fourteenth and one from the first half of the fifteenth. Only the last of these is complete, and all are derived from the same lost original, the somewhat wide discrepancies between the various manuscripts indicating that the transmission was probably oral rather than written.

The English version is interesting, not only as showing

how mediæval authors dealt with eastern subjects, but also as a welcome relief from the eternal fighting or the conventional courtly love of the majority of romances. It is a simple love story in which for once we have a Saracen setting where the characters are not regarded merely as faithless infidels. The French original seems to have been followed fairly closely, though with a constant abridgement which results in a version of only about a third of the length of the original. The descriptive passages, the illustrative scenes and episodes are usually omitted with the result that the English romance often seems disjointed, and the lack of artistic detail occasionally leads to avoidable confusion. For example, the translator tells of the disguise adopted by Floris, but omits the details which show him acting his part, and the whole episode of the discovery of the lovers is spoilt by unimaginative cutting. Occasionally these omissions improve the story, as when the artistic elaboration or philosophical moralization of the French poet are avoided, though one suspects that the improvement is unintentional.

It is not, perhaps, one of the best of the romances, but it makes pleasant reading none the less. Though it contains the usual romance ingredients—a marvellous ring which preserves the hero from sea, fire or battle, and the usual adventure and fighting, though perhaps rather less than is common—it is always the love story which is the main theme. It was the story which interested the English poet ; he usually omits the descriptive passages of his original, beautiful though they sometimes are, and when he occasionally retains them they are the weakest part of his poem. He is not particularly happy in his metre, the octosyllabic verse is too short and rapid for his theme and he uses too many rhyming tags. Nevertheless he succeeds in telling a simple unaffected story and in emphasizing the pathos which most mediæval authors found so difficult. Most of the critical passages retain their dramatic effect and are skilfully told without any of the frequent moralizing which so often spoils a mediæval tale.

These are the only romances which were certainly extant in English before 1300, though there were almost certainly others which have since been lost.[1] They are, however, fairly typical of mediæval English romance. If not in every case directly translated from the French they owe much to the influence of earlier versions in that language. Unfortunately, whilst the French romances were written for an aristocratic audience, the English versions seem to have been adapted by ruder poets for a lower class. The result is that the French emphasis on the ideals of chivalry and the conventions of courtly love is entirely absent. The different audience was interested more in adventure and fighting and cared little for the sentimental analysis so dear to the noble patronesses of the French romancers ; Lancelot, the typical hero of courtly love, never became popular in England. In the English versions the love interest is almost always quite straightforward and only rarely are the feminine characters of much importance. Whilst the sentiment is omitted or bungled the adventures are reproduced in full, often indeed even duplicated. Since the French originals have usually been adapted by mediocre poets the drastic rehandling which they felt to be necessary often resulted in clumsy and inartistic work. The main thread of the story is retained, but the imperfect appreciation of artistic detail often leads to the omission of points of vital significance, or of explanations essential to a full understanding of the story. Perhaps the commonest fault is that of over-emphasis, a fault not always absent from the French romances and carried even further in the English. The earlier romances, however, do not suffer from an invincible hero and an accumulation of marvellous and fantastic

[1] See D. Everett, ‘ A Characterization of the English Medieval Romances ’ (*Essays and Studies* xv. 98–121).

adventures to anything like the extent that the later ones do. Despite their faults the best of the English romances have the merits of good adventure stories. They are simple and direct with little of the artificial tediousness of description or sentiment which we find in the French. Artistic finish is too often lacking but the story is always there, and not crowded out of the picture by unimportant detail and conventional moralization.[1]

[1] For a full description of the metrical romances, see especially L. A. Hibbard, *Mediæval Romance in England* (New York 1924).

X

TALES AND FABLES

THE romance was by no means the only form of narrative which was developed during the mediæval period. Side by side with the longer works there also appeared short tales, both in prose and verse, which make their way into almost all types of literature. They are seized upon by religious and didactic writers and provided with an edifying moral, the result being the *exemplum*, an illustrative moral story such as is found frequently in the sermon literature of the period. The value of the *exemplum* was quickly recognized by the preachers of the day. It provided a moral in an acceptable and entertaining way and helped to keep the attention of the audience by the variety of its subjects. In England the development and use of the *exemplum* seems to have been due in great part to the newer technique of popular preaching introduced by the friars during the thirteenth century.[1] In any case its popularity was soon assured, and it maintained its position up to the end of the Middle Ages, despite the objections of Wyclif's 'poor preachers' who pleaded for a simple expounding of the scriptural text. The next stage was the collection of these *exempla* into books in which the preacher was presented with the appropriate *exemplum* for every occasion.

[1] For the development and growth of the *exemplum* see especially G. R. Owst, *Literature and Pulpit in Medieval England* (Cambridge 1933), and *Preaching in Medieval England* (Cambridge 1926) by the same author.

The earlier collections are naturally in Latin, but they were soon translated into the vernacular, and examples in Latin, French and English are frequent, the best known in England being the *Gesta Romanorum.* Such English collections are, however, comparatively late, and even individual *exempla* are not frequent in our period ; sermons in English from the thirteenth century are rare and the earlier groups of homilies from the twelfth century still follow the Old English homiletic tradition. Consequently it is not until the fourteenth century that the vernacular *exemplum* becomes common, though it was presumably in use long before.

Many of the *exempla* were elaborated into separate *contes dévots* or pious tales ; the popular liking for stories being seized upon by the clergy and used to inculcate and confirm faith. Many of the extant ones are merely collections of miracles, often so exaggerated and grotesque as to be distasteful to the modern reader. They are usually in verse and formed a regular part of the pious reading of the period. Quite a number in English are extant from the mediæval period, but only a single one in a manuscript written before 1300. The most popular subject seems to be the miracles of the Virgin Mary, sometimes in collections and sometimes treated separately. No doubt they reflect the popularity in mediæval times of the cult of the Virgin, a cult which influenced, and was influenced by, the idealization of women in the romances of chivalry. The only one extant before 1300, ' How the Psalter of Our Lady was Made ', tells how a monk was accustomed to repeat a hundred *Aves* every day. One Saturday Mary herself appeared to him in a vision, declared that he had assured himself of redemption, and directed him henceforth to repeat a hundred and fifty *Aves* daily, this being her Psalter. The first fifty were for joy of the Annunciation, the second fifty that she should bear Christ, and the third that she should go to him in bliss. In a later vision he is directed to preach her Psalter everywhere, told that he is to become an abbot and that he will die within seven years. The whole poem contains 250 three-stress verses rhyming aabccb, and is extant in two manuscripts. It is exceptional only in· the mildness of its marvels ; later the miracles become more grotesque and wonderful and the obvious moral is not always the one so carefully drawn by the narrator.

The short narrative poem was not, however, left only to the purveyors of pious reading. It was used also in a group of poems intended for the entertainment of the aristocracy. These are the *Breton lais*, romances in miniature, usually on Celtic subjects and with a strong intermixture of the supernatural, which are best represented by the *lais* of Marie de France.[1] There are eight *lais* extant in English, only two of which are translated from those of Marie, though only in fourteenth- or fifteenth-century manuscripts. No doubt earlier versions of some of them were current during our period, in one case the words of Marie seem to indicate the existence of an English *lai* at the time she was writing, but if so none of these earlier versions has survived. The French *lais* are essentially aristocratic in tone, they are full of the ideals of chivalry and the conventions of courtly love—in fact some of them are loosely connected with the Arthurian legend. Most of the English versions have, as usual, been worked over by inferior poets for the benefit of a lower class, but much of the original aristocratic atmosphere still remains.

The *exemplum*, however, was only the moralized form of a type of short narrative poem which had been developed by and for the middle class and was known as the *fabliau*.[2]

---

[1] See above, p. 79.

[2] This is the Picard dialect form of *fableau* (from *fabulellum* from *fabula*), and during the mediæval period it is regularly used instead of the Central French *fablel* because of the popularity of this type of literature in Picardy.

This type of literature first begins to appear with the development of the middle classes during the twelfth century and it flourishes with the growth of that class, most of the extant *fabliaux* apparently having been composed between the years 1150 and 1340. They seem to owe much of their popularity to the fact that they are partly the expression of a revolt against the romantic idealism of the conventional matters of romance. They are humorous tales in verse with no moral or didactic appeal, many of them in fact depending for their effect on the broadest types of humour, and, since they deal only with a single adventure of the hero, they are invariably short. The *fabliau* seems to have originated and flourished in Northern France if we are to judge from the provenance of the extant examples of the type. There is no hard and fast division between the various types of short narrative. Though written essentially for the middle classes there is evidence that the *fabliau* also found favour in other circles. Many of the themes were seized upon by the clergy and used as *exempla*; a number of the tales in the *Gesta Romanorum*, for example, are taken from the *fabliaux* with a rough and sometimes inappropriate moralization hastily added. A mixture of both the serious and humorous narrative may be unified into collections by the addition of a narrative framework, as in the *Seven Sages*, the *Decameron*, the *Confessio Amantis* and the *Canterbury Tales*. In addition *fabliau* themes are found in romance and occasionally form the subject of the later ballad poetry.[1]

One of the most surprising things in Middle English literature is the almost complete absence of single *fabliaux* as compared with the wealth of such literature in France. On the whole the omission is probably due mainly to accident and not, as has been suggested, to any innate Puritanic

---

[1] The standard work on the *fabliau* is J. Bédier, *Les Fabliaux* (Paris 1895), and see also E. Faral, ' Le fabliau latin au moyen age ' (*Romania* l. 321–85).

strain in the English character. In the first place such literature would stand comparatively little chance of being written down, except in a moralized form by the clergy. The very existence of such moral stories suggests that they were also extant in an unmoralized form. Many of the *Contes Moralisés* [1] of Nicholas Bozon, a somewhat vague figure who seems to have flourished towards the end of the thirteenth century, were taken from English originals. This is indicated by the occasional appearance of English proverbs and rhyming tags and, most of all, by the use of English names in some of the stories. The only reason for the presence of these names must be that they were already present in his original. Since he is writing in French they could hardly have been invented by him, otherwise he would presumably have invented French names. There is no reason for believing that such stories were already moralized when he made use of them. On the contrary, if they were extant in English, it is unlikely that they had even been in the hands of the clergy, in which case there was little reason for any moral. Moreover, *fabliau* themes appear in later collections of such moral tales, both Latin and English, and other evidence for the presence of this type of literature in Middle English is not altogether wanting. In 1292 the University of Oxford issued a warning against ' cantilenas sive fabulas de omasiis vel luxuriosis aut ad libidinem sonantibus ', which were no doubt tales of this type. At least half a dozen of the *fabliaux* included in the French collections seem to have been written in England. Warnings against such tales are frequent in the *Cursor Mundi*, *Piers Plowman*, and elsewhere, though it must be remembered that romances were often regarded in much the same light by the moralists. Chaucer assigns tales of the *fabliau* type to his lower-class characters, a certain indication of the

---

[1] Ed. L. Toulmin Smith and P. Meyer, *Les contes moralisés de Nicole Bozon* (Paris 1889).

kind of story popular in that class. If, as seems probable, such stories were common in England there can be little doubt that they must have been in English. After all they were composed more particularly for the lower and middle classes, the classes which would be least likely to know French and whose normal speech would be English. It is not surprising that so little of it should have survived ; it was essentially an ephemeral type of literature and one which would be unlikely to attain to a written existence.

Apart from the use of *fabliau* themes in other types of literature the only English example which has survived is *Dame Siriz*.[1] Incidentally the rhymes prove the pronunciation to have been *Sirith* despite the usual spelling with *z*. The poem is preserved in a single manuscript written, apparently, somewhere in the West towards the end of the thirteenth century. Consequently, as extant, it seems to be written in some Western dialect, but the evidence of the rhymes, of isolated forms, and the mention of the fair at Botolfston—Boston in South Lincolnshire—suggest that this is merely a later copy of a work written originally somewhere in the East Midland dialectal area. The plot itself is one of the oldest in this type of literature, and the English version of it tells how a clerk, Wilekin, falls in love with Margeri, the wife of a merchant. Whilst the husband is away at Boston Fair the clerk visits the wife, makes known his love, and begs her to take pity on him. When his advances are rejected a friend directs him to Dame Siriz who, on promise of a great reward, undertakes to help him. She procures a bitch, doses it with pepper and mustard until its eyes run, and then goes off to visit Margeri. There, after much lament, she is persuaded to tell the reason of her unhappiness. It appears that she had had a daughter, happily wedded to a good husband, who rejected the amor-

[1] Ed. G. H. McKnight, *Middle English Humorous Tales* (London 1913).

ous advances of a clerk during her husband's absence. In revenge the clerk changed her into a bitch, the very one with Dame Siriz in fact, and even now she is weeping bitterly and lamenting her former prudishness. Margeri is struck by the similarity to her own case and begins to fear the consequences of her refusal, a fear which is skilfully increased by Dame Siriz. They agree that it would be wiser for her to accept the love of the clerk, and Dame Siriz is sent in search of him. On his arrival Margeri declares her willingness to become his lover, and Dame Siriz, after bestowing good advice upon the pair, ends the tale with a brief advertisement of her own skill as a procuress.

The plot is old and widespread ; it appears in most of the western vernaculars as well as in many of the eastern languages. It seems to have originated in the Orient, where it is found fairly frequently in early Indian literature, and the idea of transformation may be due to the oriental belief in metempsychosis. A combination of two different Indian versions made its way into the *Book of Sindibad*, and it seems to have been from this work that it spread into the West. It does not appear in any of the extant versions of the *Seven Sages of Rome*—the Western version of the *Book of Sindibad*—but there seems to be some evidence that it was contained in other versions of the romance now lost. The oldest Western version of the story is contained in the *Disciplina Clericalis* of Petrus Alphonsi, a converted Spanish Jew. From this collection the theme makes its way into the *exempla* literature and is found in such collections as those of Jacques de Vitry, Nicholas Bozon and the *Gesta Romanorum*. This was, of course, the version which would be written down, but there can be little doubt that the story, without the moralization, circulated orally as a *fabliau*.

Nothing is known of the immediate source of the English *Dame Siriz*, which differs from most other Western versions in that it appears to be based directly on an Oriental version of the story. In all probability the original English was a translation from the French, but the treatment of the English tale differs considerably from that which is found in the extant French versions. It is untouched by the conventions of courtly love and the stress is laid, not on the emotional sensations of the lover, but on the trick by which the go-between accomplishes her purpose. The English tale, in fact, is frankly written as a *fabliau*, depending for its effect on the broad humour of the plot and quite untouched by the influence of other narrative literature. The versification of the poem is irregular ; the first 132 verses are in the tail-rhyme stanza and are followed by eight octosyllabic couplets. During the remainder of the poem tail-rhyme stanza and octosyllabic couplets alternate irregularly, with apparently no change in the subject-matter to correspond with the change in verse. This variation has led to the theory that the author may have been transforming, possibly from memory, an original interlude in couplets into a poem with tail-rhyme stanza, but has either become bored or found himself unequal to the task. Other evidence is available which tends to support such a theory. The amount of dialogue in the poem is considerable and often out of all proportion to its importance, the preliminary dialogue between the clerk and the wife, for example, occupying more than a quarter of the whole poem. Throughout there are remarkably few narrative verses and often enough there is no indication whatever of transitions from one speaker to another in the dialogue. Moreover an interlude, *De Clerico et Puella*, of a slightly later date and dealing with the same subject in octosyllabic couplets is actually extant. Though there are certain verbal and phraseological resemblances between the *fabliau* and the interlude, the former can hardly be based directly on the latter since, quite apart from questions of date, there are differences in the plot. The names of the characters are different and the clerk's love is a maiden and not a wife. Presumably both *fabliau* and extant interlude are based upon an earlier interlude, the differences between the two versions being due to oral transmission.

On the whole it must be admitted that the carelessness shown in the versification is evident elsewhere in *Dame Siriz*. The poem is badly proportioned, little skill is shown in the management of the narrative framework, nor is the tail-rhyme stanza particularly suitable to the theme. But despite his manifold faults the author manages to tell a story of living people. The anonymous youth, chaste wife and old woman of the sources have become living persons, Wilekin, Margeri and Dame Siriz. A touch of local colour is added by sending the merchant to Boston Fair, and it is typical of the mediæval *fabliau* that the hero of the discreditable episode should be represented as a clerk. The situations, too, are represented clearly and sharply and the characters of the various persons gradually revealed by means of a realistic dialogue, though the author is hardly so successful with Margeri as with the other two chief characters. The great success of the author is undoubtedly in the characterization of Dame Siriz, who is easily the most important character in the poem. She has been depicted by the author with considerable skill and humour, and her portrait gradually drawn from her first appearance, when she seems almost shocked at the profane suggestions of the clerk, to the final broadly humorous words where she appears in her true light. Moreover the whole poem is pervaded by an ironic humour, common in the contemporary French *fabliaux* but remarkably rare in English before the time of Chaucer. Only at the very end does the sly irony break out into open laughter.

Another type of short narrative, developed long before the mediæval period, was the fable, a short, humorous allegorical tale in which animals act in such a way as to illustrate a simple moral tale or inculcate a wise maxim.[1] It seems to have been developed in both Greece and India ; Greek fables being introduced to Western Europe by the Latin translations of Phaedrus and the Carolingian selection which goes under the name of Romulus, Indian fables by the translations of Valerius Babrius and Avianus. This type of short narrative continued popular throughout the Middle Ages, and seems to have been especially in favour in England during the twelfth and thirteenth centuries. It was during this period that the collections of Latin fables by Walterus Anglicus, Odo of Cheriton and Alexander Nequam appeared. Isolated fables are frequent also in other works, in the *Polycraticus* of John of Salisbury, in Walter Map, in the *Contes Moralisés* of Nicholas Bozon, and frequently in the Latin sermon literature of the period. No collection in English is extant, but that such tales probably existed in the vernacular is shown by the occasional quotation of English proverbs by Odo of Cheriton and Nicholas Bozon, who, we have reason to believe, drew much of their material from vernacular sources. In addition we have evidence for the existence of at least one collection in English, which has since perished. During the reign of Henry II Marie de France, the author of the *Breton lais*, produced also a collection of fables in French verse.[2] She tells us that these were translations from the English of King Alfred who, in turn, had translated them into English from the Greek of Aesop. Although we may doubt the accuracy of Marie's ascription we have no reason for doubting her statement that she is translating from English, or that such a collection of fables did, in fact, exist in Eng-

---

[1] On the general growth and development of the fable see L. Hervieux, *Les fabulistes latins* (2nd ed. Paris 1893–8), and J. Jacobs, *The Fables of Aesop* (London 1889).

[2] Ed. K. Warnke, *Die Fabeln der Marie de France* (Halle 1898).

lish at that time. They may have been written by some obscure Alfred, who was later, naturally enough, identified with the famous king. It has in fact been suggested that they may have been the work of Alfredus Anglicus who is known as a translator from Arabic into Latin during the twelfth century, and is mentioned in that connexion by Roger Bacon. Possibly, as is the case with the *Proverbs of Alured*, the popular tradition of his wisdom may have resulted in the addition of King Alfred's name to an anonymous collection. In any case, since these English fables have long since been lost, the point is of little importance, and to us the chief importance of the fable literature is due to the part it played in the development of the beast tale.

The beast tale is probably one of the most universal and popular of all types of literature. Examples of it are found in almost every language and, however it may be elaborated or shaped by individual writers, its origins are essentially popular. Naturally enough such tales will hardly appear in the early written literature. They will be written down only for another purpose than their original one of pure entertainment, as for example, when the addition of a moral converts them into fables. The difference between the fable and the beast tale is simply the difference between the *fabliau* and the *exemplum*. Just as a moralized *fabliau* theme may be used as an *exemplum*, so the fable is simply a highly specialized form of the beast tale distinguished by its moral tendency. Like the *exemplum* the fable may be used as a sermon illustration, and Odo of Cheriton tells us that his collection was drawn from the illustrations which he had used in his sermons.[1]

Knowing nothing of the thoughts or feelings of the

---

[1] On the beast tale see W. W. Lawrence, *Medieval Story* (New York 1911), pp. 143–68 ; L. Foulet, *Le Roman de Renard* (Paris 1914) ; L. Sudre, *Les Sources du roman de Renard* (Paris 1893).

animals themselves the author of a beast tale, if he is to tell any story at all, must invest his characters with human attributes. In the Middle Ages it was inevitable that the author's contemporaries should serve as his models, and that he should attribute to his animal characters the thoughts and actions which would be natural to the people of the period. Once the world of animals has been anthropomorphically conceived, the characters, under their disguise, will act and speak like the author's contemporaries. A meeting of the animals or a fight between them will be modelled on the assemblies and fights with which the author is familiar. From this it is but a short step to satire. Mirroring, as it does, the life of the author's own times, and with the different characters drawn from his contemporaries, it was inevitable that the beast tale should become the vehicle for an attack on contemporary manners and morals. This is what seems to have happened in the Middle Ages. The simple folk-tales, long current in oral form amongst the common people and as fables in more learned or pious circles, began to assume a more elaborate shape. As they expanded they grew in dramatic interest ; they no longer deal with a single situation but run to a considerable length and tell a whole series of events. The characters assume definite personalities and are given personal instead of merely general names, Reynard and Isengrim instead of the Fox and the Wolf. Originally, of course, the characterization was based on the actual characteristics of the animals themselves, but the human elements are always tending to increase. As they become more popular the characters also become more human, and in the later versions the satire is often carried to excess.

It is from these beast tales, and especially from those dealing with Reynard the Fox, that the mediæval beast epic is developed. At the same time, though usually called an epic, it must be remembered that the title is misleading in that the mediæval stories do not form a consistent whole. They are written by different men, in different places, and at different times, and so reflect differing ideas and conditions. In character they range from the *fabliau* to satire and, as we should expect, the literary merit of the different tales varies considerably. There is a close analogy between the growth of the beast epic and that of the cycles of romance. Just as, for example, the Arthurian legend is continually growing, developing new heroes, attracting new subjects and making its way into other literatures in isolated romances and not as a consistent whole, so also the beast epic is growing up in, and being borrowed into, the different literatures. Not until towards the end of the period of development is any attempt made to give a consistent history of the adventures of Reynard. The best known, though not the only one, of these collections is the French *Roman de Renart*,[1] but it must be remembered that other adventures occur which do not form part of the *Roman* though they are none the less true branches of the beast epic.

In England no complete outline of the *Roman de Renart* seems to have been written ; if it were it has certainly not been preserved. Even more surprising is it to find that only two isolated works on the subject are extant, the *Vox and the Wolf* and Chaucer's *Nun's Priest's Tale*. There is, however, some evidence which suggests that the lack of interest in the beast tale is more apparent than real, and due rather to later loss of texts than to any specific indifference to that type of literature in this country. We know of at least one other tale of Reynard which was once extant in a written form and preserved in a manuscript in the library of Dover Priory. The manuscript itself, along with most of the others formerly contained in this collection, has long since been lost, but a catalogue of the Library, drawn

[1] Ed. H. Breuer, *Roman de Renart* (Halle 1929).

243

up in 1389, still exists. According to this catalogue one of the items contained in the manuscript numbered 170 was a ' Fabula de Wlpe medico in anglicis ' of which the opening words, ' Hit byful whylem ', confirm the statement that the work was in English.[1] It is impossible to do more than guess at the subject of the tale. It may have been that which tells how the animals all gathered to condole with the sick lion. The fox alone is absent, a fact duly emphasized by Isengrim the Wolf. However, when the fox does arrive, he avenges himself on Isengrim by advising the lion to have himself wrapped in the newly flayed skin of a wolf. Another, which forms the subject of one of Marie's fables, tells how the fox prescribed the heart of a hare for the sick lion, and there are others of the exploits of Reynard to which the title could be applied. Nothing is known of the English tale except the title and the first three words and, had not the catalogue describing the manuscript in which it is written happened to have been preserved, we should not even have known of the existence of such a story.

The importance and popularity of the fable in twelfth- and thirteenth-century England also suggests an interest in the beast tale. Occasionally the introduction of English into these fables suggests that, though written in Latin, they may have been based on popular beast tales in English. In one of his fables Odo of Cheriton tells of the wolf who wished to become a priest and, at the end of the fable, quotes the English :

> Thai thu Wolf hore hodi te preste,
> tho thu hym sette Salmes to lere,
> evere beth his geres to the groue-ward.[2]

---

[1] M. R. James, *The Ancient Libraries of Canterbury and Dover* (Cambridge 1903), p. 460.

[2] L. Hervieux, *op.cit.* II. 611 ; variants are given by T. Wright, *Latin Stories* (Percy Society viii), 55, 229, and the above by B. J. Whiting in *Speculum* ix. 219, n. 2.

The heading of the fable, *De Ysingryno*, suggests connexion with the beast epic, and the lines themselves seem to fall into passable alliterative verse of the popular type as found in the *Proverbs of Alured* or the *Bestiary*. It seems quite within the bounds of possibility that Odo is quoting from some lost beast tale in alliterative verse, upon which he has based his fable. Since the quotation varies slightly in the different manuscripts of the fables it may indicate that the English was extant only in an oral, and not in a written, form. Nicholas Bozon tells the widespread beast tale of the animal—in his case, strangely enough, a sheep—which, seeing the moon reflected in the waters of a well, falls into it in the attempt to obtain what he takes to be a cheese. Here, too, the sheep is represented as lamenting in English :

> Was it nevere my kynd
> Chese in wellez grond to fynde,[1]

a fact which indicates an English source for the fable, and suggests the former existence of an English poem on the subject. Mention of Reynard the fox, of Ysengrim the wolf and of Tibert the cat in Odo, Bozon and the Latin sermon literature also indicates a widespread acquaintance with the beast epic in England. Mediæval carvings of the cowled fox are to be found in churches and occasionally a scene from one of his exploits. It seems probable enough that the *Vox and the Wolf* is only the fortunate survivor of a once considerable literature, and that the beast tale was as popular in England as elsewhere. When we consider the character of the *Roman de Renart*, which has aptly been called the romance of disillusion, with its occasional coarse episodes and invariable satire of everyone and everything, and remember that practically all the manuscripts from this early period are monastic productions, we can only be surprised that a single tale should have survived and must

[1] L. Toulmin Smith and Paul Meyer, *op.cit.*, p. 151.

consider ourselves fortunate that monastic librarians were not always so conscientious nor copyists so fastidious as perhaps might have been expected.

The only extant representative of the beast tale in English before Chaucer, the *Vox and the Wolf*,[1] is preserved in the same manuscript as *Dame Siriz*. Like the latter it seems to have been copied out in a western dialect some time during the second half of the thirteenth century, but the rhymes indicate that it must have been originally composed in some dialect in which South-Eastern and East Midland forms were to be found side by side. The story which it tells is a well-known one, found in the *Roman de Renart* and later treated by Henryson.[2] A hungry fox makes his way into a hen-roost belonging to a monastery, succeeds in despatching three hens out of the five which he finds there and has a long argument with Chauntecler the cock explaining, unsuccessfully, that he would feel all the better for a little blood-letting. Feeling thirsty he goes to a well which has two buckets over a pulley, gets into one of them and goes down to the bottom of the well, where he loudly repents of his greed. Then Sigrim the wolf, also hungry and thirsty, appears on the scene and, hearing the lamentations of Reneward, comes to see what the matter may be. The fox, seeing a chance of escape, tries to persuade the wolf that he is dead and in Paradise. 'Are you really dead?' says the wolf. 'When did you die? It isn't three days ago that you and your wife and children all dined with me.' 'I'm dead all right,' says the fox, 'and I thank God for it. I wouldn't return for all the wealth in the world. There there is nothing but care and woe, filth and sin, but here are joys which it is impossible to

---

[1] Ed. G. H. McKnight, *Middle English Humorous Tales* (London 1913).

[2] H. Harvey Wood, *Robert Henryson, Poems and Fables* (Edinburgh 1933), pp. 24 ff.

count, and any amount of sheep and goats.'   Overcome by hunger the wolf begs to be allowed to join his friend, but is refused until he shall have confessed all his sins.   After some half-hearted objections the wolf agrees.   He repents that all his life he has received the just curses of widows and killed over a thousand sheep.   Worse still he has even repeated slanders against his friend the fox and, having caught him in bed with his wife, had even suspected that there might be some truth in those slanders.   Now he repents of all his wicked thoughts and asks the forgiveness of the fox.   This, in words of due solemnity, is granted to him and, feeling himself now purified, he asks how he shall join his friend.   He is told to get into the other bucket and on his way down meets the fox coming up.   Reneward cynically regrets that the wolf's profit is likely to be small but, happy that he is duly absolved and in a pure state of life, promises to have the soul-knell rung and masses said for him.   In the morning the wolf is discovered by the monastic gardener, pulled out and hunted away with blows.

It seems probable that the English tale depends ultimately on some French version, but the exact original is not extant. It is, however, closely related to the version which appears in the *Roman de Renart* and both probably derive ultimately from the same original.   The tale seems to have been popular in England, versions of it are found in Odo and Bozon, and a passing allusion to the ' tale of the fox and the wolf in the well-buckets ' in the *Summa Predicantium* of John Bromyard indicates that he expected it to be well known to his readers.

If the original tale were anything like the version to be found in the *Roman de Renart* it would seem that the Eng-lish adaptor, as is the case in the romances translated from the French, has not bothered to reproduce the artistic detail of his original.   In the English tale the simple way in which Reneward is trapped is not what we expect from the hero of the beast epic. A much more satisfactory explanation is given in the French. It is a clear starlight night, and as he looks over the rim of the well he sees his reflection looking up towards him. He takes it to be his wife Hermeline at the bottom of the well, and the echo of his voice he takes to be her voice replying to his questions. Consequently he gets into the bucket and goes down to see what is wrong. Moreover, in the French, Sigrim is persuaded to get into the bucket in a much more plausible way. In the English Sigrim accepts without question this strange method of a descent into heaven, but in the French Reneward explains the two buckets as being God's balance of good and evil in which souls are weighed, and Sigrim too must be weighed in the balance before he can enter into Paradise. In addition a certain inartistic cutting is evident in the hen-roost episode. From later references we gather that Reneward has succeeded in disposing of some of the hens, probably three, but no mention is made of this in the episode itself. Nor is it particularly relevant to the main plot and, occupying as it does about a quarter of the whole poem, it is certainly out of proportion. For all that we would not willingly lose the conversation between the fox and the cock; the somewhat pompous disapproval of the cock at the slaughter of the hens, and the hopeful attempt of the fox to entice him from the beam and add him to his bag. In fact the characterization throughout is excellent; the watering mouth of the wolf when Reneward describes the unlimited food in ' heaven ', the cringing manner in which he apologizes for believing his own eyes when he saw Reneward misconducting himself with his wife and the sanctimonious smugness with which the fox forgives him for his all too well-founded suspicions. The way in which Reneward insists on hearing the wolf's confession is characteristic of the hero of the beast epic. Eagerly hoping to persuade Sigrim to get into the bucket he cannot, even at the risk of arousing his suspicions, lose the chance of humiliating his old enemy. The English poem lacks some of the artistic detail which we should have expected to be present in the French original, but the dialogue is always natural and straightforward and the octosyllabic metre is in perfect keeping with the subject-matter. Popular proverbs are used ; after all it was part of the game that the beast tale should be outwardly as moral as the most pious literature. Throughout, the English poem has a buoyancy and lightness of touch which can bear comparison with Chaucer's essay in the beast tale, and leaves it as no unworthy representative of the French *Roman de Renart*.

XI

LYRIC POETRY

NO lyric poetry is extant from the Old English period, though the title is sometimes applied to a small group of poems which are better classed as elegies. It is impossible to tell whether this lack is due to the accidents of a later loss of texts or not. Practically all the extant Old English poetry seems to be the result of a purely literary development in the monastery, or in the halls of the great nobles. Since it was mainly written with the object of making Christian teaching and ideals familiar to the people, or of extolling the ancestors of noble families and the great heroes of the past, it is unlikely that the lyric ever did develop in this poetry. In this respect the extant texts probably reflect the contemporary poetry fairly accurately, especially since the structure of that poetry, the conventional vocabulary, the alliterative metre with its traditional stress on scenes of violence, would be against the development of the lyric. But, side by side with this literary and conventional poetry, there probably flourished a more popular type with a looser structure and a vocabulary nearer to the everyday speech of the common people. Such popular poetry has, however, left behind it only the barest trace of its existence. Whether it dealt with the same subjects as the aristocratic poetry, or whether a lyric strain had been developed in it, are questions which must remain unanswered.

There is no direct evidence for the existence of lyric

poetry in England before the twelfth century, and even then only odd fragments of it have been preserved before the following century. When it does appear in writing it is already in many respects highly developed and its ultimate origins are not to be traced. Some of the influences which have gone to its development are obvious enough; there can be no doubt, for example, that it has been influenced to a considerable extent by the lyric poetry in French and Latin, though whether it owes its primary inspiration to these two literatures is a different question. There is little in the Middle English lyric which we can claim as an unmistakable development from Old English, but since we know nothing of Old English lyric poetry—not even whether it existed or not—the fact that we can trace no connexion is of little value as evidence.

Whatever may have been the origin of the Middle English lyric there can be no doubt of its close connexion with the contemporary French lyric and with the Latin accentual poetry. It is much more doubtful whether the courtly lyric, which had been developed in Provençal at the beginning of the twelfth century, exerted any direct influence.[1] There was considerable commercial intercourse during the early Middle English period between England and the south of France—the Bordeaux wine-trade, in fact, flourished during the greater part of the Middle Ages. A goodly proportion of southern France formed part of the Angevin empire of Henry II, and some of it remained under the English kings until the middle of the fifteenth century. Richard I had some reputation as a troubadour and had relationships, hostile or friendly, with most of the leading troubadours of the period. There can be no doubt that southern literary influences must have been strong at the courts of the first two Plantagenets, though, since those

[1] See H. J. Chaytor, *The Troubadours and England* (Cambridge 1923).

courts were rarely in England, the fact loses much of its significance. Henry III and Edward I married wives from the south of France, and these were attended to their new homes by so many of their countrymen that their numbers and influence became one of the standing grievances of the English. For all that little evidence can be produced for any direct influence from the Provençal courtly lyric on Middle English poetry. The considerable influence which undoubtedly was exerted by the Provençal lyric seems to have reached England through northern France in which, during the second half of the twelfth century, the courtly lyric of the south had become acclimatized. Here all the well-worn mannerisms of the troubadours, the ideals of courtly love, the constant references to spring and to the nightingale, are repeated in another language and in turn make their way into English. At the same time that influence, in the latter literature, is restricted in many ways. Whilst some of the ideals of courtly love may occasionally be reflected in the Middle English lyric, the technical vocabulary of love is largely absent and there is not the same delight in sentimental analysis. The influence of the Provençal lyric is more apparent in such technical details as the construction of the stanza or the distribution of the rhymes.

Undoubtedly one of the most important of the contributions to the development of the Middle English lyric was that made by the *carole*, the vogue of which as a social pastime seems to have been especially great during the early part of the Middle Ages.[1] The later development of the term is apt to lead to some confusion, but the evidence of mediæval descriptions and illuminations allows us to say with some certainty what exactly the mediæval writers understood by the term *carole*. Essentially it seems to have been a dance accompanied by a song. A chain of dancers moved to the accompaniment of the voice under

[1] R. L. Greene, *The Early English Carols* (Oxford 1935).

the direction of a leader whose duty it was to sing the various stanzas, the whole company replying with the refrain. In most countries during the Middle Ages a type of lyric seems to have been developed which owed its form to the fact that it had been originally sung in such dances. It varied in detail in the different countries, but the essential characteristic, the sharp division into stanza and refrain, is the same in most. It was a type of poetry which persisted long after its almost complete separation from the conditions which gave it birth.

There can be no doubt that this type of song-accompanied dance was popular on the continent long before the Norman Conquest—the repeated ecclesiastical decrees against it are evidence enough of its existence. Nor does the complete silence of Old English literature on the subject necessarily indicate its absence in this country. When the *carole* does begin to appear in England the nature of the allusions suggests that it already had a long history behind it. The Latin writer of the *De Gestis Herewardi Saxonis* tells us that the country women were singing of the deeds of that hero in their dances, and the *cantilenae* dealing with themes from Old English history and legend, which were known to William of Malmesbury and Henry of Huntingdon, had perhaps developed from, or into, the same kind of thing. The earliest English lyric of which we know, the song of Canute on the monks of Ely, seems to have become the refrain of a *carole*. The twelfth-century chronicler, Thomas of Ely, tells how Canute, whilst rowing near the Isle of Ely, was attracted by the song of the monks. He thereupon composed a song in English of which Thomas has preserved the first four lines :

> Merie sungen ðe Munekes binnen Ely.
> ða Cnut ching reu ðer by.
> Roweð cnites noer the land.
> and here we þes Muneches sæng.

and other verses which follow, which even today are sung publicly in dances and remembered in the sayings of the wise.[1]

However difficult we may find it to believe in Canute as the first composer of lyric poetry in English, and whatever may have been the original form of the song—for there is no reason to suppose that it was originally composed as a *carole*—there can be no doubt that it was in use as one by the twelfth century. Whatever these examples may suggest it must be admitted that they provide no definite proof for the existence of the *carole* in Anglo-Saxon England. There can, however, be no doubt that there was certainly dancing in England very soon after the Conquest, maybe due to the introduction of the French *carole*, but possibly merely the continuation of a custom as long established in England as in France. Certainly music, the indispensable accompaniment of the *carole*, seems to have attained to a considerable pitch of development at a comparatively early date in England. This is suggested, in a tale told by Simeon of Durham, by the eagerness with which Turgot, a nobly born Northumbrian, was received by King Olaf of Norway in 1074 and appointed as teacher in psalmody to the king himself.[2] Giraldus Cambrensis tells us that music was flourishing in England in the twelfth century, especially in the north. After describing the development of part-singing in Wales, he continues :

In the Northern districts of Britain, beyond the Humber in Yorkshire, the people who dwell there make use of the same kind of symphonic harmony, but with less variety ; singing only in two parts, one murmuring in the bass, the other warbling in the treble.

Neither of the two nations has acquired this peculiarity by art, but by age-long tradition, which has rendered it natural and familiar. The practice is now so firmly-rooted in them that it

[1] D. J. Stewart, *Liber Eliensis* (London 1848), p. 202.
[2] Simeon of Durham, *Historia Regum* (Rolls Series 75), ii. 203.

is unusual to hear a simple melody, but among (the Welsh) it is rendered in manifold parts, and among the (northern English) it is rendered in two parts. Even the boys, and, what is still more surprising, the youngest children, observe the same modulations in their singing.[1]

Where music and part-singing have been so well developed as this there must already have been careful patterns of stanza and, were the *carole* absent from Old English literature, it must have found a ready welcome on its introduction from France.

None of the songs used in these twelfth-century *caroles* has survived, though there is a certain amount of evidence for their former existence. William FitzStephen, in his description of London, probably speaks of ring-dances, and a tale told by Giraldus Cambrensis suggests that some, at any rate, of the songs used in such dances may have been in English. In the *Gemma Ecclesiastica*[2] he includes a chapter against the custom of using churches and churchyards for songs and dances. As an illustration of the evils which may arise from such a practice he tells of a wake which was kept up all the night long in a churchyard in the diocese of Worcester, the dancers continually repeating the words of the refrain as they danced. The result was that the priest, who had had it ringing in his ears all night, could not get it out of his mind when he came to celebrate Mass the next morning. Consequently, instead of beginning with *Dominus vobiscum*, he repeated the refrain of the *carole*, *Swete lamman dhin are*, ' Sweetheart, have mercy ', a happening which caused a great scandal in the district and led the then Bishop of Worcester to pronounce an anathema upon any person who should in future sing that song anywhere within the diocese. The English words quoted by

---

[1] Giraldus Cambrensis, *Descriptio Kambriae* (Rolls Series 21), vi. 189.
[2] Rolls Series 21, ii, 120.

Giraldus are actually found in an extant English lyric, but since it was not written down until about a century later there is not much probability that it is anything like the *carole* which led to the scandal. Other evidence provided by the thunderings of the clergy against such vain and worldly songs is even more significant. Incidentally it is rather ironical that, so often, only the fragments of these songs quoted by them in sermon or moral illustrations have survived. In an early thirteenth-century sermon we hear how

when wanton women and foolish men in this country go into the ring, amongst many other songs worth little, which they sing, so they say thus :

> Atte wrastlinge mi lemman i ches
> And atte ston-kastinge i him forles.[1]

But the ' many other songs ' known to the priest have all been lost and only these two lines have survived from what must have been a flourishing literature. These allusions, of course, refer to the dances of the country people, and not to the courtly *carole* as practised in the halls of the nobles. These latter were presumably imported directly from France, though they probably had little to distinguish them, beyond a greater dignity and restraint, from the ring-dances of the common people from which they were ultimately derived.

These seem to be the main influences which can be discerned in the early Middle English lyric poetry, and there can be no doubt that French influence is pre-eminent. Though the *carole* may possibly have been known in this country before the Conquest much of its later popularity was probably due to the vogue of similar French poetry. It was mainly due to the popularity of the *carole* and of

[1] Ed. M. Förster, ' Kleinere mittelenglische Texte ' (*Anglia* xlii. 152).

similar amusements that the poetical art of France came to be dominant over the greater part of Northern Europe, and that the French type of lyric was transported into so many different languages. The courtly lyric from the south makes its way into Northern France and from there into England where, in turn, it exerts its influence on the native poetry. Almost as important as the influence of the French lyric is that of the accentual Latin verse which, from its original use in the songs of the peasants and the soldiers of Rome, had been adopted by the Church and developed into the mediæval hymn. Here the influences and interactions are complex and felt both indirectly, through the French, and directly. The hymns influence the religious and secular lyrics both directly and through the goliardic poems. In turn the vernacular love lyrics influence the goliardic poetry and through it the secular and religious Latin poetry.

Any discussion of the lyric poetry of the Early Middle English period is rendered difficult by the uncertainty as to what exactly we should include. The beginning presents no difficulty, but towards the end it is usually impossible to say definitely of the individual poems whether we should date them as late thirteenth or early fourteenth century, since palæographical evidence is usually all that is available. For example, one of the most important collections of Middle English lyric poetry, MS. Harley 2253, was written somewhere about 1320 so that some of the lyrics contained in it should probably come within our period, others just after it, and any distinction of date must be largely tentative. The most satisfactory course seems to be to deal only with those lyrics which have been edited by Professor Carleton Brown in his *English Lyrics of the XIIIth Century*,[1] even though other scholars have attributed some of them to the fourteenth century.

There is probably no need to labour the undoubted fact

[1] Oxford 1932.

that only a small proportion of the lyric poetry which was actually composed during this period has been preserved. This is especially true of the secular poetry, as indeed, considering the conditions of survival, we should expect to be the case. Copies of some of the religious lyrics occasionally exist in more than one manuscript, but the secular lyrics are invariably extant only in a single version indicating that the field of selection must have been wide. Practically no lyric poetry has survived from the twelfth century though, from occasional allusions in other types of literature, it is clear that much must have existed. The impression that the extant remains are only the survivors of a much more extensive literature is heightened when we consider the different places in which these lyrics have been preserved. Much of our knowledge of Middle English lyric poetry is due to the chance survival of two or three manuscript collections, but, apart from these, odd snatches of lyric may appear anywhere. We find them in sermons, in Latin or English books of devotion, in moral tales or chronicles, and scribbled on the margins or fly-leaves of manuscripts dealing with very different subjects. They appear in the most unsuitable places, on the back of a papal bull or scratched on the wall of a ruined church. In odd places here and there we can catch glimpses of a rich lyric literature, most of which has since perished.

If we could trust the chronicler of Ely, Middle English lyric poetry could claim a royal origin, and the name of Canute would head the list of English lyricists. As it is we must make do with a saint and that distinction must go to Godric, the hermit of Finchal. Thanks to his biographers we know a good deal about him personally. In his youth he led an adventurous life as a sailor and a merchant and, on his conversion, made pilgrimages to many of the famous shrines including Jerusalem, finally settling down as a hermit at Finchal where he died *c.* 1170. Three short lyrics composed by him have been preserved, two four-line stanzas in honour of the Virgin, a couplet spoken to him in a vision by his dead sister, and a four-line stanza in honour of his patron, St Nicholas.[1] These, alone of his works, have been preserved in the Latin biographies and chronicles of the period, but are obviously far too brief to allow us to say anything of his lyrical gifts, on which question we must accept the verdict of his contemporaries. It is not, however, until the second half of the thirteenth century that English lyrics become at all frequent, or rather that they at last have a chance of being written down and so preserved. For, despite the lack of texts, there can be no doubt of the existence of lyric poetry in the twelfth century. As an addition to the examples quoted above we may note that, according to his biographer, Becket, when on an embassy to the French king, was preceded into the French towns and villages by a company of youths, singing in their own language according to the custom of their country.[2] Naturally enough it is usually the religious lyrics which have been preserved from this early period, since they were the lyrics which would most readily find favour in the monasteries and so stood the best chance of being written down. Out of the ninety-odd lyrics printed by Carleton Brown only about a dozen can be classed as secular. The earliest of these is the well-known lyric

> Sumer is icumen in,
> Lhude sing cuccu !
> Groweþ sed and bloweþ med
> and springþ þe wde nu.
> Sing cuccu !

This was written by some monk belonging to the Abbey of Reading in his commonplace book some time between

---

[1] Ed. with full references by J. Hall, *Selections from Early Middle English* (Oxford 1920), I. 5 ; II. 241–5.

[2] William FitzStephen, *Life of Becket* (Rolls Series 67), III. 31.

the years 1230 and 1240. The elaborateness of the music, which accompanies the words, has persuaded some critics that it is a literary rather than a popular composition. But we know from Giraldus that even popular music had attained to a surprisingly high pitch of development by this time, and the freshness and simplicity of the lyric certainly suggest the folk-song rather than the consciously literary work. Love and the coming of spring, the song of the nightingale and the pangs of the forlorn lover are as constant themes in the English as in the contemporary French lyric. They range, too, from the folk-song to the purely literary, almost courtly, composition, and the patterns of the stanza metre vary as much as the subject. On a purely spring theme is the following of which the opening is reminiscent of that which we find in the debate between the *Thrush and the Nightingale* :

> Lenten ys come wiþ loue to toune,
> wiþ blosmen & wiþ briddes roune,
>   þat al þis blisse bryngeþ ;
> dayes-eȝes in þis dales,
> notes suete of nyhtegales,
>   vch foul song singeþ.
> þe þrestelcoc him þreteþ oo ;
> away is huere wynter woo,
>   when woderoue springeþ.
> þis foules singeþ ferly fele,
> ant wlyteþ on huere wynter wele,
>   þat al þe wode ryngeþ.

The more usual method of treatment, however, is to begin with a description of the coming of spring, pass on to the charms of the loved one and end with the pangs of unrequited love. Alternatively the grief of the lover may follow immediately on the opening description of spring as in the following :

> When þe nyhtegale singes þe wodes waxen grene,
> Lef & gras & blosme springes in aueryl, y wene,
> ant loue is to myn herte gon wiþ one spere so kene,
> nyht & day my blod hit drynkes, myn herte deþ me tene.

In any case the spring opening is as conventional in the English lyrics as it is in the French. Sometimes a refrain is used, but it is improbable that such a poem as 'Alisoun' was ever danced in a *carole*; it strikes one rather as being a literary development of the popular *carole* :

> Bytuene mersh & aueril
> when spray biginneþ to springe,
> þe lutel foul haþ hire wyl
> on hyre lud to synge.
> ich libbe in louelonginge
> for semlokest of alle þynge ;
> He may me blisse bringe,
> icham in hire baundoun.
>> An hendy hap ichabbe yhent
>> ichot from heuene it is me sent—
>> from alle wymmen mi loue is lent,
>> & lyht on Alysoun.

The opening lines of another lyric have all the freshness of a folk-song :

> Blow, northerne wynd,
> sent þou me my suetyng !
> blow, norþerne wynd,
> blou ! blou ! blou !

But this is followed by the conventional catalogue of the beauties of the loved one and a description of the despair of the lover, characteristic rather of the courtly than of the popular lyric :

> for hire loue y carke ant care,
> for hire loue y droupne ant dare,
> for hire loue my blisse is bare,
>> ant al ich waxe won ;
> for hire loue in slep y slake,
> for hire loue al nyht ich wake,
> for hire loue mournyng y make
>> More þen eny mon.

Pleasant and successful though the lyric undoubtedly is, it is thoroughly artificial and has little affinity with the opening lines. In all probability the refrain of a popular *carole* has been taken as the theme of a courtly lyric, a practice found elsewhere during the Middle English period. These examples all come from the Harley MS. 2253 in which is to be found most of the best of the lyric poetry which has been preserved. It is written throughout in a single hand and probably comes from the priory of Leominster, so that the lyrics included in it have been copied in a Western dialect. It is unlikely, however, that, as is the case with the alliterative poetry, the West was also the home of the lyric in the Middle English period. It is certain enough that the work of many different authors is represented in the collection in the Harley manuscript, and an examination of the rhymes indicates that many different dialects have been drawn upon. The fact that so many of the extant lyrics are written in a Western dialect is probably due merely to the chances of survival.

The influence of the courtly lyric, though easily perceptible, is much less well defined than it becomes in the following century. The lyrics are still essentially English and not French in spirit as in technique. Most of the special types, as elaborated by the troubadours, are absent, though occasional examples are to be found. In a Bodleian manuscript is to be found a *reversaris*, a poem of contradictions or antitheses in which the Provençal poets had elaborated a convenient device for describing a lover's distractions :

> Loue is sofft, loue is swet, loue is goed sware.
> Loue is muche tene, loue is muchel kare.
> Loue is blissene mest, loue is bot ȝare.
> Loue is wondred and wo, wiþ for to fare.

But the very elaborateness of this lyric and its obvious debt to foreign influences make us suspect that it is a comparatively late production. An early lyric with the refrain :

> Nou sprinkes þe sprai,
> al for loue icche am so seeke
> that slepen i ne mai.

has certain affinities with the Provençal *pastorela* and there is extant a similar French lyric which affords a close parallel. For all that the English lyric reads much more like a popular *carole* than a literary composition based on a French original. The fact that a comparatively large number of the thirteenth- as compared with the fourteenth-century lyrics, are provided with music indicates that they were composed to be sung rather than to be read. In England the fourteenth century is the real age of the literary lyric. In the earlier period the English, as compared with the contemporary French lyrics, are much more direct in expression and genuine in sentiment. Many of the stanza forms and some types of conventional phraseology have been borrowed, but a new and more vigorous life has been breathed into them.

Comedy is slenderly, though successfully, represented by a single poem on ‘ The Man in the Moon ’. In it the poet pityingly apostrophizes the supposed inhabitant.

You don’t seem to be very happy. I wonder how you got there. I suppose some hayward has caught you cutting sticks and taken a surety from you. Never mind, bring your bundle home. We’ll invite the hayward to our house, make him comfortable and give him plenty to drink. Then, when he’s as drunk as a drowned mouse, we’ll go and redeem your pledge from the baliff.

This is the only surviving example of the humorous lyric, but the lightness of touch which we find in it, and its general success, indicate that the author was no novice to this type of poetry.

The religious lyrics generally owe much, as we should expect, to Latin hymns and to Latin religious poetry.

Occasionally they are simply translations from the Latin, as in the English version of the *Stabat iuxta Christi crucem*. Frequently they borrow the metres and the phraseology of their exemplars. Sometimes they are written in a mixture of two or three languages, but it is rare that such macaronic poetry is more than a literary curiosity. Only occasionally do the different languages blend, as in the following:

> Of on þat is so fayr and briȝt
>   velud maris stella,
> Briȝter þan þe day-is liȝt,
>   parens & puella,
> Ic crie to þe, þou se to me,
> Leuedy, preye þi sone for me
>   tam pia,
> þat ic mote come to þe,
>   maria. . . .

> Leuedi, flour of alle þing,
>   rosa sine spina,
> þu bere ihesu, heuene-king,
>   gratia diuina.
> Of alle þu berst þe pris,
> Leuedi, quene of parays
>   electa,
> Mayde milde Moder es
>   effecta.

The influence of other religious poetry is occasionally obvious in the religious lyrics. In one of them the ideas and sentiments of the *Poema Morale* reappear so unmistakably that we can hardly doubt that the author knew, and wrote under the influence of, that poem. Another has a close affinity with the Worcester *Debate of the Body and the Soul*. Much of it tells of regret for a misspent life, of a contempt for worldly things, and of the hopes of the Christian religion. It is the melancholy of the Old English elegies, with the final appeal to Christ or the Virgin often very much of an afterthought. Through a whole class of such poetry runs the old idea of the transitoriness of worldly things, though the moral is not now that fame and a good name are alone worth striving for, but rather the contemplation of a future life. It is characteristic that Friar Thomas of Hales, on being asked to write a love poem for a certain maiden, should take the opportunity of emphasizing the vanity of the world and dwelling on the everlasting love of Christ. Nothing is known of the author except that he seems to have been a Franciscan and that the poem, since it has mention of 'Henry vre kyng' must have been written before 1272. Presumably he was a native either of the town of Hales in Gloucestershire or of Halesowen in Worcestershire. Seldom have the old ideas been better expressed than in some of the stanzas of his 'Loue Ron':

> Hwer is paris & heleyne
>> þat weren so bryht & feyre on bleo,
> Amadas & dideyne,
>> tristram, yseude and alle þeo,
> Ector, wiþ his scharpe meyne,
>> & cesar, riche of wordes feo,
> Heo beoþ i-glyden vt of þe reyne
>> so þe schef is of þe cleo.

> Hit is of heom also hit nere
>> of heom me haueþ wunder itold.
> Nere hit reuþe for to heren
>> hw hi were wiþ pyne aquold,
> & hwat hi þoleden a-lyue here?
>> al is heore hot iturnd to cold
> þus is þes world of false fere—
>> fol he is þe on hire is bold.

> þeyh he were so riche mon
>> as henry vre kyng,
> And al so veyr as absalon
>> þat neuede on eorþe non euenyng,
> Al were sone his prute a-gon,
>> hit nere on ende wrþ on heryng.
> Mayde, if þu wilnest after leofmon
>> ich teche þe enne treowe king.

It is not surprising that the poem was one of the few thirteenth-century lyrics still remembered and imitated at the
end of the fourteenth century. But the question :

> Uuere beþ þey biforen vs weren,
> Houndes ladden and hauekes beren
> And hadden feld and wode ?
> þe riche leuedies in hoere bour,
> þat wereden gold in hoere tressour
> Wiþ hoere briʒtte rode.

and the answer :

> Al þat ioye is went away,
> þat wele is comen te weylaway,
> To manie harde stoundes.

provided a theme for religious poets throughout the Middle
Ages and was not unknown to the Elizabethans. Another
favourite theme was the Crucifixion; in fact one of the
earliest and most perfect of the religious lyrics is a simple
quatrain to which its editor has given the title ' Sunset on
Calvary ' :

> Nou goth sonne vnder wod—
> me reweth, marie, þi faire rode.
> Nou goþ sonne vnder tre—
> me reweþ, marie, þi sone and þe.

Other poems on the same subject, ' Stond wel, moder,
ounder rode ', and ' Hi sike, al wan hi singe ', quite apart
from the usual technical excellence of the metre, have an
invariable dignity and pathos which it would be difficult to
surpass.

The contemporary secular lyric seems to have exerted a
considerable influence on the religious poetry. The conventions of the former are often carried over into the latter.
We find again the spring morning, the song of the nightingale, hear the youth telling of the beauty of his mistress

and lamenting his own unworthiness, or the maiden longing for her lover. But the subjects here are Christ and the Virgin Mary, though there is little in the phraseology to indicate this, for the phraseology and the conventions of the secular love lyrics have been deliberately borrowed. In part this was no doubt due to the activity of the *scholares vagantes*, who borrowed the ideas and phraseology of the secular and amorous lyrics for the service of the Church as readily as they provided satirical and irreverent words for the music of the church offices. In part, too, it was due to a deliberate attempt of the church to turn the vain and foolish songs of the people to the service of God ; a tendency evident in Old English times and continued long afterwards. It had led to the Christianization of the old pagan epics and, conversely, to the arming of the saints. We hear how Aldhelm, in an attempt to instil Christian teaching into his barbarous flock, had disguised himself as a minstrel and gradually introduced moral and salutary words into the epic lays with which he attracted the attention of his audience. According to William of Malmesbury some of these songs were still remembered in the twelfth century.[1] In the same way Thomas of Bayeux, who died Archbishop of York in 1100 : ' nec cantu nec voce minor, multa ecclesiastica composuit carmina. Si quis in auditu ejus arte joculatoria aliquid vocale sonaret, statim illud in divinas laudes effigiare(t).' [2] Similarly a Latin religious poem has been added below the Middle English Cuckoo Song as a substitute for the more worldly sentiments there expressed. Other examples of religious lyrics written side by side and in imitation of secular lyrics are not wanting. The best illustration of this tendency comes from an Irish manuscript of the fourteenth century. In it are to be found some sixty

[1] William of Malmesbury, *Gesta Pontificum* (Rolls Series 52), 336.
[2] *op.cit.* p. 258.

Latin hymns, which we are told were expressly written to take the place of the vain and worldly songs of the people. They were intended to be sung to the same tunes as those used with the secular songs, and the opening words of a dozen of them have been scribbled down as a guide to the special tunes. Apart from this the vernacular lyrics have all been lost, though we would willingly have given all the sixty Latin substitutes for the complete texts of the dozen vernacular fragments which remain.

Very little of the poetry dealing with contemporary political events has survived. It is reasonable enough to suppose that a good deal of such verse must have been composed, and an appreciable amount in Latin and French is still extant, but works in these languages had a much better chance of a written existence, and so of later preservation, than similar poems in English. Occasional allusions to it still remain; one of the charges brought against William of Longchamp, Bishop of Ely, and Chancellor under Richard I, was that ' hic ad augmentum et famam sui nominis, emendicata carmina et rhythmos adulatorios comparabat, et de regno Francorum cantores et joculatores muneribus allexerat, ut de illo canerent in plateis : et jam dicebatur ubique, quod non erat talis in orbe '.[1] If such songs were to be intelligible to the common people they must have been in English, though, considering Longchamp's fall and exile soon afterwards, it is not surprising that none of them has been preserved. A single stanza of a poem dealing with one of the contemporary political questions, and of a type such as must have been common during the Middle English period, has been preserved by Walter of Hemingburgh. He tells how Edward I, whilst holding a parliament on one occasion, asked the sons of the magnates what they talked about whilst their elders were in council. After making sure that the king would

[1] Roger of Hoveden, *Chronica* (Rolls Series 51), III. 143.

not be offended at his frankness, one of them replied by quoting the following lines, evidently a stanza from some popular song of the period:

> Le roy cuvayte nos deneres
> E la Rayne nos beau maners
> E le Quo voranto
> Sale mak wus al to do.[1]

The dislike which the nobles felt for the statute *Quo Warranto* is expressed in other anecdotes from contemporary sources, but these four lines are all that remain of what must have been a considerable, if in the main ephemeral, literature in the vernacular on this and on similar subjects. Soldiers' songs are a similar class of poetry which has left very little trace behind it. Such verse is essentially oral and popular and has little chance of a written existence, so that it is only by accident that occasional fragments of it have survived. The earliest example of which we have any knowledge is part of a song said to have been sung by the followers of Geoffrey de Mandeville, Earl of Essex, during the ravaging of the Fen district. In one of the manuscripts of the *Historia Anglorum* of Matthew Paris there is preserved the tradition that the earl and his followers sang mockingly of their wild deeds:

Facti enim amentes cantitabat unusquisque Anglice,

> I ne mai a liue
> For Benoit ne for Iue.[2]

The references are apparently to the destruction of the town of St Ives, and to the seizure and fortification of the Benedictine monastery of Ramsey. The same chronicler gives two lines of a song said to have been sung, apparently as a *carole*, by the gallants who had joined the Flemish

---

[1] Walter of Hemingburgh, *Chronicon* (London 1848), II, 7.
[2] J. H. Round, *Geoffrey de Mandeville* (London 1892), p. 213.

mercenaries of the Earl of Leicester, when they ravaged the countryside in 1173 :

> Qui etiam, quando ad aliquam planitiem gratia pausandi diver-
> terant, choreas ducentes patria lingua saltitando cantabant,
>
> > Hoppe, hoppe, Wilekin, hoppe, Wilekin,
> > Engelond is min ant tin.[1]

But by far the greater number of such remains as have survived are those which deal with the wars against Scotland. Parts of songs composed by both Scots and English against each other have been preserved, mainly in the later chronicles. A number of these, usually translated into French, are to be found in the Anglo-French verse chronicle of Peter of Langtoft, and occasionally, when he seems to have tired of the work of translation, the Middle English original still remains. When Robert Mannyng translated Peter of Langtoft's chronicle into English verse, he gave an English translation of these songs, and the fact that he occasionally adds further stanzas not included in his original indicates that the songs must have been known to him and that he is not merely giving a translation of the French of Peter of Langtoft. Both these chronicles were written at the beginning of the fourteenth century ; similar songs are quoted in the fifteenth century in the *Brut* and in Fabyan's *Chronicle*, and it is reasonable to suppose that those dealing with the Scottish wars of Edward I must have been current in the thirteenth century. Amongst them are fragments of songs supposed to have been sung by the English at the siege of Dunbar, and on the execution of Wallace, and by the Scots after the relief of Berwick :

> What wenys kynge Edwarde with his lange shankys
> To have wonne Berwyck all ure unthankys.[2]

---

[1] Matthew Paris, *Historia Anglorum* (Rolls Series 44), I. 381.
[2] *Fabyan's Chronicle*, ed. Ellis, p. 398.

Farther north we find similar fragments in Wyntoun, one of the earliest of the Scottish vernacular chroniclers, which presumably refer to our period. He gives us part of a popular lament for the death of Alexander III:

> Qwhen Alexander our kynge was dede,
>   þat Scotlande lede in lauche and le,
> Away was sons of alle and brede,
>   Off wyne and wax, of gamyn and gle.[1]

and also four lines of a song made by the English against Black Agnes of Dunbar.[2]

These are all only the remains of what must have been a once extensive literature, most of which has since perished. Today, of this political poetry, only two complete poems remain from a period earlier than the fourteenth century, one on the *Battle of Lewes* and a second on *The Follies of Fashion*. The latter is a denunciation of the extravagances of women's dress, written in an elaborate stanza form further complicated by the addition of alliteration, and more interesting from the social than from the literary viewpoint. The *Song of Lewes*, which must have been composed some time after the date of that battle in 1264 and before the defeat and death of Simon de Montfort at Evesham in the following year, is much more interesting. It was evidently composed by some partisan of Montfort at a time when their opponents were no longer feared, but could be treated with good-humoured contempt. A roar of laughter pursues them after their defeat, with a special contempt for Richard, Earl of Gloucester, the elected king of the Romans, who is looked upon as the evil counsellor of the young Prince Edward. His ignominious flight from the battle, his refuge in a windmill and subsequent capture by the Barons are

---

[1] F. J. Amours, *Wyntoun's Original Chronicle* (Scottish Text Society 1903–14), vii. 3620 ff.

[2] *op.cit.* viii. 4993 ff.

related with much glee and considerable accuracy, every stanza ending with the complacent couplet:

> Richard, þah þou be euer trichard,
> Trichen shalt þou neuer more.

The much-debated question of the origin of the ballad need not detain us here since the ballad proper does not appear before the fifteenth century; there is evidence for the existence of a considerable ballad literature during the fourteenth century, but none of it has been preserved. A poem on Judas, telling how he was led to betray Christ because of the theft by his sister of thirty pieces of silver which had been entrusted to him, has been preserved from the thirteenth century. It is usually called the earliest of the ballads, but has little, beyond a narrative content, in common with the later ballads. Yet there is some evidence which suggests that, even in the thirteenth century, the genuine ballad may already have been flourishing. Records exist of a law-suit which took place in the fourteenth century between Lord Neville of Raby and the Prior of Durham. Apparently, as a rent for his lands at Raby, Lord Neville was supposed to bring a stag to the monastery on September 4th, and a dispute seems to have grown up concerning the manner in which this offering was to be made. The Prior said that Lord Neville should come with a few servants, hand over the stag and go away again. Lord Neville, on the other hand, claimed that the stag should be brought into the cathedral to the sound of the horns of his followers; afterwards he and his servants should take possession of the prior's house and feast there for the following day and night. In 1290 the offering led to a regular battle between Lord Neville's men and the monks, in which the latter, armed with the great candlesticks used in the service, succeeded in driving away the former and retaining possession of the stag. After this, during the lifetime of that

Lord Neville, the custom was abandoned, and the proposal
of his son to revive it led to a law-suit in 1331. In the
course of the case the Prior, who incidentally won it, brought
forward an interesting piece of evidence to show that the
offering had once been made on Holy Rood Day. This
was the fragment of a lament which, he said, had been
sung after the death of Lord Neville's great-grandfather,
Robert de Neville, *c.* 1280:

> Wel, qwa sal thir hornes blau
> Haly Rod thi day?
> Nou is he dede and lies law
> Was wont to blaw thaim ay.[1]

In this odd stanza we can perceive the authentic note of the
ballad, appearing long before the earliest written examples,
and suggesting the existence of a thirteenth-century ballad
literature which is completely lost, or preserved only in
much later copies.

Altogether there are probably less than a hundred vernacular lyrics of all kinds, which can be confidently assigned
to a date before 1300. Casual allusions bear witness to the
fact that these are but a small proportion of what was
actually composed. In this lyric poetry the influence of
contemporary French literature is obvious and important;
from Old English the only borrowings which we can distinguish are a sense of the transitoriness of worldly things
and a fondness for alliteration. Occasionally we find
alliteration and rhyme used side by side in stanzas whose
complexity reminds us of the similar mixture in the *Pearl*.
A certain platitudinous dullness and insipidity is occasionally to be found in some of the religious lyrics, but on the
whole the vernacular lyric poetry disappoints us less frequently than any other type of mediæval literature, and a
surprisingly high proportion of it, especially of the secular
love lyrics, is really great poetry. Of all Middle English

[1] Raine, *Hist. Dun. Scrip. Tres.* (Surtees Society ix), p. 112.

273

literature it is this which strikes the most modern note and is the easiest for a modern reader to appreciate. Moreover, the mere technical achievement of these early poets is amazing. Most of the simple stanza forms, and many of the more complex ones, are handled with considerable skill and mastery, and the maturity of this technique is one of the most surprising things about Middle English literature.[1]

[1] For fuller references to some of the lost lyrical poetry, see R. M. Wilson, ' More Lost Literature ' [Leeds Studies in English v. 1 ff.]

XII

THE BEGINNINGS OF THE DRAMA

THE religious drama[1] which developed during the mediæval period seems to owe little or nothing to the classical drama of Rome or of Greece; either to the literary drama or to that more popular type to be found in the Roman mime. The former practically disappears with the fall of Rome not to appear again until the Renaissance. Though many of the texts survived it is doubtful whether the Middle Ages ever realized that the plays had been written to be acted and not merely to be read. Some of the plays of Terence remained in favour as a school book, and in the tenth century they served as a model for Hrotsvitha, a Benedictine nun of Gandersheim, who produced half a dozen plays in Latin prose which were designed to inculcate the virtues of chastity and to glorify the sufferings of the martyrs. But this remained an isolated experiment, and it is doubtful whether the plays of Hrotsvitha were ever meant to be acted; certainly some of the scenes in them would seem to be remarkably unsuited to presentation in the cloister, when all allowance has been made for the freer manners of a more primitive time. The interpretation which the Middle Ages attached to the terms *tragoedia* and *comoedia* shows how completely all knowledge

---

[1] On the origins of mediæval drama see especially Karl Young, *The Drama of the Medieval Church* (Oxford 1933), and E. K. Chambers, *The Mediæval Stage* (Oxford 1903).

of the Roman literary drama had vanished. Both were regarded simply as forms of narrative ; tragedy, dealing with people of high degree, begins happily but ends in misfortune, whilst comedy dealing with ordinary people commences with complication and misfortune, but ends happily. The other Roman dramatic tradition, the mime, fell under the ban of the Church. Its members, the acrobats, conjurers and tumblers, formed part of the mediæval crowd of wandering entertainers and probably handed on little more of the dramatic tradition beyond the practice of some sort of impersonation and imitation. A different type of drama, totally unconnected with any of the traditions of classical drama, was that which developed out of the ceremonies of the common people of mediæval Europe, who made dramatic performances—often going back to a remote and pagan past and lasting until almost modern times in the various Mummers' plays.

These various traditions, however, seem to have exerted little if any influence on the beginnings of mediæval drama. They were usually denounced by the Church, which originated and fostered a drama of its own. It did not, perhaps, entirely avoid reflecting the influence of its rivals, but in general it advanced on its own path. There was much in the liturgy of the Church which offered an obvious approach to drama, but these dramatic phenomena in the liturgy cannot be regarded as the effectual origins of the genuine mediæval drama. The Mass, after all, despite its dramatic possibilities, was essentially a re-creation and not a dramatization, and the *Horae*, being designed as devotional exercises, exhibit no intention of representing actual events and never gave promise of any development into drama. Some of the special ceremonies of Holy Week, the Palm Sunday Procession and the Adoration of the Cross, could have been transformed into plays easily enough, and similarly the ceremonies at the sepulchre, the *Depositio* and the *Elevatio*, promised more in a dramatic way than they ever succeeded in accomplishing. The arrangements for stage-setting were ample enough, but the utterances remain the familiar liturgical forms of the season accompanied by no more dialogue than is usual in normal daily worship, and spoken with no effort of impersonation. For this after all is the essential test of drama, not dialogue nor gesture but impersonation. The actor must pretend to be the person whose words he is speaking and whose actions he is imitating, and show, either by his costume or by other means, his intention of resembling that person.

The plays of the Church did not, then, arise directly or primarily from the elaboration of elements present in the traditional forms of worship, but out of deliberate literary additions to the liturgical text. Such additions can be traced back to the wordless sequences or choral elaborations of the final vowel of the Alleluia of the Mass. These long musical phrases came to be supplied with words appropriate to the particular feasts. Notker, a monk of St Gall, tells us how he heard of this innovation somewhere about 875 and became a composer, the words helping him and the other singers to memorize the music. The earliest additions were in prose with a separate syllable to each note of music, but elaboration soon set in. The variety of such embellishments, usually called *tropes*, is large and they sometimes became so lengthy as to dwarf the authorized text to which they were attached. Often the attachment is completely severed and the elaborations stand forward as self-contained and apparently independent compositions, the longest group of this kind being known as *sequences* or *proses*. The development seems to have started comparatively early, but it was not until the Carolingian period that the *trope* became at all popular or widely spread. During the literary revival which took place at that time it began to take an increasingly important place in public worship in certain communities in France and in the neighbouring countries. Many of the *tropes* included pieces of dialogue and show distinct signs of dramatic promise; they only needed impersonation to become diminutive plays. But, so far as we know, only one of these *tropes*, originally no more impressive or dramatic than many of the others, achieved this further advance. This was the prose *trope* which had become attached to the Introit of the Mass of Easter, of which the simplest (though not the earliest) version extant is to be found in a tenth-century manuscript from the monastery of St Gall, and which has tentatively been ascribed to the monk Tutilo who died in the year 912:

INTERROGATIO : Quem quaeritis in sepulchro, Christicolae ?
RESPONSIO : Iesum Nazarenum crucifixum, o coelicolae.
Non est hic, surrexit sicut predixerat ; ite nuntiate quia surrexit de sepulchro.

This is not in itself a play, of course, and it only very gradually became one. From Monte Cassino during the eleventh century come certain directions for the action. A priest, robed in white, stands before the altar and addresses the *Quem quaeritis* to the choir. Two priests in the choir then give the answer. The priest at the altar delivers the *Non est hic*, whereupon the other two turn to the choir and say *Alleluia, resurrexit Dominus*. Here the altar already has something of the character of a dramatic setting, and in other versions dialogue seems to have been carried on across it. Nevertheless, so long as the *trope* remained attached to the Mass, the dramatic development was slight and there seems to be no instance of impersonation.

But gradually the *trope* became detached from the Mass and was given a place in the canonical office between the last Responsory of Matins and the Te Deum. In this new position it achieved a generous amount of literary freedom and its dramatic possibilities began to be realized. It was brought into association with two other observances of a dramatic character, the *Depositio* and the *Elevatio*, and, as the *Visitatio Sepulchri*, it develops into the authentic Easter Play with impersonation added to the dialogue. The simple form of the play demands two priests in white *cappae*, who go behind the altar and act as Angels. Two deacons in dalmatics, carrying incense in thuribles and with their heads veiled, signify the two Marys visiting the tomb with spices. The dialogue having been spoken, the two Marys uncover the altar cloths and, turning to the monks, sing the Antiphon. But already by the tenth century a more elaborate production is to be found at Winchester in the *Regularis Concordia* of St Æthelwold. There the Marys are three in number and the sepulchre is hidden by a curtain on a ring.

In this way the Easter play gradually developed, but it must be emphasized that the forward movement was not regular over the whole field. The simple form may appear later than the more elaborate ones, and the logical order may be very different from the historical. The Church, after all, was not interested in drama for its own sake, but was simply seeking for vivid methods of expressing its great mysteries and of enforcing their meaning to the common people. The Angels are apparently first provided with wings in a version from Narbonne, and the Roman soldiers appear, in dumb show only, at the Sainte Chapelle in Paris. The Unguentarius, the spice-seller from whom the Marys purchase their offerings, appears in a speaking part at Prague; and, in a comparatively late version from Coutances, the Roman soldiers appear to have been allowed to extemporize. The simple form, which included only the Angels and the Holy Women, was in use throughout the whole period from the second half of the tenth to the fifteenth or even the sixteenth century, but in other versions the scope of the play is increased by the inclusion of the visit of Peter and John to the tomb. A third form, which seems to have been unknown before the late twelfth century, included also the risen Christ and the scene with Mary Magdalene.

Other plays, which dealt with the events before and after Easter, were also gradually developed. Four especially are of considerable elaboration and seem in certain characteristics to look forward to the later religious drama of the laity. These are the *Peregrinus*, dealing with the journey to Emmaus and later enlarged to include the doubting of Thomas and even the scene with Mary Magdalene at the tomb, the *Ascension*, *Pentecost* and the *Passion Play*, of which latter there seems to have been no dramatization before the beginning of the thirteenth century. The Christmas observances were almost as popular as those at Easter and there too the drama was gradually developed, probably in imitation of the Easter plays and from a *trope* which had been influenced by the Easter *Quem Quaeritis*. The *Officium Pastorum* grew out of the Christmas *trope*, *Quem quaeritis in praesepe*, which, like the Easter *trope*, had eventually been transferred from Mass to Matins. In course of time the episode of the Magi combined with the play of the Shepherds to form the *Officium Stellae*. This was of considerable interest in that it introduced, probably during the eleventh century, the figure of Herod whose furies became so popular a feature of the later vernacular mediæval drama. Old Testament scenes make their entrance with the *Ordo Prophetarum*, which was ultimately derived from a sermon that the Middle Ages ascribed to St Augustine. In this play each prophet in turn testifies to the truth of the Christian faith, and it is possible to see in this the germ of the cycle of religious plays which later became popular in secular performances.

And so, within a period of less than three centuries, the drama of the Church had grown up and attained almost to its final development. The Easter dialogue had originated somewhere about the year 900, and by the end of the century had already become a true play provided with impersonation and an adequate setting. Most of the important plays known to the Church, versions of the Easter and Epiphany plays, the *Passion Play*, the dramatization of subjects from the Old Testament, the *miracula* of St Nicholas, and the treatment of subjects from eschatology, had all been composed by the end of the thirteenth century. Not that dramatic composition within the Church ceased with the year 1300; a few dramatic ceremonies such as the Feast of the Presentation of the Virgin Mary and the Assumption did not come into existence until towards the end of the mediæval period. But by the beginning of the fourteenth century the more important themes of church drama had received full and characteristic treatment.

This drama dealt with a great variety of subjects and very probably extended over the whole of sacred history. Comparatively few plays dealing with Old Testament subjects still remain and the earliest is one which deals with Jacob and his sons. There is no reason, however, to suppose that examples of all the plays which were composed during this period have been preserved, and it is possible enough that they reached back to the story of Adam. Naturally enough the greatest attention is given to incidents from the life of Christ, especially to the Nativity and to the Resurrection, but on the whole, judging from the texts still preserved and from those whose existence can be inferred, it would seem that the Church dramatized sacred history with generous inclusiveness.

As we should expect, the plays differ considerably amongst themselves both in the general nature of their content and in their attachment to the liturgy. Some of them are definitely liturgical in content and form an indispensable part of public worship; but as a rule they arose, not from a dramatization of essential parts of the liturgy, but as deliberate additions to it. This is especially the case with the Easter plays where the original dialogue, composed as an addition to the liturgy, has been gradually extended for dramatic purposes through the addition of passages drawn from sacred sources, from commentaries and from the Fathers, and eventually of verses composed imaginatively. A similar development can be traced for the Christmas *Officium Pastorum* and no doubt others arose in the same way. Not, of course, all of them ; when a drama has once been developed, then the dramatization of other subjects will proceed imaginatively, and many of the more elaborate plays were probably composed originally as definite plays.

In England itself little is known of the Latin drama of the Church before 1300. Presumably this country took its share in the general development, though few of the texts are extant. The religious drama, however, was essentially international and occasional allusions indicate that, as we should expect, it was being staged in England as in the rest of Western Europe. The earliest reference to it in England appears to belong to the very beginning of the twelfth century. A certain Geoffrey, a Norman clerk and schoolmaster to the Abbey of St Albans, prepared a *ludus de Sancta Katerina* at Dunstable. For it he borrowed from the Abbey certain copes which, unfortunately, were accidentally burnt. This appears to have affected him so keenly that he became a monk and by 1119 had become Abbot of St Albans.[1] William FitzStephen, in a description of London prefixed to his life of Becket written *c.* 1180, tells us ' Londonia pro spectaculis theatralibus, pro ludis scenicis, ludos habet sanctiores, repræsentationes miraculorum quae sancti confessores operati sunt, seu repræsentationes passionum quibus claruit constantia martyrum ',[2]

---

[1] Thomas Walsingham, *Gesta Abbatum Monasterii Sancti Albani* (Rolls Series 28, iv), I. 73.

[2] William FitzStephen, *Vita Sancti Thomae* (Rolls Series 67), III. 9.

though we hear nothing more of any plays in London until a couple of centuries later. The Cathedral statutes of Bishop Hugh of Lichfield (1188–98) provide for the *Pastores* at Christmas and the *Quem quaeritis* and the *Peregrini* at Easter. During the thirteenth century other references indicate the acting of plays at Beverley, Lincoln, Salisbury and York, and there is no reason to suppose that such references apply to the earliest production of plays in these towns.

Why examples of the liturgical drama of the Church should be so rare in England is not an easy question to answer. No doubt the ravages at the dissolution of the monasteries have much to answer for, and probably another reason is that, by the middle of the fourteenth century, drama had passed into the hands of the lay people and this secular and vernacular drama had taken the place of the earliest liturgical drama of the Church. For this later drama, numerous examples of which have been preserved in the various cycles of Mystery plays, was very different from the earlier. It was spoken and not sung, it used the vernacular instead of Latin, was played out of doors not in the church, and was a specifically national development of the former international literature. After the fourteenth century, though all the plays had a common background, and drew on common sources in Scripture, legend and ecclesiastical exegesis, the several countries of Europe showed significant variation in literary form, choice of theme and methods of presentation. This secularization, as it may be called—though the themes were still essentially religious, took place approximately during the century between 1250 and 1350, and by the latter date the drama had mostly passed out of the hands of the Church. So long as the plays remained closely attached to the liturgy they were necessarily restricted in various ways and could not be allowed to develop indefinitely. There was, however, an increasing desire for elaboration, especially a popular desire for the elaboration of the comic element which, though the germs of it were present already in the liturgical plays, could be freely developed only in secular surroundings. The increasing length and elaboration made the former presentation indoors impossible, so they were moved, first of all to the precincts of the church, then to the churchyard, and finally to the market-place or other open space of the town. Similarly a larger number of actors became necessary than could be provided by the Church, even when near some large monastery, so that lay people had to be allowed to take part. This led in turn to the gradual abandonment of the Latin of the liturgy for the language of everyday life. Already vernacular passages had been present in some of the Latin plays, sometimes as a translation of the Latin, sometimes as an independent dramatic unit. The result is a body of transitional plays in each of which one of the vernaculars is either prominent or predominant, but in which the elements inherited from the church plays are still conspicuous. These transitional pieces are eventually succeeded by vernacular religious plays covering the whole range of sacred history, and sometimes requiring several days for their performance. Moreover the increasing secularization leads to the taking over of them by the laity, and the performance is financed by special bodies—in England usually by the town guilds. The tendencies towards secularization which became evident towards the end of the thirteenth century were, in all probability, greatly strengthened by the sermon literature of the period. The sermon, in the hands of the friars, had already led the movement from the church to the market-place, and from Latin to the vernacular, and in it the comic element was already well developed.

When the plays began to be produced out of doors, the climatic conditions became important, and, as their increasing elaboration had led to the loosening of their bonds with the feast which they commemorated, there was a natural tendency to play them as far as possible during the summer months. Whitsuntide early became a favourite date, but during the fourteenth century, especially in England and in Spain, the recently established feast of Corpus Christi became the usual one. The plays were more or less attached to the religious procession, originally the leading ceremony of the day. This, however, was gradually thrust into a very minor position as the mere herald of the following mystery plays.

In English literature there is little of interest dramatically before the appearance of the full cycles of vernacular plays towards the end of the fourteenth and during the fifteenth century. The transitional type of drama was presumably present here as elsewhere, but it has left little trace of its existence, though we hear of a play on the Resurrection performed in the churchyard at Beverley in 1220.[1] The earliest extant example of the transitional type of drama is a fragment which has been found written down on the back of a manorial roll from Rickinghall in Suffolk.[2] It contains a single complete stanza in French and English, in which the speaker announces that he is a king, and part only of a following stanza in which he addresses a messenger ; the stage directions being, as usual, in Latin. The fragment seems to have been a waste scrap, discarded because of mistakes by the copyist, and afterwards economically used for manorial accounts. Both the writer's original and his own copy have long since disappeared, and only this accidental scrap is left to bear witness to a vanished cycle of mystery plays. It was apparently written in the early fourteenth century, and there is nothing to tell us of its

[1] *Miracula alia Sancti Johannis Episcopi* (Rolls Series 71), I. 328.
[2] J. P. Gilson, 'A Fourteenth Century Fragment' (*Times Literary Supplement* 1921, p. 340) ; see also pp. 356, 373.

original provenance, though Bury St Edmunds seems a likely enough guess. Another fragmentary text of this type has been discovered at Shrewsbury,[1] though it was apparently not written before the fifteenth century. It contains the part, with cues, of a single actor in three plays, the *Pastores*, *Quem Quaeritis* and *Peregrinus*, and shows how the Latin text was first sung by a group of performers and then expanded separately by them in the vernacular. Though late the fragment is interesting as showing the transition, not only from Latin to the vernacular, but also from the sung to the spoken drama. Equally important is the much earlier Anglo-French *Jus d'Adam*,[2] which appears to have been composed in Normandy some time between 1150 and 1160, but survives only in an Anglo-French manuscript. It is an elaboration of the Christmas *Prophetae* type of play, and as extant falls into three divisions, the Fall of Man, the murder of Abel, and the *Ordo Prophetarum* from Abraham to Nebuchadnezzar. The procession of prophets must have continued as far as John the Baptist so that presumably the remainder of the play has been lost. Apparently it was played by Latin-speaking clerics for the benefit of the common people. The greater part of the text is in Anglo-French octosyllabic couplets, but the stage directions, the prophecies and the lections, of which the Anglo-French is a translation, are in Latin. The stage directions are especially full and valuable and indicate that the work must have been played in the open air. This and a fragmentary play on the *Resurrection*,[3] also in Anglo-French and written about fifty years after the *Jus d'Adam*, are the only transitional texts which have been preserved from our period. Since this survey closes with

[1] Ed. O. Waterhouse, *The Non-Cycle Mystery Plays* (EETS Extra Series 1909), pp. 1–7.

[2] Ed. P. Studer, *Le Mystère d'Adam* (Manchester 1918).

[3] Ed. J. G. Wright (Paris 1931).

1300, in the middle of the transitional period, we could hardly expect any plays written entirely in English, and could hope only for the transitional type in which English and Latin were used side by side, but if examples of these ever existed they must have long since disappeared.

CONCLUSION

THERE are many periods of English literary history for which their admirers have attempted to claim an importance and significance not willingly conceded by other scholars. But even the most inveterate despiser of mediæval literature must recognize the importance of the period which sees the birth of the lyric, the beginnings of the vernacular drama, the appearance in English literature of Reynard the Fox, of Charlemagne, and of the Arthurian legend with all that it implies. Obviously the literary characteristics of two centuries are not to be summed up in a single phrase. We can call it an age of transition, a period which sees the change from Old to Middle English, from the earlier, more specifically Germanic to the later more international literature in which many of the traditional Germanic characteristics have been transformed by the all-pervading influence of French literary models. Such a title, however, means very little ; every age is inevitably in some sense an age of transition, a period of which the beginning differs from the end and in which the intervening years indicate the connexion between the two. However inevitable or true a title such as this might be it can hardly serve to differentiate the period with which we are concerned from the centuries which follow.

In any case there is little to differentiate the remainder of the eleventh century from that part of it which preceded the Conquest. The line of Cerdic no longer occupied the throne of Wessex ; England was ruled by a foreigner and formed a part only of his domains. The same thing had happened before, and had left apparently little trace on the culture or institutions of the country. Swegen had imposed on England a Danish dynasty, and Canute had founded a great northern maritime empire. But on the death of Canute's sons the throne had reverted to a descendant of Alfred, and England remained an Anglo-Saxon England with but few traces left of any foreign domination. In the early years of the Conquest who was to say that Norman rule would survive the Conqueror? Scandinavian settlement had been far more intensive and widespread than that of the Norman emigrants in the years following the Conquest, yet Scandinavians and Anglo-Saxons had practically become one and there was no reason why their Norman kinsmen should not also be absorbed—as indeed they eventually were. One of the ' ifs ' of history is the question of the difference in the history of England had Robert Curthose proved a successful duke of Normandy and founded a dynasty strong enough to repel the designs of its English kindred on the Norman heritage. Certainly to the literary historian the date of the Conquest has no immediate significance. In the remainder of the eleventh century the Anglo-Saxon tradition persists in literature. The standard West Saxon is still the literary language of the country, though warnings of change are implicit in the reforming activities of Lanfranc and Anselm.

The twelfth century is that in which the change from Old to Middle English finally takes place. The continued union of England and Normandy, and—equally important —the later French empire of the Angevin kings, had opened the way for the unrestricted entrance of French literary influence into England. No doubt that influence would have been considerable even in an Anglo-Saxon England, as it was in fact in thirteenth-century Norway, but matters were simplified by the presence of a foreign aristocracy in Church and State. In any case its victory is very gradual and far from complete ; Old English literature had attained to such a pitch of development that foreign influences, however strong, could only transform and not extinguish many of the characteristic features. The change is slow ; sometimes we can actually see it taking place, as in the historical and homiletic prose, at others the later loss of texts has gone far to obscure the essential continuity. Much of the later ' Matter of England ' must have existed in some form or other during the Old English period ; vernacular treatments of it have survived only in the later mediæval romances so that the gradual change from epic to romance has been obscured. Oriental ideas and subjects have appeared already in Old English, and the almost complete absence of such subjects in the vernacular during the twelfth century produces an apparent gap which we have no reason to suppose did in actual fact exist. Lyric poetry appears in the thirteenth century already technically perfect, and in the hands of poets completely at home in this new type of literature. Consequently there is a tendency to ignore the scattered evidence for a twelfth-century lyric literature and to look upon the English lyric as an importation, already technically mature, from the continent. Undoubtedly the comparatively little evidence which still exists does suggest that the transition from Old to Middle English, in both literature and language, was a gradual development and not the sudden change introduced by a conquering army, which it is sometimes presumed to be. The ultimate effects of the Conquest on English literature, either for the better or the worse, were exceptionally important, but today it is the essential continuity between Old and Middle English literature, rather than any difference, which needs emphasis.

In England, as elsewhere in Europe, the twelfth century is probably one of the most remarkable and significant of all the periods of mediæval history. Politically it opens with the statesmanlike figure of Henry I, initiating many of the reforms and policies of his greater grandson, under whom English and Normans are fast becoming one people. During the anarchy of Stephen's reign it experienced the worst aspects of mediæval feudalism, whilst the second half of the century saw the early promise and greatness of the Angevin empire pass into disappointment and disruption. Intellectually England takes its full share in the renaissance of learning which spreads over Europe. This is especially evident from the number of English scholars who received preferment abroad. Amongst them we find such names as John of Salisbury, Bishop of Chartres ; John of Poitiers, Archbishop of Lyons ; Ralph de Serris, Dean of Rheims ; Nicholas Breakspear, the only Englishman to become Pope ; Robertus Pullus, Chancellor of the Apostolic See ; Thomas Brown, the great financial minister of Roger of Sicily. These are only some of those who achieved the highest preferment ; it is far from being a complete list. In John of Salisbury England possessed the greatest classical scholar of the century. Much of the new learning was introduced to the West by English translators working in Spain and in Sicily, whilst in Adelard of Bath was to be found the most original and the greatest of the twelfth-century scientists. Under Henry II England possessed perhaps the most learned king of the West [1] and at his court were to be

---

[1] At any rate Peter of Blois thought so. Writing to the Archbishop of Palermo, ' Your king,' he says, ' is a good scholar, but ours is far better ; I know the abilities and accomplishments of both. You know that the king of Sicily was my pupil for a year ; you yourself taught him the elements of verse-making and literary composition ; from me he had further and deeper lessons, but as soon as I left the kingdom he threw away his books and took to the easy-going ways of the court. But with the King of England there is school every day, constant conversation of the best scholars and discussions of questions.' On Henry's literary accomplishm· its see W. Stubbs, *Lectures on Medieval and Modern History* (Lc on 1886), pp. 118 ff.

found that brilliant company of Latin writers, whose works are amongst the few mediæval Latin works that the modern age can read with interest and amusement. In Latin poetry, although England produced nothing to compare with the great religious poetry of the continent, with Adam of St Victor, with Abaelard, or with the magnificent *De Contemptu Mundi* of Bernard of Morlaix, which gave to the Middle Ages one of the seven great mediæval Latin hymns, yet it produced one of the best of the mediæval Latin epics and a considerable number of secular lyrics of the type usually known as Goliardic poems, poems of bitter satire on the evils of the times, love lyrics and drinking songs ; the most modern in spirit of all the mediæval Latin verse. Nor were the literary achievements of the century confined only to Latin. At its beginning the Old English traditions and language were still being carried on ; by the end they have been almost forgotten and a new tradition is being established. But despite the numerous difficulties, the diversity of dialects and the lack of any fixed orthography, literary artists are at work whose genius is evident and for whose works there is no need to make allowance. In the *Peterborough Chronicle* the anarchies of Stephen's reign are not unworthily described by the last of that series of English chroniclers whose work, historically and artistically, is the especial glory of Anglo-Saxon England. In the *Ancren Riwle* is produced perhaps the greatest and most influential of the vernacular prose works in the Middle English period. In the *Owl and the Nightingale* the first of the modern poets is at work, whose intermingling of the best of the literary traditions of France and England produces an artistic unity not unworthy of his great successor two centuries later. Moreover Anglo-French, a newly developed literary language, has given to us one of the best of the mediæval treatments of the story of Tristram and Iseult and the delightful *lais* of Marie de France.

Great in achievement the twelfth century is still greater in promise. The vernacular lyric, present already in French and Provençal, is not absent from England, though complete examples of it survive only from the following century. Drama is already beginning to break away from the bonds of the church, and the extant Anglo-French examples in the vernacular foreshadow the later mystery plays. Most important of all are the themes which have appeared, some already treated in contemporary literature, others awaiting development in the not too distant future. Reynard the Fox, the 'Matter of England', allegory, all the greatness of the Arthurian legend, Lancelot and Guinevere, Tristram and Iseult, the quest of the Holy Grail, the glory of the Round Table and the mystery and tragedy of the last great battle, all are already present in the twelfth century, along with other themes from Geoffrey of Monmouth, King Lear, Cymbeline, and others, later to become famous.

Inevitably the thirteenth century, despite its undoubted achievements, must follow as an anticlimax. Much of the promise of the preceding century is fulfilled, yet it is perhaps inevitable that promise should outrun performance. There is no doubt of the importance of the period politically ; the century which sees the signing of the Great Charter and the summoning of the first Parliament is obviously one of the most significant in English history. But it is full of sordid squabbles in which we can feel little sympathy for any of the protagonists. The century opens with the loss of Normandy and the civil wars of John, in which the figure of the great archbishop, Stephen Langton, casts over the party of the barons the shadow of a patriotism and dignity to which they themselves could lay little claim. The civil wars during the following reign, when the king and his French favourites are for a time humbled by the barons under the leadership of Simon de Montfort, the latter undoubtedly an able, honest and patriotic, but not somehow very sympathetic, figure. Probably the greatest man of the century, omitting the scholars, was Edward I, a strong king, an able ruler and the first soldier of his age. Almost alone amongst Norman and Plantagenet kings he was able to resist the lure of continental conquest, that fatal inheritance of the Norman Conquest, and to return to the policy of the Anglo-Saxon kings in their concentration on the union of Britain. That he should fail was perhaps inevitable, the forces of nationalism are becoming too strong, but his partial failure does not detract from the greatness of a conception that was not to be accomplished until nearly 300 years after his death.

In literature, as in religion, the century is essentially that of the friars : in England of the Franciscans, on the continent of the Dominicans. It is the century of scholasticism, reaching its peak in England in the figure of Duns Scotus, thereafter declining in the hands of less able disciples. It is above all the century of Grosseteste and Roger Bacon ; of the introduction of Greek and the synthesization of the whole of mediæval science by the greatest of all mediæval scientists. The vernacular literature, still employed mainly for entertainment and in the edification of the ignorant, is increasing in volume and has a better chance of preservation. Most of the themes present in the twelfth century have received a treatment which still survives. A dozen secular lyrics bear witness to the charm and unexpected maturity of a type of literature of which the greater part has been lost. In the *Vox and the Wolf* we have the only surviving example before Chaucer of the tales of Reynard the Fox, and the ' Matter of England ' is receiving adequate treatment in both French and English. The change from Old to Middle English, which had taken place during the preceding century, is now well-established, and English is gradually and unobtrusively preparing the way for its final victory in the following century as the language of literature in England.

It must be admitted that much of the surviving literature from this post-Conquest period is of comparatively little interest to the modern reader. Indeed, one suspects that some of the interminable handbooks of pious reading were too much even for the mediæval audience. But, as we have perhaps too frequently pointed out during the preceding pages, there is no reason to suppose that the proportions of the extant literature are at all representative of that which was actually composed. On the contrary we can often catch glimpses of a rich literature, which has since vanished, rarely religious in tone, more frequently secular, and such as is preserved only in rare examples or not at all. The rich lyric literature of the twelfth century, which scattered scraps of evidence proves to have existed, has almost completely vanished. The cycle of Reynard is represented by a single surviving tale and occasional hints of others long since lost. The early romances of the ' Matter of France ', the ' Matter of Britain ' and the ' Matter of England ', to say nothing of the innumerable other themes of mediæval romance, have nearly all perished. From accidental allusions here and there we can occasionally catch tantalizing glimpses of the richness and variety of.this lost literature, but we can never know how much has vanished without leaving a single trace behind it. No doubt an appreciable proportion of the religious literature has disappeared too, worn to shreds by the hands of generations of pious readers, but it always had a much better chance of survival than the purely secular literature. It was assured of a written existence, and of continual copying, whilst much of the latter was probably never written down at all but depended entirely on oral tradition. Some of it probably lingered long in the memories of the common people, Leland in the sixteenth century found some of the mediæval tales still remembered, but how little of it ever achieved a written existence, even in late and unrepresentative versions. Religious literature was assured of a peaceful existence in the seclusion of the monastic libraries, and if it survived being carted away for fuel, or for wrapping-paper, at the dissolution, it might eventually pass into one of the great national or private collections. Secular literature had the same dangers to contend with, and many others which were peculiarly its own. The surprising thing is rather the amount which has been preserved than that which has perished. Yet unless, as far as possible, we take this lost literature into account we are apt to obtain an entirely false impression of the early literature. As Professor Chambers, the first to appreciate its full significance, has pointed out :

. . . it is safe to say that if the lost poetry had been preserved, the whole history of English literature, prior to Chaucer and Langland, would appear to us in a different light. The homilies and lives of saints, which bulk so largely in Medieval English verse and prose, would subside till they occupied a just, and a small, proportion of our attention.[1]

During the two and a half centuries with which we are concerned vernacular literature is steadily increasing in importance throughout Western Europe. It is not yet a serious rival of Latin, but is continually strengthening its hold and quietly preparing for the time when, in the different countries, it shall take first place, not only in the literature of entertainment and edification but also in that of learning and original scholarship. Moreover, by the end of the period, the vernacular of almost every country already has some special contribution to make to the development of European literature. That of France is obvious enough ; it is from French that the rest of Western Europe borrows the romance, the shorter narrative exemplified on the one

[1] R. W. Chambers, ' The Lost Literature of Medieval England ' (*Transactions of the Bibliographical Society*, v. 294).

hand by the *fabliau* and on the other by the Breton *lai*, the beast epic and allegory. However firmly such literary forms may be naturalized in other countries they always depend, directly or indirectly, on French models. The success or failure of the individual works usually depends on the achievement of the author in assimilating and reproducing the atmosphere of his French originals. To the south of France we are indebted for the troubadour lyric. From these it passes into other vernaculars, each of which impresses it with its own special stamp, but in every case owing the initial inspiration to Provençal.

Apart from French perhaps the most important vernacular in literature during this period is that of German. The late twelfth and early thirteenth centuries produce the *Nibelungenlied* and see the appearance of four poets, Hartmann von Aue, Gottfried von Strassburg, Wolfram von Eschenbach and Walther von der Vogelweide—a group which no contemporary vernacular can equal. Strongly influenced by French, they retain an amazingly individual and personal quality and transform foreign literary forms and subjects into a thoroughly national literature. Italy, before the fourteenth century, is too dependent on Provençal, and only towards the end of the period, with the immediate predecessors of Dante, can we perceive the emergence of a truly national literature. Yet it is from the Italy of the thirteenth century that European literature derives the sonnet, one of the most important of literary forms. In the far north Iceland has developed a narrative prose which leaves the Sagas without an equal in their particular department of literature. At the other end of Europe Spain can show only one really great work before the fourteenth century—the *Poema del Mio Cid* ; her contribution depends rather on her position as an intermediary through which the Middle Ages learnt most of what they were to know of Greek science and philosophy.

Until after 1300 England has comparatively little to show as compared with continental vernacular literatures. In the international learning expressed in Latin it takes, as has been shown above, an important and sometimes a leading part. Its contribution to the vernacular literature is not so easily determined. The commanding position which that literature had gained during the Old English period has been largely lost, and it has had to start again with added handicaps such as were not known elsewhere. Yet there were compensations; the development of Anglo-French, though it helped to retard the development of English, nevertheless made possible a more intimate fusion of the two literatures, and the *Owl and the Nightingale* shows the possibilities inherent in the mingling of the strains. One of the great subjects of mediæval romance—the Arthurian legend—had its origin in England and owed much of its initial development to English authors—though writing usually in Latin or Anglo-French rather than in English. The possession of a distinctively national alliterative poetry helped to avoid monotony by providing an alternative system of prosody, though its greatest triumphs were not to appear before the fourteenth century. On the whole the importance of English literature in the twelfth and thirteenth centuries, as compared with vernacular literature on the continent, depends more on its promise of future development than in any specific achievement of its own. The native elements in it, the alliterative poetry and the homiletic prose, were to show themselves capable of great things in the future. The facility with which it had made literary forms borrowed from the continent its own was to bear fruit in the later development of the lyric and the drama.

INDEX

Printed in Great Britain by
Butler & Tanner Ltd.,
Frome and London